INDIA
OF THE NORTH
PACIFIC COAST

THE CARLETON LIBRARY SERIES

A series of original works, new collections and reprints of source material relating to Canada, issued under the supervision of the Editorial Board, Carleton Library Series, Carleton University Press Inc. Ottawa, Canada.

INDIANS OF THE NORTH PACIFIC COAST

Studies in Selected Topics

Edited and with an Introduction
by

Tom McFeat

Carleton University Press
Ottawa
University of Washington Press
Seattle

First published in 1966 by McClelland and Stewart Ltd., Toronto, Ontario, Canada

First University of Washington Press edition 1967

Second printing 1971
Third printing 1973
Fourth printing 1976
Fifth printing 1980
Sixth printing 1989
Seventh printing 1992
Eighth printing 1995

Canadian Cataloguing in Publication Data

Main entry under title:
Indians of the North Pacific Coast

(The Carleton library, ISSN 0576-7784; no. 25)
Includes bibliographical references.
ISBN 0-88629-058-9

1. Indians of North America—Northwest Coast of North America.
I. McFeat, Tom, 1919- II. Series.

N78.M34I64 1987 971.1′00497 C87-090187-7

Library of Congress Cataloguing-in-Publication Data

Indians of the North Pacific coast.

Bibliography: p.
1. Indians of North America—Northwest Coast of North America.
I. McFeat, Tom.

E78.N78155 1988 971.1′00497 88-20675
ISBN 0-295-74095-7

Printed and bound in Canada.

CONTENTS

Introduction

This book is about Indians of the Northwest Coast who lived between Yakutat Bay in Southeastern Alaska and Juan de Fuca Strait. It is the Northwest Coast that Boas knew, although the culture area has, since Boas's time, been extended into northern California. In order to avoid confusion, I have used the phrase "North Pacific Coast" to designate only those Coastal Indians living north of Washington State: the Coast Salish, the Nootka, the Kwakiutl, the Bella Coola, the Tsimshian, the Haida and the Tlingit. Some of the papers I have selected for this volume deal with problems of a special kind. These problems, aptly called "puzzles" by Dr. Wike,[1] are concerned with subjects peculiar to the groups I have named, and not to those south of them. The problems arise out of considerations of the Potlatch and of the class and ranking system; they also include discussions of individual attitudes and behaviour which are related to apparently mysterious conditions specific to the area.

The interpretation of the behaviour and institutions of these people of the North Pacific Coast has received an unusual amount of attention. One has the impression of a uniqueness that is, on the surface at least, greater than that found anywhere else in North America. As long ago as 1923, Kroeber[2] convincingly demonstrated the relative "aloofness" and separateness of these cultures when, having ordered sets of culture traits in terms of their recency or remoteness in time, he was able to identify those which were shared between the North Pacific Coast and the rest of North America or Asia and by this means to document both the quality of "aloofness" and its great historical

[1] Wike, Joyce, "More Puzzles on the Northwest Coast," *American Anthropologist*, n.s., 59 (April 1957), 301-17.

[2] Kroeber, Alfred L., "American Culture and the Northwest Coast," *American Anthropologist*, n.s., 25 (January 1923) 1-20.

depth. The problems of interpretation are, therefore, viewed here as arising, in part, from the relative isolation of these cultures from others. The people of the North Pacific Coast developed along their own lines for a considerable time; they had the opportunity to evolve distinctive patterns of behaviour and institutions. The reason for isolation from some areas is obvious: the Pacific Ocean lies on one side, the coast ranges on the other. But it is not so obvious why the area should have been isolated from the south, which extends without conspicuous barriers into California and on to Mexico. The ocean and the mountain ranges are clearly not the only causes of isolation.

The settlement patterns of the North Pacific Coast communities were, in fact, themselves a reflection of conditions of isolation. As these peoples focused their interests on river mouths for the lucrative runs of salmon and herring, they accordingly ranged their communities along discontinuous stretches of beach. Behind them stood the walls of the plunging coastal ranges on the mainland; in front of them was the sea. On the islands, as well as on the mainland, an inland flora grew that was rich and gross, springing up and growing thick and then rotten in its self-imposed darkness. Travel this way was awkward in the extreme. Living on a beach, with mountains and impenetrable forest on one side and the open sea on the other, leaves little alternative for the inhabitants but to become isolates – unless, that is, they can find the means of making contact with other groups. Assuming that the means by which original settlement had been made had disappeared, geographical isolation based on island living would result in every beach community becoming a universe unto itself.

The people of the North Pacific Coast, on the other hand, did not actually become total isolates. They constructed efficient sea-going craft which they used to maintain contact at least with their neighbours, and in some cases with groups much more distant. One might expect that regular and more or less equally distributed contacts between beach communities within any region of the area as a whole would have been maintained, and that these contacts would have included, as part of a general flow of interaction between groups, contacts with the peoples across the Strait of Juan de Fuca and down the coast through California. There is little doubt, however, that the unitary character of the culture developed toward the north, and not toward the south, of Juan de Fuca and the Columbia River. In spite of the fact that they had good water-craft, the people of the North Pacific Coast remained relatively isolated from the people to the south. Clearly, boats were a necessary, but not a sufficient, condition of communication between groups.

Bringing about a system of contacts between peoples requires a number of related attributes and accomplishments. The Massim Melanesians,[3] for example, like the people of the North Pacific Coast, were constituted of widely separated units. They too had good sea-going craft. A particular mechanism was required, however, to sustain regular contacts between groups which tended to be foreign to one another, and it was specifically through the agency of the Kula, the mechanism of exchange which they evolved, that the Trobrianders, the Dobuans and others from a score of islands throughout the district were able to keep in touch at regular intervals. Within the Kula as a whole, the Trobrianders provided what might be called the mainspring of the system. Because of the abundance of their natural resources, their willingness to accumulate large surpluses, and the social organization by which their resources could be consolidated and channelled into overseas exchange,[4] the Trobrianders seem to have been the key group in maintaining the system and in keeping otherwise over-populated islands

[3] See Bronislaw Malinowski, *Argonauts of the Western Pacific* (New York: E. P. Dutton & Co., 1922; paperback reprint, 1961).

[4] The ability of the Trobrianders to marshal large resources efficiently for overseas exchange was, to a considerable extent, a result of their recognition of a relationship between a man and his sister's husband, known as *urugubu*, whereby the man was obliged to grow the better half of all his produce for his brother-in-law. In this way a man's interest in his sister's children was maintained and satisfied (it was his sister's children, not his own, over whom he maintained authority and who would inherit from him). Should a chief possess fifty or more wives and thus receive the produce from fifty or more brothers-in-law, while giving in turn only to one or two, he could accumulate and store his produce, in the end using it to organize the great overseas expeditions.

supplied with food and other needs. Other islanders who formed overseas partnerships-in-exchange were able to participate on an equitable basis because the main exchange commodities (arm bands for bracelets and bracelets for arm bands) were produced independently of food and constituted major valuables that were sought by all partners.

Among the groups of the North Pacific Coast there was no direct counterpart to the key role of the Trobrianders among the Massim Melanesians. All groups participated more or less equally in the system of exchange that bound them together. But many of the other conditions that made the Kula possible supported in like manner the institution of the Potlatch, which was the "binding" equivalent of the Kula on the North Pacific Coast. The natural resources were there in both cases. The Trobrianders grew yams and taros well in excess of their needs and stored them against particular occasions. The people of the North Pacific Coast, for their part, fished with great efficiency, drawing into their storage facilities quantities of salmon which most of them took twice a year; and they were also sea-hunters of note. It is true they were poor land-hunters, and they knew nothing about cultivation. Nonetheless, they had a surplus of food, and an abundance of good straight-grained cedar out of which they could build fine sea-going craft. The coast Indians, moreover, developed a system of chieftainship which, like its counterpart in Melanesia, made sense only in the context of the crucial overseas relationships recurrently expressed in great exchanges. As I have already suggested, however, these exchange relationships did not extend southward; the mechanism which bound together the island-like settlements of the North Pacific Coast did not broaden to bring others into the community of participants.

Both the Kula Ring (as it was called) and the Potlatch were binding institutions. The Potlatch was binding in two ways. First, it brought together groups which would not otherwise, as far as can be determined, have had anything to do with one another except through warfare or marriage. Second, the Potlatch was, like the Kula Ring, an elaborately ceremonial way of bestowing gifts – and, therefore, of requiring a return. In principle, neither institution could ever come to a halt since one gift implied another. One Potlatch closed one set of obligations only to open another. Nothing short of a radical intrusion of new conditions could close the cycle.

It is said that the Kula Ring collapsed when the authorities in their wisdom judged it sinful for Trobrianders to have more than one wife, and certainly sinful beyond measure for one man to have more than fifty. Whether or not the Kula machinery was as deftly jammed as this comment suggests, one can hardly think of a more cleverly indirect way of bringing the mechanism to a halt. The Potlatch, in contrast, was subjected to a plainly frontal attack by the authorities in charge of enlightenment: it was simply outlawed. One must read Boas and Barnett, in this volume, and Charlie Nowell's account of his brother's purchase of a Potlatch "copper," to understand the significance of that bludgeoning act of prohibition.

Considerable attention is given, in the pages which follow, to the many functions of the Potlatch which were associated with its role as an exchange agent between groups. However, its function as a standardizing agent throughout the various sub-cultures of the coast Indians, under conditions of relative isolation, is not generally examined. In order to clarify the nature of this latter function, I should like to explain what I meant by the use of the term "relative isolation."

Island cultures are inherently isolated cultures. As illustrated by the cultures of the Maori or the Tikopians, which disengaged themselves eventually from the main influences of greater Polynesia, they become increasingly differentiated from the base to which their ancestors belonged, developing consistently in one way while the remainder develop in another. This pattern of divergence does not seem surprising when one considers the effects of reproductive isolation in biological groups. When a "gene pool" is divided, one expects divergence in development. Viewed internally, cultures are characterized by the continuous diffusion of information (i.e., of knowledge, beliefs and habits) across an area – a process of transmission which leaves its evidence in the distribution of culture traits among the various groups of people involved. The ethnological model of diffusion is this: unless barriers occur which prevent the exchange of information, its movement will be continuous and unbroken. This one might call the *isometric pattern* of diffusion in cultures. At some point trait diffusion fades out: information is not exchanged or passed along a particular cultural route. When none of the traits of one culture are found to have developed as a result of information exchange with others, that culture may be said to be isolated. Relative isolation, then, is an intermediate case which occurs when the exchange of information is intermittent. The condition usually arises where considerable distances are involved or in the presence of some substantial barrier, such as that of a mountain range or an ocean. If one were to locate the available examples of cultures along a continuum of isolation, island cultures would be found to occupy the extreme position of minimal contact. And this is precisely the kind of diffusion-zone condition with which both the Kula and the Potlatch had to contend. The fact that the Potlatch did not bridge the gap between the Indians of the North Pacific Coast and the Indians to the south defines their mutual isolation.

The outstanding examples of cultural isolation were drawn by Kroeber[5] from the cultures of Southampton Island and Easter Island. Since these were island cultures, like the cultures of Tikopia and the Maori and the North Pacific Coast, the vicissitudes which they suffered could perhaps be seen as common to all island cultures, but in a more extreme form. Kroeber observed two results in the cases of isolation which he studied. One might be called a case of cultural impoverishment; this was the case of Southampton Island, where the culture became, generation by generation, an increasingly barren version of the original, exhibiting not merely an arrest in cultural achievement but actually a failure to reach the level of technical competence (the only type of evidence available from a prehistorical culture) which characterized the areas from which it had derived. Easter Island proved to be a different case, and in all respects

[5] Kroeber, Alfred L., *Anthropology* (New York: Harcourt, Brace and Co., Inc., 1948), pp. 376-78.

like the cases with which we are familiar among living cultures. Here the groups evolved rapidly, manifesting intensive development in restricted aspects of their cultures, as though some inherent potential for behaviour, which might have been held in check under the influence of isometric diffusion, had begun to dominate their activities.

It is conceivable that something similar to the latter process underlies the problem of interpretation which Dr. Wike describes as a series of puzzles. The institutions and behaviour patterns of the people of the North Pacific Coast (and, more especially, the Potlatch and the intimately related system of rank and class) might well be looked upon as, in part, developing over the long run out of conditions of relative isolation and, indeed, as a specific adjustment to these conditions. In this connection, close attention should be paid to Drucker's essay on the Kwakiutl and Tsimshian Potlatches which faced the sudden difficulty, under conditions of acculturation, of ordering into a single ranking or class system groups which had not previously been in contact.

Partner to the problem of the interpretation of institutions is the problem of the interpretation of behaviour. Here I refer the reader to the final group of papers, those which concern the behaviour of individuals, whether in day-to-day affairs or in relation to the more specific questions of ranking and potlatching. It may be recalled that one of Ruth Benedict's more exotic examples of behavioural deviation throughout the world came from the Indians of the North Pacific Coast. She referred to these peoples (the Kwakiutl especially) as *megalomanic* in their behaviour – both in their attitudes toward one another's actions and in their interpretation of events, more particularly of events involving crisis. In raising the question of the relativity of normal and abnormal behaviour, and in contending that definitions of such states are local and the product of the community's culture, Benedict painted a lurid picture of suspicion, mutual distrust and extreme self-aggrandizement in a culturally relativistic frame. What is interesting, however, is that her position was not (as are some more recent ones) that this behaviour was a response to disorganization resulting from

group movements following contact, but rather that it was endemic to the culture of the North Pacific Coast. Though she was not, of course, the only one to comment thus on this behaviour, she was alone in dealing with it at length and in finding in it material of theoretical significance. If her generalizations were overdrawn, it does not follow that they were unwarranted.[6] I am, consequently, inclined to believe that part of the difficulty of interpreting these behavioural patterns lies, as does the difficulty of analysing the institutions of class and of the Potlatch, in the fact of their origin in previous conditions of isolation, and that this circumstance, in turn, tended to bring about both the uniqueness and the narrow concentration of effort or of focus which characterizes the culture of the North Pacific Coast.

A book of essays on a single culture area is unusual, but necessary, since it is difficult for an undergraduate in a huge class – or for any non-professional reader – to find the writings represented here. He is fortunate in having easy access to Drucker's work, but will not likely find Boas, Sapir or Swanton, and he is even less likely to find writings of earlier observers, such as Sproat, or the eighteenth-century captive at Nootka Sound, John Jewitt. As he reads the work of men and women who have done outstanding work in the North Pacific Coast, he will find more penetrating interpretations than a single chapter in a book dealing with several culture areas could provide. In this kind of book there will not likely be consensus at every point. If depth of insight sometimes results in conflicting interpretations, then the reader should be stimulated to read more deeply the literature of the area and to search it with specific problems in mind.

No single anthropologist has ever been expert in all branches of the field as they apply to the North Pacific Coast, nor has any been intimately conversant with all subareas or with all problems of interpretation or theory. The present book makes use of expert testimony, as do all books

[6] It is a pity that Seymour Parker's recent paper, "The Kwakiutl Indians: 'Amiable' and 'Atrocious'," *Anthropologica*, n.s., vi (1964), 131-58, was published too late for inclusion in this volume.

of this kind, but since it must draw its material from the existing literature, it runs the risk of lacking overall consistency. This deficiency I have tried to offset by the imposition of a series of limitations of my own making. I have limited the book, first, to a single ethnographic area; it should be a more serviceable book as it is than if it were devoted to a consideration of the Indian cultures of the whole of North America. I have also restricted the coverage of sub-fields of anthropology; there are no papers on the archaeology, the linguistics or the physical anthropology of the area. Finally, and within this restricted view of the North Pacific Coast, I have imposed further limitations on the topics covered: the centre of gravity of this book is the Potlatch and the class or ranking system of the coast Indians. I hope that these limitations will not obscure for the reader what is or was generally prevalent in the culture of the North Pacific Coast. As a safeguard I have included sections of Drucker's comprehensive trait list which covers the groups in question and from which the reader may gain useful leads to the generality of a given topic. For the reader as yet unfamiliar with the literature of the North Pacific Coast, several summaries, listed at the back under Suggestions for Further Reading, should be a helpful complement to this book.

In order to keep this book to a manageable size, I have omitted all of the footnotes in the original texts except for explanatory notes and references connected with direct or indirect quotations. Also in the interests of space a number of the selections have had to be condensed. All omissions in the text are indicated by ellipses.

TOM MCFEAT
University of Toronto
November, 1965

PART ONE

AN INTRODUCTION TO THE AREA

The Indian Tribes of the North Pacific Coast

FRANZ BOAS

The Pacific Coast of America between Juan de Fuca Strait and Yakutat Bay is inhabited by a great many Indian tribes distinct in physical characteristics and distinct in languages, but one in culture. Their arts and industries, their customs and beliefs, differ so much from those of all other Indians that they form one of the best defined cultural groups of our continent.

While a hasty glance at these people and a comparison with other tribes emphasize the uniformity of their culture, a closer investigation reveals many peculiarities of individual tribes which prove that their culture has developed slowly and from a number of distinct centers, each people adding something to the culture which we observe at the present day.

The region inhabited by these people is a mountainous coast intersected by innumerable sounds and fiords and studded with islands, large and small. Thus intercourse along the coast by means of canoes is very easy, while access to the inland is difficult on account of the rugged hills and the density of the woods. A few fiords cut deep

---

Source: Franz Boas, *The Social Organization and Secret Societies of the Kwakiutl Indians*. Reports of the United States National Museum (Washington, D.C., 1895), pp. 317-322. Reprinted by permission of the Smithsonian Institution.

into the mainland, and the valleys which open into them give access to the heart of the high ranges which separate the coast from the highlands of the interior, forming an effectual barrier between the people of the interior and those of the coast. These fiords and their rivers and valleys offer comparatively easy access to the coast, and along these lines interchange of culture has taken place. Extending our view a little beyond the territory defined above, the passes along which the streams of culture flowed most easily were Columbia River in the south and the pass leading along Salmon and Bella Coola rivers to Dean Inlet and Bentinck Arm. Of less importance are Chilcat Pass, Stikine River, Nass and Skeena rivers, and Fraser River. Thus it will be seen that there are only two important and four less important passes, over which the people of the coast came into contact with those of the interior. Thus they have occupied a rather isolated position and have been able to develop a peculiar culture without suffering important invasions from other parts of America.

As the precipitation all along the coast is very great, its lower parts are covered with dense forests which furnish wood for building houses, canoes, implements, and utensils. Among them the red cedar (*Thuya gigantea*) is the most prominent, as it furnishes the natives with material for most manufactures. Its wood serves for building and carving; its bark is used for making clothing and ropes. The yellow cedar, pine, fir, hemlock, spruce, yew tree, maple, alder, are also of importance to the Indians. The woods abound with numerous kinds of berries, which are eagerly sought for. The kelp and seaweeds which grow abundantly all along the shore are also utilized.

In the woods the deer, the elk, the black and grizzly bear, the wolf, and many other animals are found. The mountain goat lives on the higher ranges of the mainland. The beaver, the otter, marten, mink, and fur seal furnish valuable skins, which were formerly used for blankets. The Indians keep in their villages dogs which assist the hunters.

The staple food of the Indians is, however, furnished by the sea. Seals, sea lions, and whales are found in considerable numbers; but the people depend almost entirely upon various

species of salmon, the halibut, and the oulachon or candlefish (*Thaleichthys pacificus*, Girard), which are caught in enormous quantities. Various specimens of cod and other sea fish also furnish food. Herrings visit the coast early in spring. In short, there is such an abundance of animal life in the sea that the Indians live almost solely upon it. Besides fish, they gather various kinds of shellfish, sea urchins, and cuttlefish.

The people are, therefore, essentially fishermen, all other pursuits being of secondary importance. Whales are pursued only by the tribes of the west coast of Vancouver Island. Other tribes are satisfied with the dead carcasses of whales which drift ashore. Sea lions and seals are harpooned, the barbed harpoon point being either attached to a bladder or tied to the stern of the canoe. The harpoon lines are made of cedar bark and sinews. The meat of these sea animals is eaten, while their intestines are used for the manufacture of bowstrings and bags. Codfish and halibut are caught by means of hooks. These are attached to fish lines made of kelp. The hook is provided with a sinker, while the upper part is kept afloat by a bladder or a wooden buoy. Cuttlefish are used for bait. The fish are either roasted over or near the fire or boiled in wooden kettles by means of red-hot stones. Those intended for use in winter are split in strips and dried in the sun or over the fire. Salmon are caught in weirs and fish traps when ascending the rivers, or by means of nets dragged between two canoes. Later in the season salmon are harpooned. For fishing in deeper water, a very long double-pointed harpoon is used. Herring and oulachon are caught by means of a long rake. The oulachon are tried in canoes or kettles filled with water, which is heated by means of red-hot stones. The oil is kept in bottles made of dried kelp. In winter, dried halibut and salmon dipped in oil is one of the principal dishes of the tribes living on the outer coast. Clams and mussels are collected by the women; they are eaten fresh, or strung on sticks or strips of cedar bark and dried for winter use. Cuttlefish are caught by means of long sticks; sea eggs are obtained by means of round bag nets. Fish roe, particularly that of herring, is collected in great quantities, dried, and eaten with oil.

Sea grass, berries, and roots are gathered by the women. The sea grass is cut, formed into square cakes, and dried for winter use. The same is done with several kinds of berries, which when used are dissolved in water and eaten mixed with fish oil. Crab-apples are boiled and kept in their juice until late in the winter. They are also eaten with fish oil. The food is kept in large boxes which are bent of cedar wood, the bottom being sewed to the sides.

In winter, deer are hunted. Formerly bows and arrows were used in their pursuit, but these have now been replaced by guns. The bow was made of yew wood or of maple. The arrows had stone, bone, and copper points. Bows and arrows were carried in wooden quivers. Deer are also captured by being driven into large nets made of cedar bark, deer sinews, or nettles. Elks are hunted in the same way. For smaller animals traps are used. Deer and bears are also caught in large traps. Birds were shot with arrows provided with a thick blunt point. Deer-skins are worked into leather and used for various purposes, principally for ropes and formerly for clothing.

The natives of this region go barelegged. The principal part of their clothing is the blanket, and this was made of tanned skins or woven of mountain-goat wool, dog's hair, feathers, or a mixture of both. The thread is spun on the bare leg and by means of a spindle. Another kind of blanket is made of soft cedar bark, the warp being tied across the weft. These blankets are trimmed with fur. At the present time woollen blankets are most extensively used. At festive occasions "button blankets" are worn. Most of these are light blue blankets with a red border set with mother-of-pearl buttons. Many are also adorned with the crest of the owner, which is cut out in red cloth and sewed onto the blanket. Men wear a shirt under the blanket, while women wear a petticoat in addition. Before the introduction of woollen blankets, women used to wear an apron made of cedar bark and a belt made of the same material. When canoeing or working on the beach, the women wear large water-tight hats made of basketry. In rainy weather a water-tight cape or poncho made of cedar bark, is used.

The women dress their hair in two plaits, while the men

wear it comparatively short. The latter keep it back from the face by means of a strap of fur or cloth tied around the head. Ear and nose ornaments are used extensively. They are made of bone and of abalone shell. The women of the most northern tribes (from about Skeena River northward) wear labrets.

A great variety of baskets are used – large wicker baskets for carrying fish and clams, cedar-bark baskets for purposes of storage. Mats made of cedar bark, and in the south such made of rushes, are used for bedding, packing, seats, dishes, covers of boxes, and similar purposes.

In olden times work in wood was done by means of stone and bone implements. Trees were felled with stone axes and split by means of wooden or bone wedges. Boards were split out of cedar trees by means of these wedges. After the rough cutting was finished, the surface of the wood was planed with adzes, a considerable number of which were made of jade and serpentine bowlders, which materials are found in several rivers. Carvings were executed with stone and shell knives. Stone mortars and pestles were used for mashing berries. Paint pots of stone, brushes, and stencils made of cedar bark formed the outfit of the Indian painter. Pipes were made of slate, of bone, or of wood.

Canoes are made of cedar wood. The types of canoes vary somewhat among the different tribes of the coast, depending also largely upon whether the canoe is to be used for hunting, travelling, or fishing. The canoe is propelled and steered by means of paddles.

The houses are made of wood and attain considerable dimensions. The details of construction vary considerably among the various tribes, but the general appearance is much alike from Comox to Alaska, while farther south the square northern house gives way to the long house of the Coast Salish. . . .

The physical characteristics of the Indians of this region show that they are by no means a homogeneous people. So far as we know now, we may distinguish four types on the coast of British Columbia: The northern type, embracing the Nisqa′ and Tsimshian; the Kwakiutl type; that of Harrison Lake; and the Salish of the interior, as represented by

the Okanagan, Flathead, and Shuswap. . . . The northern Indians are of medium stature. Their arms are relatively long, their bodies short. The head is very large, particularly its transversal diameter. The same may be said of the face, the breadth of which is enormous, as it exceeds the average breadth of face of the North American Indian by 6 mm. The height of the face is moderate; therefore its form appears decidedly low. The nose is very low as compared to the height of the face, and at the same time broad. Its elevation over the face is also very slight only. The bridge is generally concave, and very flat between the eyes.

The Kwakiutl are somewhat shorter, the trunks of their bodies are relatively longer, their arms and legs shorter than those of the first group. The dimensions of the head are very nearly the same, but the face shows a remarkably different type, which distinguishes it fundamentally from the faces of all the other groups. The breadth of the face exceeds only slightly the average breadth of face of the Indian, but its height is enormous. The same may be said of the nose, which is very high and relatively narrow. Its elevation is also very great. The nasal bones are strongly developed and form a steep arch, their lower end rising high above the face. This causes a very strongly hooked nose to be found frequently among the Kwakiutl, which type of nose is almost absent in all other parts of the Pacific Coast. This feature is so strongly marked that individuals of this group may be recognized with a considerable degree of certainty by the form of the face and of the nose alone.

The Harrison Lake type has a very short stature. The head is exceedingly short and broad, surpassing in this respect all other forms known to exist in North America. The face is not very wide, but very low, thus producing a chamæprosopic form, the proportions of which resemble those of the Nass River face, while its dimensions are much smaller. In this small face we find a nose which is absolutely higher than that of the Nass River Indian with his huge face. It is, at the same time, rather narrow. The lower portion of the face appears very small, as may be seen by subtracting the height of the nose from that of the face, which gives an approximate measure of the distance from septum to chin.

The Salish of the interior have a stature of 168 cm. Their heads are shorter than those of the tribes of Northern British Columbia or of the Indians of the plains. Their faces have the average height of the Indian face, being higher than that of the northern type of Indians, but lower than that of the Kwakiutl. The nose is high and wide, and has the characteristic Indian form, which is rare in most parts of the coast.

Primary Forms of Material Culture: Living and Eating

JOHN R. JEWITT

It may, perhaps, be as well in this place to give a description of Nootka; some account of the tribes who were accustomed to visit us; and the manners and customs of the people, as far as I hitherto had an opportunity of observing them.

The village of Nootka is situated in between 49 and 50 degrees north latitude, at the bottom of Friendly Cove, on the west or northwest side. It consists of about twenty houses or huts, on a small hill, which rises with a gentle ascent from the shore. Friendly Cove, which affords good and secure anchorage for ships close in with the shore, is a small harbour of not more than a quarter or half a mile in length, and about half a mile or three quarters broad, formed by the line of coast on the east, and a long point or headland, which extends as much as three leagues into the sound, in nearly a westerly direction. This, as well as I can judge from what I have seen of it, is in general from one to two miles in breadth, and mostly a rocky and unproductive soil, with but few trees. The eastern and western shores of this harbour are steep, and in many parts rocky, the trees growing quite to the water's edge, but the bottom to the north and northwest is a fine sandy beach of half a mile or more in extent.

From the village to the north and northeast extends a plain, the soil of which is very excellent, and with proper

Source: John R. Jewitt, *A Narrative of the Adventures and Sufferings of John R. Jewitt, only survivor of the Ship Boston, during a captivity of nearly three years among the savages of Nootka Sound; with an account of the manners, mode of living, and religious opinions of the natives.* (Edinburgh: Constable, 1824), pp. 65-79. Title supplied by editor.

cultivation may be made to produce almost any of our European vegetables; this is but little more than half a mile in breadth, and is terminated by the sea-coast, which in this place is lined with rocks and reefs, and cannot be approached by ships. The coast in the neighbourhood of Nootka is in general low, and but little broken into hills and valleys. The soil is good, well covered with fine forests of pine, spruce, beech, and other trees, and abounds with streams of the finest water, the general appearance being the same for many miles around.

The village is situated on the ground occupied by the Spaniards, when they kept a garrison here; the foundations of the church and the governor's house are yet visible, and a few European plants are still to be found, which continue to be self-propagated, such as onions, pease, and turnips, but the two last are quite small, particularly the turnips, which afforded us nothing but the tops for eating. Their former village stood on the same spot; but the Spaniards finding it a commodious situation, demolished the houses, and forced the inhabitants to retire five or six miles into the country. With great sorrow, as Maquina* told me, did they find themselves compelled to quit their ancient place of residence, but with equal joy did they repossess themselves of it when the Spanish garrison was expelled by the English.

The houses, as I have observed, are above twenty in number, built nearly in a line. These are of different sizes, according to the rank or quality of the *Tyee,* or chief, who lives in them, each having one, of which he is considered as the lord. They vary not much in width, being usually from thirty-six to forty feet wide, but are of very different lengths; that of the king, which is much the longest, being about one hundred and fifty feet, while the smallest, which contain only two families, do not exceed forty feet in length. The house of the king is also distinguished from the others by being higher.

Their method of building is as follows: They erect in the ground two very large posts, at such a distance apart, as is intended for the length of the house. On these, which are of equal height, and hollowed out at the upper end, they lay

* Having been taken prisoner, Jewitt became this chief's slave.–[ed.]

a large spar for the ridge-pole of the building, or if the length of the house requires it, two or more supporting their ends by similar upright posts; these spars are sometimes of an almost incredible size, having myself measured one in Maquina's house, which I found to be one hundred feet long, and eight feet four inches in circumference. At equal distances from these two posts, two others are placed on each side, to form the width of the building; these are rather shorter than the first, and on them are laid, in like manner, spars, but of a smaller size, having the upper part hewed flat, with a narrow ridge on the outer side to support the ends of the planks.

The roof is formed of pine planks, with a broad feather edge, so as to lap well over each other, which are laid lengthwise from the ridge-pole in the centre, to the beams at the sides, after which, the top is covered with planks of eight feet broad, which form a kind of coving projecting so far over the ends of the planks that form the roof, as completely to exclude the rain. On these they lay large stones to prevent their being displaced by the wind. The ends of the planks are not secured to the beams on which they are laid by any fastening, so that in a high storm, I have often known all the men obliged to turn out and go upon the roof to prevent them from being blown off, carrying large stones and pieces of rock with them to secure the boards; always stripping themselves naked on these occasions, whatever may be the severity of the weather, to prevent their garments from being wet and muddied, as these storms are almost always accompanied with heavy rains. The sides of their houses are much more open and exposed to the weather; this proceeds from their not being so easily made close as the roof, being built with planks of about ten feet long and four or five wide, which they place between stancheons or small posts of the height of the roof; of these, there are four to each range of boards, two at each end, and so near each other, as to leave space enough for admitting a plank. The planks or boards which they make use of for building their houses, and for other uses, they procure of different lengths, as occasion requires, by splitting them out, with hard wooden wedges, from pine logs, and afterwards dubbing them down

with their chisels, with much patience, to the thickness wanted, rendering them quite smooth.

There is but one entrance; this is placed usually at the end, though sometimes in the middle, as was that of Maquina's. Through the middle of the building, from one end to the other, runs a passage of about eight or nine feet broad, on each side of which, the several families that occupy it live, each having its particular fire-place, but without any kind of wall or separation to mark their respective limits; the chief having his apartment at the upper end, and the next in rank, opposite on the other side. They have no other floor than the ground; the fire-place, or hearth, consists of a number of stones loosely put together; but they are wholly without a chimney, nor is there any opening left in the roof, but whenever a fire is made, the plank immediately over it is thrust aside, by means of a pole, to give vent to the smoke. The height of the houses in general, from the ground to the centre of the roof, does not exceed ten feet; that of Maquina's was not far from fourteen; the spar forming the ridge-pole of the latter was painted in red and black circles alternately, by way of ornament, and the large posts that supported it had their tops curiously wrought or carved, so as to represent human heads, of a monstrous size, which were painted in their manner. These were not, however, considered as objects of adoration, but merely as ornaments.

The furniture of these people is very simple, and consists only of boxes, in which they put their clothes, furs, and such things as they hold most valuable; tubs for keeping their provisions of spawn and blubber in; trays from which they eat; baskets for their dried fish and other purposes, and bags made of bark matting, of which they also make their beds, spreading a piece of it upon the ground when they lie down, and using no other bed-covering than their garments. The boxes are of pine, with a top that shuts over, and instead of nails or pegs, are fastened with flexible twigs; they are extremely smooth and high polished, and sometimes ornamented with rows of very small white shells. The tubs are of a square form, secured in the like manner, and of various sizes, some being extremely large, having seen them that were six feet long by four broad and five deep. The trays

are hollowed out with their chisels from a solid block of wood, and the baskets and mats are made from the bark of trees.

From bark they likewise make the cloth for their garments, in the following manner: A quantity of this bark is taken and put into fresh water, where it is kept for a fortnight, to give it time to completely soften; it is then taken out and beaten upon a plank, with an instrument made of bone, or some very hard wood, having grooves or hollows on one side of it, care being taken to keep the mass constantly moistened with water, in order to separate, with more ease, the hard and woody from the soft and fibrous parts, which, when completed, they parcel out into skeins, like thread. These they lay in the air to bleach, and afterwards dye them black or red, as suits their fancies, their natural colour being a pale yellow. In order to form the cloth, the women, by whom the whole of this process is performed, take a certain number of these skeins, and twist them together, by rolling them with their hands upon their knees into hard rolls, which are afterwards connected by means of a strong thread, made for the purpose.

Their dress usually consists of but a single garment, which is a loose cloak or mantle (called *Kutsack*) in one piece, reaching nearly to the feet. This is tied loosely over the right or left shoulder, so as to leave the arms at full liberty.

Those of the common people are painted red with ochre, the better to keep out the rain, but the chiefs wear them of their native colour, which is a pale yellow, ornamenting them with borders of the sea-otter skin, a kind of grey cloth, made of the hair of some animal which they procure from the tribes to the south, or their own cloth wrought or painted with various figures in red or black, representing men's heads, the sun and the moon, fish and animals, which are frequently executed with much skill. They have also a girdle of the same kind, for securing this mantle, or *Kutsack*, around them, which is in general still more highly ornamented, and serves them to wear their daggers and knives in. In winter, however, they sometimes make use of an additional garment, which is a kind of hood, with a hole in it for the purpose of admitting the head, and falls over the

breast and back, as low as the shoulders; this is bordered both at top and bottom with fur, and is never worn, except when they go out.

The garments of the women vary not essentially from those of the men, the mantle having holes in it for the purpose of admitting the arms, and being tied close under the chin, instead of over the shoulder. The chiefs have also mantles of the sea-otter skin, but these are only put on upon extraordinary occasions; and one that is made from the skin of a certain large animal, which is brought from the south by the Wickanninish and Kla-iz-zarts. This they prepare by dressing it in warm water, scraping off the hair and what flesh adheres to it carefully with sharp muscle-shells, and spreading it out in the sun to dry, on a wooden frame, so as to preserve the shape. When dressed in this manner, it becomes perfectly white, and as pliable as the best deer's leather, but almost as thick again. They then paint it in different figures, with such paints as they usually employ in decorating their persons: these figures mostly represent human heads, canoes employed in catching whales, &c.

This skin is called Metamelth, and is probably got from an animal of the mouse kind; it is highly prized by these people, is their great war dress, and only worn when they wish to make the best possible display of themselves. Strips or bands of it, painted as above, are also sometimes used by them for girdles or the bordering of their cloaks, and also for bracelets and ankle ornaments by some of the inferior class.

On their heads, when they go out upon any excursion, particularly whaling or fishing, they wear a kind of cap or bonnet in form not unlike a large sugar loaf with the top cut off. This is made of the same materials with their cloth, but is in general of a closer texture, and, by way of tassel, has a long strip of the skin of the metamelth attached to it, covered with rows of small white shells or beads. Those worn by the common people are painted entirely red, the chiefs having theirs of different colours. The one worn by the king, and which serves to designate him from all the others, is longer and broader at the bottom; the top, instead of being flat, having upon it an ornament in the figure of a

small urn. It is also of a much finer texture than the others, and plaited or wrought, in black and white stripes, with the representation in front of a canoe in pursuit of a whale, with the harpooner standing in the prow prepared to strike. This bonnet is called *Seeya-poks*.

Their mode of living is very simple – their food consisting almost wholly of fish, or fish spawn fresh or dried, the blubber of the whale, seal, or sea-cow, muscles, clams, and berries of various kinds; all of which are eaten with a profusion of train-oil for sauce, not excepting even the most delicate fruit, as strawberries and raspberries. With so little variety in their food, no great secret can be expected in their cookery. Of this, indeed, they may be said to know but two methods, *viz.* by boiling and steaming, and even the latter is not very frequently practised by them. Their mode of boiling is as follows: Into one of their tubs they pour water sufficient to cook the quantity of provision wanted. A number of heated stones are then put in to make it boil, when the salmon or other fish are put in without any other preparation than sometimes cutting off the heads, tails, and fins, the boiling, in the meantime, being kept up by the application of the hot stones, after which it is left to cook until the whole is nearly reduced to one mass. It is then taken out and distributed in the trays. In a similar manner they cook their blubber and spawn, smoked or dried fish, and, in fine, almost everything they eat, nothing going down with them like broth.

When they cook their fish by steam, which are usually the heads, tails, and fins of the salmon, cod, and halibut, a large fire is kindled, upon which they place a bed of stones, which, when the wood is burnt down, becomes perfectly heated. Layers of green leaves, or pine boughs, are then placed upon the stones, and the fish, clams, &c. being laid upon them, water is poured over them, and the whole closely covered with mats, to keep them in the steam. This is much the best mode of cooking, and clams and muscles done in this manner are really excellent. These, as I have said, may be considered as their only kinds of cookery; though I have, in a very few instances, known them dress the roe, or spawn of the salmon, and the herring, when first taken, in a different

manner; this was by roasting them, the former being supported between two split pieces of pine, and the other having a sharp stick run through it, with one end fixed in the ground. Sprats are also roasted by them in this way, a number being spitted upon one stick; and this kind of food, with a little salt, would be found no contemptible eating even to an European.

At their meals, they seat themselves upon the ground, with their feet curled up under them, around their trays, which are generally about three feet long by one broad, and from six to eight inches deep. In eating, they make use of nothing but their fingers, except for the soup or oil, which they lade out with clam-shells. Around one of these trays, from four to six persons will seat themselves, constantly dipping in their fingers, or clam-shells, one after the other. The king and chiefs alone have separate trays, from which no one is permitted to eat with them, except the queen, or principal wife of the chief, and whenever the king, or one of the chiefs, wishes to distinguish any of his people with a special mark of favour on these occasions, he calls him, and gives him some of the choice bits from his tray. The slaves eat at the same time, and of the same provisions, faring, in this respect, as well as their masters, being seated with the family, and only feeding from separate trays.

Whenever a feast is given by the king, or any of the chiefs, there is a person who acts as a master of ceremonies, and whose business it is to receive the guests as they enter the house, and point out to them their respective seats, which is regulated with great punctiliousness as regards rank; the king occupying the highest, or the seat of honour, his son or brother sitting next him, and so on with the chiefs according to their quality; the private persons belonging to the same family being always placed together, to prevent any confusion. The women are seldom invited to their feasts, and only at those times when a general invitation is given to the village.

As, whenever they cook, they always calculate to have an abundance for all the guests, a profusion in this respect being considered as the highest luxury, much more is usually set before them than they can eat. That which is left in the

king's tray he sends to his house for his family, by one of his slaves, as do the chiefs theirs, while those who eat from the same tray, and who generally belong to the same family, take it home as common stock, or each one receives his portion, which is distributed on the spot. This custom appeared very singular to my companion and myself; and it was a most awkward thing for us, at first, to have to lug home with us, in our hands or arms, the blubber or fish that we received at these times; but we soon became reconciled to it, and were very glad of an opportunity to do it.

Boatmanship

GILBERT MALCOLM SPROAT

Canoes are made on this coast principally of cedar, and are well shaped, and managed with great skill by men, women, and children. They are moved by a single sail or by paddles, or in ascending shallow rapid streams, by long poles. I have seen an Indian boy with a single pole make good way with a small laden canoe against a stream that ran at the rate of six miles an hour. Canoes are of all sizes, but of a uniform general shape, from the war-canoe of forty feet long to the small dug-out in which children of four years old amuse themselves. Outriggers are not used, but the natives sometimes tie bladders or seal-skin buoys to the sides of a canoe to prevent it from upsetting in heavy weather. The sail – of which it is supposed, but rather vaguely, that they got the idea from Meares some eighty years ago – is a square mat tied at the top to a small stick or yard crossing a mast placed close to the bow. It is only useful in running before the wind in smooth water. The management of a canoe by natives in a heavy sea is dexterous; they seem to accommodate themselves readily to every motion of their conveyance, and if an angry breaker threatens to roll over the canoe, they weaken its effect quickly by a horizontal cut with their paddles through the upper part of the breaker when it is within a foot of the gunwale. Their mode of landing on a beach through a surf shows skill and coolness. Approaching warily, the steersman of the canoe decides when to dash for the shore; sometimes quickly countermanding the movement, by strenuous exertion the canoe is paddled back. Twenty minutes may thus pass while

Source: Gilbert Malcolm Sproat, *Scenes and Studies of Savage Life* (London: Smith, Elder and Co., 1868), pp. 82-87. Title supplied by editor.

another chance is awaited. At length the time comes; the men give a strong stroke and rise to their feet as the canoe darts over the first roller; now there is no returning: the second roller is just passed when the bow-paddler leaps out and pulls the canoe through the broken water; but it is a question of moments: yet few accidents happen. The paddles used by the Ahts [Nootka] are from four to five feet long, and are made of crab-apple or yew. Two kinds are used; the blade of one is shaped like a leaf, and the other tapers to a sharp point. The sharp-pointed paddle is suitable for steering, as it is easily turned under water. It was formerly used as a weapon in canoe-fighting for putting out the eye – a disfigurement which many of the old Aht natives show. In taking a seat in a canoe, the paddler drops on his knees at the bottom, then turns his toes in, and sits down as it were on his heels. The paddle is grasped both in the middle and at the handle. To give a stroke and propel the canoe forward, the hand grasping the middle of the paddle draws the blade of the paddle backwards through the water, and the hand grasping the handle pushes the handle-end forward, and thus aids the other hand in making each stroke of the paddle: a sort of double-action movement. As a relief, the paddler occasionally shifts to the handle the hand grasping the middle of the paddle, and *vice versa*. Such a position looks awkward, but two natives can easily paddle a middle-sized canoe forty miles on a summer day. The Strait of Juan de Fuca is about fifteen miles wide, and trading canoes often cross during the summer season to the American shore. The Indians paddle best with a little wind ahead; when it is quite calm, they often stop to talk or look at objects in the water. It is useless to hurry them: they do quite as they please, and will sulk if you are too hard upon them. In a small canoe, when manned by two paddlers, one sits in the stern and the other in the bow. The middle is the seat of honour for persons of distinction. An Indian sitting in the stern can propel and steer a canoe with a single paddle. In crowded war-canoes the natives sit two abreast. No regular time is kept in the stroke of the paddles unless on grand occasions, when the canoes are formed in order, and all the paddles enter the water at once and are worked with regularity. The most skilful canoe-

makers among the tribes are the Nitinahts and the Klah-oh-quahts. They make canoes for sale to other tribes. Many of these canoes are of the most accurate workmanship and perfect design – so much so that I have heard persons fond of such speculations say that the Indians must have acquired the art of making these beautiful vessels in some earlier civilized existence. But it is easy to see now, among the canoes owned by any tribe, nearly all the degrees of progress in skilful workmanship, from the rough tree to the well-formed canoe. Vancouver Island and the immediately opposite coast of the mainland of British Columbia have always supplied the numerous tribes to the northward with canoes. The native artificers in these localities have in the cedar (*Thuja gigantea*) a wood which does not flourish so extensively to the north, and which is very suitable for their purpose, as it is of large growth, durable, and easily worked. Savages progress so slowly in the arts, that the absence of such a wood as cedar, and the necessity of fashioning canoes with imperfect implements from a hard wood like oak, as the ancient people of Scotland did, might make a difference of many centuries in reaching a stated degree of skill in their construction.

The time for making canoes in the rough is during the cold weather in winter, and they are finished when the days lengthen and become warmer. Few natives are without canoes of some sort, which have been made by themselves, or been worked for, or obtained by barter. The condition of the canoe, like an Englishman's equipage, generally shows the circumstances of the possessor. Selecting a good tree not far from the water, the Indian cuts it down laboriously with an axe, makes it of the required length, then splitting the trunk with wedges into two pieces, he chooses the best piece for his intended canoe. If it is winter, the bark is stripped and the block of wood is dragged to the encampment; but in summer it is hollowed out, though not finished, in the forest. English or American tools can now be easily procured by the natives. The axe used formerly in felling the largest tree – which they did without the use of fire – was made of elkhorn, and was shaped like a chisel. The natives held it as we use a chisel, and struck the handle with a stone, not

unlike a dumb-bell, and weighing about two pounds. This chisel-shaped axe, as well as large wooden wedges, was also used in hollowing the canoe. The other instruments used in canoe-making were the gimlet and hand-adze, both of which indeed are still generally used. The hand-adze is a large mussel-shell strapped firmly to a wooden handle. The natural shape of the shell quite fits it for use as a tool. In working with the hand-adze, the back of the workman's hand is turned downward, and the blow struck lightly towards the holder, whose thumb is pressed into a space cut to receive it. The surface of the canoe, marked by the regular chipping of the hand-adze, is prettier than if it were smooth. The gimlet, made of bird's bone, and having a wooden handle, is not used like ours: the shaft is placed between the workman's open hands brought close together, and moved briskly backwards and forwards as on hearing good news; in which manner, by the revolution of the gimlet, a hole is quickly bored. Thus, also, did the natives formerly produce fire, by rubbing two dry cedar sticks in the same way. A few slits, opening on one side, were made in a dry flat stick, and on the end of the rubbing stick being inserted into one of these, and twirled round quickly between the palms, a round hole was made, at the bottom of which ignition took place among the wood dust. When the wood was in bad order for lighting, two or three natives were sometimes employed successively in the work, before fire was obtained. The making of a canoe takes less time than has been supposed. With the assistance of another native in felling and splitting the tree, a good workman can roughly finish a canoe of fifteen or twenty feet long in about three weeks. Fire is not much used here in the hollowing of canoes, but the outside is always scorched to prevent sun-rents and damage from insects. After the sides are of the required thinness, the rough trunk is filled with fresh water, which is heated by hot stones being thrown into it, and the canoe, thus softened by the heat, is, by means of cross-pieces of wood, made into a shape which, on cooling, it retains. The fashioning is done entirely by the eye, and is surprisingly exact. In nine cases out of ten, a line drawn from the middle of the extremities will leave, as nearly as possible, the same width all along on each side of the line.

To keep the canoe in shape, light cross-pieces fastened to the inside of the gunwales are placed about four feet apart, and there remain. The gunwale is turned outwards a little to throw off the water. The bow and stern pieces are made separately, and are always of one form, though the body of the canoe varies a little in shape according to the capabilities of the tree and the fancy or skill of the maker. Red is the favourite colour for the inside of a canoe, and is made by a mixture of resin, oil, and urine; the outside is as black as oil and burnt wood will make it; the bow and stern generally bear some device in red. The natural colour of the wood is, however, often allowed to remain. The baling-dish of the canoes is always of one shape – the shape of the gable-roof of a cottage – and is well suited to its purpose.

Nootka Whaling

PHILIP DRUCKER

That the prestige value of whaling outweighed its economic importance is clear from modern accounts, and substantiated by Jewitt's interesting journal. It was only the great whalers of ancient traditional times who killed ten whales a season. Recent whalers, though they hunted diligently and had improved equipment, got but few in their entire careers.

The informant áLiyū was one of the last of the Ahousat whalers. In his generation, he averred, there were eight Ahousat men who went whaling; only he and one other, a classificatory cousin of his, called Ahousat Amos, were successful. áLiyū killed three whales in his career; he lost several that escaped after he had struck them, owing to defects in the gear or, in his opinion, to laxness of certain of his crews in observing the ritual preparation. Amos got one, and the others killed none at all. In the preceding generation there had been three whalers: the informant's father's elder brother, who killed 13 whales over a period of 12 years (the informant's father assisted this man, captaining the second crew); Amos' father, who killed 3; and another man, who also killed 3. Before these men began whaling, the art had been neglected for several generations by the Ahousat.

The procedure, both practical and ritual, had been kept alive in the families of the chiefs, being passed down by word of mouth, áLiyū averred.

Jewitt gives a good deal of information on "Maquina's"

Source: Philip Drucker, *The Northern and Central Nootkan Tribes* (Washington, D.C.: Bureau of American Ethnology, 1951), Bulletin 144, pp. 49-53. Reprinted by permission of the publisher. Title supplied by editor.

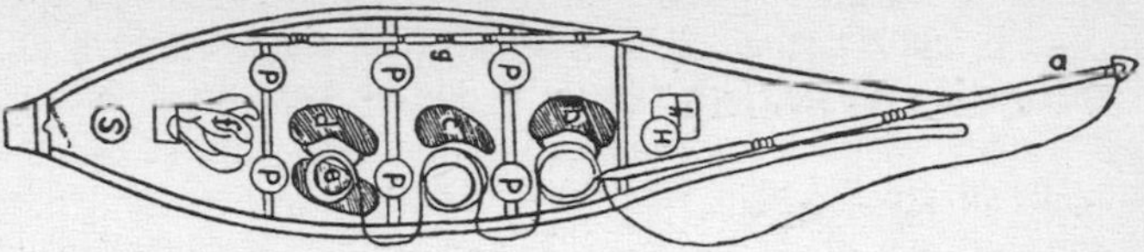

Crew stations and stowage of gear for whale hunt. *H*, harpooner; *P*, paddlers; *S*, steersman. *a*, Rigged harpoon; *b*, first float and small coil of line; *c*, second float and large coil of line (laid on top of line basket (la'ac)); *d*, third float and large coil, on top of *e*; *e*, fourth float (on mats on top of food and gear boxes); *f*, spare floats, deflated, water buckets; *g*, spare harpoon shaft, lance, spade; *h*, whaler's tackle boxes, etc.

hunting, mainly because it affected his lot considerably: after a long period of bad luck the chief would be "very cross" and his white slaves' lot was harder than usual. During the one partial and two complete whaling seasons that Jewitt reports on (1803, 1804, and 1805), the chief devoted himself energetically to the hunt, but the box score is not impressive. It reads: Days hunted, 53; struck and lost, 8; killed, 1. Four more whales were killed by Moachat chiefs during the same time, presumably after the investment of a similar amount of time and effort[1]. Clearly the economic reward in proportion to the expenditure of time and energy was slight.

The clearest account of the mode of stowing gear in the whaling canoe was that given by ȧLiyū. According to him, the eight members of the crew and the equipment were arranged in the following manner. (See illustration on this page.) The harpooner (ō'ōtah) stood in the bow, his harpoon lying to his right, point forward over the prow. The head was set firmly and the lanyard was caught to the shaft by means of a yellow cedar-bark string (maLhsum). The first float lay behind him in the first compartment, close at the feet of the first paddler (tcimi-

[1] Jewitt, John R. *A Journal kept at Nootka Sound by John R. Jewitt, one of the survivors of the crew of the ship Boston during a captivity among the Indians from March, 1803 to July 1805.* Reprinted from the original edition, Boston, 1807. With an introduction and a check list of later accounts of Jewitt's captivity by Norman L. Dodge. (Boston: C. E. Goodspeed and Co., 1931).

tsȧqs), whose duty it was to throw it overboard as the harpooner made his strike. The line ran over the thwart on the right of the first paddler, the first section being coiled on a mat on top of the large basket in the compartment behind him. From this coil the line ran over the thwart to the right of the third paddler (tsisiłhsi). His specific task was to thrust his paddle under the line to aid it as it ran out. The second section of the line was coiled behind him on top of mats laid over boxes of food and water. The fifth paddler (ū'ūhs) had to see that this part of the line paid out smoothly. The second paddler (qatsȧqs) had to paddle with a deep hard stroke to steady the canoe, the fourth and sixth (both called ʟitcciłsī) backed water to turn the canoe to port as soon as the strike was made. The steersman (ʟītca) made a hard stroke with an outward thrust to turn the canoe. The arrangement of gear depends on the fact that the whale was to starboard when struck, and the canoe sheered off sharply to port so that the line paid over the starboard side.

When everything was in readiness, and the ritual preparation had been completed, the chief (for it was invariably a chief who owned the gear and acted as harpooner) announced the fact to his crew. The gear was stowed and the canoe launched. A whaling canoe was never dragged down the beach, it was carried down to the water. One or more similarly fitted and manned vessels went along to assist in the hunt; often they were captained by younger kinsmen of the head whaler. The latter, however, was always highest in rank, and it was his prerogative to strike first. Usually a party of two or three in a swift sealing canoe accompanied the chief to carry the news to the village when the whale was struck. The expedition set out before sunset to the whaling grounds. There were some differences in procedure depending on the kind of whale sought: ma'ak were usually found closer inshore than the humpbacks; for the former the canoes sometimes stood by not far from the village beach. On arriving at the grounds the gear was checked, and the floats blown up. At dawn the hunt began. The canoes separated in order to cover a wider area. On sighting a whale one of the crew signaled to the other canoes by waving his paddle overhead. All hands set to paddling hard

but noiselessly, except the harpooner, who laid his paddle in the water and took his position for striking. The fifth paddler recovered the paddle. The harpooner stood with his right foot on the forward thwart, his left on the gunwale close to the prow piece. He held the harpoon ready, his right hand palm down, his left farther up the shaft, palm upward. The lanyard lay to his right. Poised and tense, he stood waiting for the whale to come up again so that the canoe could dart in close for the strike. If the cetacean was first sighted at some distance, the canoeman made for the place where they expected him to come up. If luck was on their side, the animal came up nearby. Sometimes it took a long time to close up on the quarry. A whale feeding undisturbed comes up to blow, submerges slowly and lazily and emerges to blow again, repeating the process "usually four times," informants say. Then he sounds and is gone for a long while.

When the whale was finally overtaken, the crew sought to bring the harpooner alongside at just the proper moment, coming up along the whale's left side from the rear outside the creature's field of vision. It was necessary to come very close, for the harpoon was thrust, being too heavy to throw. The trick was in laying alongside just as the whale was submerging, his flukes well under water. If the strike was made prematurely, that is, while the whale was still rising, the canoe was likely to be stove in as the creature thrashed about with his "tail." Coolness and good timing were indispensable at this critical moment. The success of the harpooner depended to a great extent on the skill of his crew, particularly that of his steersman. A whale swims by moving his flukes pendulum fashion. The strike had to be made when the flukes were to port (to the canoe) so that they would be thrust away from the canoe. From his post, the harpooner could not see the "tail"; it was the steersman's duty to watch its position and give the signal for the thrust. He gave a sharp exclamation, and, to make doubly sure, the first paddler touched the harpooner on the leg with the tip of his paddle. Aiming at the side, just behind the flipper, the hunter lunged with all his strength. Were he experienced, he would give the line a quick jerk to break the cedar strands and free

the shaft, but this was not essential, for the shaft would come loose of itself in a short time, owing to its weight and the whale's struggles. After the strike, the harpooner dropped into the compartment before the forward thwart, crouching there until the danger of being hit by or caught in the line was past. The crew swung the canoe sharply to port to get in the clear and let the line pay out. Owing to its stiffness, it usually ran smoothly, having little tendency to kink or foul. The moments from the strike until the line was out were the most dangerous ones; anything might happen. The least the crew could expect was a wetting as the wounded creature thrashed about. Had one of them been careless about his preparatory ritual, the canoe would be capsized or even struck by the whale and smashed, or a man might be caught in a loop in the line and dragged out to his death.

The initial struggles of a wounded whale are said to be most violent. Informants tell of having seen whales jump almost out of the water "like a salmon" trying to shake off the stinging harpoon. After his titanic rushes the animal usually sounded for a long time. The harpooner went back amidships where he sat resting; the first, third, and fourth paddlers blew up more floats and laid the second line; the rest of the crew paddled after the quarry, whose progress was marked by the fourth float, which was never drawn under water. The harpoon shaft was recovered, usually to be sent ashore by an assistant's canoe to notify the people a whale had been struck, although some men used the same shaft for the second harpoon. There may have been various individual usages, depending on the whaler's ritual. The second harpoon line was shorter than the first. The aide in the second canoe came up to plant his harpoons when the whale reappeared. Impeded by the weight of the lines and floats, worn by his desperate struggles, and seriously wounded, the whale began to weaken. The whalers recovered the ends of their lines, to attach the droguelike line basket, or held them to make their prey tow the canoe. As he dived less deeply each time, and stayed on the surface longer, a canoe would run in close to bend on additional floats.

Sometimes a whale ran far out to sea. This was usually taken to mean that the whaler had been careless in his

ceremonial preparations. Songs and prayers were resorted to, to make the creature turn back landward. A Hesquiat informant maintained that when the whale was quite weak the supernatural power of songs and prayers might be supplemented by going in front of the animal, shouting and splashing water and even poking it in the head with a lance to turn it. It would not be killed while it was far out at sea unless there seemed to be no chance of turning it. The harpoon wounds were seldom immediately fatal; the killing was done with a lance. When the time came for the kill, the first paddler took the lance with the broad, flat blade to cut the main tendons controlling the flukes, so that they dropped down useless. When the whale had been thus hamstrung, the same man drove the other lance in under the flipper. The great animal rolled and spouted blood, then died.

It was necessary to tie the whale's mouth shut as soon as it died to prevent the carcass from filling with water and sinking. One of the crew – the task was not assigned to any particular member – dived and cut one hole through the whale's mandible behind the bone and another through the upper lip, through which a rope was passed binding the two together. Often one or two floats were attached to this loop to help support the head, and other floats were brought up close around the carcass to make it ride high in the water. The main tow line was fastened to the loop through the jaw. The end was brought lengthwise under the canoe, being brought up and tied to the forward thwart on the starboard side, with a short guide or "preventer" over the port side at the stern. This tow was less likely to capsize the canoe, especially if the whale should sink.

PART TWO

SOCIAL ORGANIZATION

The Social Organization of the West Coast Tribes

EDWARD SAPIR

The social groupings that prevail among the West Coast Indians may be classified under four heads: groupings according to rank, groupings based on kinship, local groupings, and ceremonial or ritualistic groupings. The last of these may hardly be considered as coming within the scope of social organization; but among certain of the West Coast tribes, more particularly the Kwakiutl, they have become so intimately connected with the social structure that it is difficult to exclude entirely a reference to ceremonial groups. These four types of social units naturally intercross in a great many different ways, so much so that it becomes no easy matter to present a thoroughly intelligible picture of the social structure of a typical West Coast tribe.

Before examining each of these types of organization somewhat more closely, it will be well to acquaint ourselves briefly with the distribution of the tribes we are considering. The northernmost of the tribes generally included under the term of West Coast Indians, are the Tlingit, who occupy the long strip of coast forming the panhandle of southern Alaska. They are subdivided into a large number of distinct tribes, among the better known of which are the Yakutat,

---

Source: *Proceedings and Transactions of the Royal Society of* Canada, Section 2, Series 3, Vol. 9 (Ottawa, 1915), pp. 355-374. Reprinted by permission of the publisher.

Chilcat, and Sitka Indians. These speak a number of mutually intelligible dialects forming a linguistic unit that is only very remotely related to certain other American languages. The Haida Indians occupy the Queen Charlotte Islands and part of the Prince of Wales archipelago north of these. These Indians formerly inhabited a large number of villages distributed along the coasts of the Islands; but are now almost entirely reduced to the two villages of Skidgate and Massett in the Queen Charlottes, and a number of villages in the Prince of Wales archipelago, occupied by the Kaigani. South of the Tlingit, on the mainland, are the Tsimshian, who inhabit the region of Nass and Skeena rivers. They are divided into three closely connected dialectic groups which form one of the isolated linguistic stocks of America, at least so far as is at present known. The Haida and Tlingit languages, on the other hand, can be shown to be distantly related. South of the Tsimshian are the Bella Coola, in many respects a peculiar tribe, that form an isolated offshoot of the great Salish family which has representatives as far south as Columbia river. The northwestern, northern, and northeastern shores of Vancouver Island and the mainland opposite are occupied by a large number of tribes that are closely connected linguistically and may be embraced under the general term of Kwakiutl, which term, however, applies strictly speaking only to the Indians of Fort Rupert in northern Vancouver Island. The more northern of the Kwakiutl tribes, such as the Bella Bella and Kitamat, offer a contrast in social organization to their southern neighbours, being more closely allied in several important respects to the linguistically unrelated Tsimshian. The western coast of Vancouver Island is inhabited by a number of tribes grouped together under the term Nootka. The Nootka language is genetically related to Kwakiutl, though only fairly distantly so. Finally, in the southeastern part of Vancouver Island and on the mainland opposite, there are a considerable number of linguistically quite divergent but related tribes making up the bulk of the Coast Salish, as far as they are represented in Canada. From our present point of view the Tlingit, Haida, Tsimshian, Bella Coola, and northern Kwakiutl, are to be grouped together in contrast to the southern Kwakiutl, Nootka, and

Coast Salish. The former of these may be considered as the more typical in regard to social organization. It is interesting to observe that the broad line of division runs through a linguistic group, an example of the failure of linguistic and cultural classifications to coincide such as we have numerous parallels of in America, and indeed all over the world.

All these tribes are characterized by a clear development of the idea of rank; indeed, it may be said that nowhere north of Mexico is the distinction between those of high and those of low birth so sharply drawn as in the West Coast tribes. Three classes of society may be recognized – the nobility, the commoners, and the slaves. It is not practicable to distinguish between chiefs and nobles, as has been done for instance by Hill-Tout for the Coast Salish, as the lesser chiefs or nobles grade right in continuously with the head chiefs. Intermarriages between nobles and commoners or slaves, and between commoners and slaves, were in theory quite impossible, and in earlier days could at best have been but rare. We learn here and there from their legends that individuals of low rank were sometimes raised to a higher rank by marriage into a chief's family; but the very point made in such case serves to emphasize the essential differences of rank. High rank is determined primarily by descent – whether in the male or female line depends on the tribe. A very important factor, furthermore, in determining rank is wealth, as illustrated more particularly by the distribution of great quantities of property at ceremonial feasts generally known as potlatches. It is not enough for one of high birth to rest in his hereditary glory. If he wishes to preserve the respect of his fellow tribesmen, he must at frequent intervals reassert his rank by displays of wealth, otherwise he incurs the risk of gradually losing the place that properly belongs to him on the score of inheritance. We read, indeed, of cases in which men of lower rank have by dint of reckless potlatching gained the ascendency over their betters, gradually displacing them in one or more of the privileges belonging to their rank. Among the West Coast Indians, as in Europe, there is, then, opportunity for the unsettling activities of the parvenu.

A necessary consequence of the division of the village

community into a number of large house-groups is that, associated with each chief, there is, besides the immediate members of his own family, a group of commoners and slaves, who form his retainers. The slaves are immediately subject to his authority and may be disposed of in any manner that he sees fit. The commoners also, however, while possessing a much greater measure of independence, cannot be considered as unattached. Everything clustered about a number of house-groups headed by titled individuals, and in West Coast society, as in that of mediaeval feudalism, there was no place for the social free-lance. If the number of commoners and slaves connected with a chief's family grew too large for adequate housing under a single roof, one or more supplementary houses could be added on to the first; but they always remained under its sphere of influence. In this way we can understand how even a group of houses forming an outlying village might be inhabited entirely by people of low birth, who were directly subject to one or more chiefs occupying houses in the mother village. From this point of view the whole tribe divides into as many social groups as there are independent chiefs.

The rank of chief or noble is connected in most cases with a certain degree of personal power, but real communal authority is naturally vested in only the highest chief or chiefs of the village, and then not always as absolutely as we might be inclined to imagine. Even the highest chief is primarily always associated with a particular family and house, and if he exercises general authority, it is not so much because of his individual rank as such, as because the house-group that he represents is, for one reason or another, the highest in rank in the community. In legendary terms this might be expressed by saying that the other groups branched off from or attached themselves to that of the head chief.

Fully as characteristic of high rank as the exercise of authority is the use of a large variety of privileges. The subject of privileges among the West Coast Indians is an exceedingly complex one and cannot be adequately disposed of here. Privileges include not only practical rights of economic value, such as the exclusive or main right to a particular

fishing ground or the right to receive a certain part of a whale which has drifted on to the tribal shore; but also, and indeed more characteristically, many purely ceremonial or other non-material rights. It is these which form the most important outward expression of high rank, and their unlawful use by those not entitled to them was certain in every case to bring about violent friction and not infrequently actual bloodshed. One of the most important of these privileges is the right to use certain carvings or paintings, nearly always connected with the legendary history of the family which the chief represents. We shall have somewhat more to say of these crests later; here I wish to point out that from our present point of view the crests are but one of the many privileges that are associated with high rank. A further indication of such rank is the right to use certain names. The right to the use of any name is, properly speaking, determined by descent, and the names which have come to be looked upon as higher in rank than others naturally descend only to those that are of high birth. These names comprise not only such as are applied to individuals and of which a large number, some of higher, others of lower rank, are at the disposal of the nobleman; but also names that he has the exclusive right to apply to his slaves, to his house, very often to particular features of his house, such as carved posts and beams, and in some cases even names applied to movable objects such as canoes or particularly prized harpoon-heads or other implements. Further indicative of rank is the right to perform particular dances both in secular feasts or potlatches and, though perhaps to a somewhat less extent, also at ritualistic performances.

Perhaps the clearest outward manifestations of rank is in the place given a chief whenever it is necessary to arrange in some order the various participants in a public function. Thus, in a public feast or potlatch, those of high rank are seated in certain parts of the house that are preserved exclusively for the nobility. These are the rear of the house and the halves of the sides which are nearest the rear. These seats are graded as to rank, and it is perhaps not too much to surmise that the obvious grading made visible to the eye by a definite manner of seating at feasts was in a large

measure responsible for the extension of the idea of grading of ranks and privileges generally. The exact seat of honour differed somewhat with the different tribes. In some it was the centre of the rear; in others that seat on the right side of the house, as one faces the door, which was the nearest the corner. Other arrangements into series which could give a concrete idea of the ranking enjoyed by an individual are the order in which gifts are distributed to the chiefs at a potlatch; furthermore, the order in which they are called out when invited by a representative of another tribe to attend a feast which is to be given some time in the near future by the latter. The ranking orders thus arrived at by seating, distribution of gifts, invitations to feasts, and in various other ways that it is not necessary to enter upon here, might be expected to coincide. To a certain extent they do tend to approximate, and the highest in rank in a community will nearly always be found to head any such list that might be constructed. In practice, however, one finds that the various orders do not necessarily strictly correspond, in other words, that a person might individually be of lesser rank than another from the point of view of seating, but would have a prior claim to be invited, say. This curious state of affairs shows clearly enough that at last analysis rank is not a permanent status which is expressed in a number of absolutely fixed ways, but is rather the resultant standing attained by the inheritance of a considerable number of theoretically independent privileges which do, indeed, tend in most cases to be associated in certain ways, but may nevertheless be independently transmitted from generation to generation.

Nowhere in America is the idea of the grading of individuals carried to such an extent as among the West Coast Indians. It applies, however, only to the nobility, the commoners and the slaves not being differentiated among themselves with regard to rank. It has already been indicated how the ceremonial seating, for instance, of the nobility is expressive of their higher or lower status relatively to each other. In those tribes, like the Haida and Tlingit, that are subdivided into phratries and clans, a matter that we shall take up presently, this grading of chiefs represents some-

thing of a political or administrative basis, inasmuch as subsidiary to the town chief we have a number of clan heads. Subordinate to these, in turn, are the heads of the various house-groups. Here again, however, it is important to notice that the town chief is always at the same time the chief of the particular clan that is dominant in that village and that the clan chief is at the same time the head of the particular house-group that forms the nucleus of, or is the highest in rank in, the clan. In other words, ranking is not so much of a political or administrative character as it is determined by the handing down of status and privilege from holder to heir. It follows that the political organization, such as it is, impresses one as superimposed on the house-group or family organization by inner growth of the latter. So strong a hold has the idea of ranking taken upon the Indians that we find it operative even in cases where it would naturally not be expected to find application. Thus, it is often customary for a number of invited tribes as such, as represented of course by certain chiefs, to be assigned definite ceremonial seats and thereby by implication to be ranked relatively to each other – at times a somewhat risky proceeding. Furthermore, in some tribes it is even customary for medicine men to be organized on the basis of rank, such ranking not necessarily depending entirely on the individual supernatural powers displayed by the medicine men as on the fact that they are entitled by inheritance of medical lore to such and such honours.

As already indicated, the subject of privileges is a vast one, and a complete enumeration of all the economic, ceremonial, and other privileges of one high in rank would take a long time. To a certain extent a man has the right to split his inheritance, in other words, to hand down to one of his sons or nephews, as the case might be, certain privileges, to another certain others. Very often such a division is reductible to the association of privileges with definite localities, a point which is of primary importance in connection with the village community as the fundamental unit in West Coast organization. Thus, if one by the accidents of descent has inherited according to one line of descent a number of privileges associated with village A, in which he

is no longer resident, and a number of other privileges according to another line of descent originally associated with village B, in which he is resident, it would be a quite typical proceeding for him to bring up one of his heirs, say the one naturally highest in rank, to assume control of one set of privileges, a younger heir of the other. If the privileges originally connected with village B, let us say, tend to give one a higher place in the tribe than those connected with village A, the chances are that the first heir will be induced to take up his permanent residence in that village, while the transmitter may take the younger heir down to the more distant village and take up residence for a period in order to introduce his heir, as it were, to the privileges designed for him. In other words, there is a more or less definite tendency to connect honours with definite villages and, indeed, no matter how much rights of various sorts may become scattered by the division of inheritances, by the changes of residence due to intermarriage, and by other factors which tend to complicate their proper assignment, a West Coast Indian never forgets, at least in theory, where a particular privilege originated or with what tribe or clan a particular right, be it name, dance, carving, song, or what not, was in the first instance associated. In short, privileges are bound to the soil.

This brings us to what I believe to be one of the most fundamental ideas in the social structure of these Indians, that is, the idea of a definite patrimony of standing and associated rights which, if possible, should be kept intact or nearly so. Despite the emphasis placed on rank, I think it is clear that the individual as such is of very much less importance than the tradition that for the time being he happens to represent. The very fact that a man often bears the name of a remote ancestor, real or legendary, implies that the honours that he makes use of belong not so much to him individually as to his glorious ancestry, and there is no doubt that the shame of falling behind, in splendour and liberality, the standard set by a predecessor, does much to spur him on to ever greater efforts to increase his prestige and gain for himself new privileges. There is one interesting fact which clearly shows the importance of the family patri-

mony or of the standing of a particular line of descent as such, as distinct from the individual who happens to be its most honoured representative. This is the merging of various persons belonging to three or four generations into a single unit that need not be further differentiated. Among the Nootka Indians, for instance, an old man, his oldest son say, the oldest son of the son, and, finally, the infant child of the latter, say a daughter, form, to all intents and purposes, a single sociological personality. Titularly the highest rank is accorded, among the Nootka, to the little child, for it is always the last generation that in theory bears the highest honours. In practice, of course, the oldest members of the group get the real credit and do the business, as it were, of the inherited patrimony; but it would be difficult in such a case to say where the great-grandfather's privileges and standing are marked off against those of his son, or grandson, or great-granddaughter. In some cases even a younger son, who would ordinarily be considered as definitely lower in rank than his elder brother, might represent the standing of his father by the exercise of a privilege, say the singing of a particular song in a feast, that belongs to the patrimony of the family. "For men may come and men may go," says the line of descent with its distinctive privileges, "but I go on forever." This is the Indian theory as implied in their general attitude, though there is no doubt that tremendous changes have in many instances gradually evolved by the dying out of particular lines of descent and the taking over of their privileges by other groups only remotely perhaps connected with them by kin, by the introduction of a new privilege gained say as a dowry, and by numerous other factors. The best way to gain a concrete idea of such a structure of society is to think of the titled portion of the tribe as holding up a definite number, say fifteen or more, honoured names, or occupying that number of seats, that have descended from the remote past. The classification of the tribe according to kin intercrosses with that based on rank, as by it individuals are brought together who, from the latter point of view, would have to be kept apart. It is clear that not all the members of a large family group can inherit the standing and all the privileges that belong to it. There must be a large number,

particularly the younger sons and daughters and those decended from them, who are less favoured than their elders and who will inherit only some, probably the lesser, privileges. In the course of time, as their relationship to the heads of the family or clan becomes more and more remote, they must be expected to sink lower and lower in the general social scale, and there is no doubt that a large proportion of the commoners are to be considered as the unprivileged kinsmen of the nobles. This is no doubt the attitude of at least some of the Indian tribes, such as the Nootka, among whom such a notion of the relation between the classes of society as we find among the castes of India, say, is certainly not found. There is no doubt, however, that with the growth of power attained by the chiefs and with the increasing remoteness of the ties of kinship binding them with most of the commoners, the chasm between the two would gradually widen. The slaves must be left out of account in this connection. They do not enter into the genealogical framework of the tribe, but seem to a large extent to have been recruited from captives of war.

Indian legend, at least among the Nootka and Kwakiutl, generally conceives of the village community as having grown up out of the small family immediately connected in the remote past with a legendary ancestor. All the members of the village community are therefore looked upon as direct descendants of a common ancestor and must therefore, at least in theory, bear definite degrees of relationship to one another. Whether or not the members of a village are actually so connected is immaterial, the essential point being that even in those tribes where there is no clan organization properly so-called, there is, nevertheless, a distinct feeling of kinship among all or most of the members of each of its village communities. This is borne out by the fact that individuals are taught to address each other by certain terms of relationship, even where the appropriateness of such terms is not obvious to them. Thus, a man well advanced in years might call a little child his older brother, for the reason that they are respectively descended from ancestors who stood to each other in that relation. Naturally intermarriages would bring about intercrossings of all sorts, and in course of time

the more remote degrees of relationship would be forgotten and new ones, brought nearer home by more recent marriages, take their place.

Let us suppose that a village community is strictly homogeneous in structure, that is, contains no members that cannot count their descent in either the male or female line from the common ancestor. It is obvious that this state of affairs cannot last indefinitely. The accidents of war will doubtless bring it about that sooner or later some neighbouring village community, that has suffered considerably at the hands of an enemy and that finds itself subject to extermination at their hands will seek protection from the first village community and, in order to gain this end, will receive permission to take up residence in it. It is immediately apparent that the new enlarged village community, provided it is permanent, will have increased in complexity of structure. Their adherence to their respective traditions will be such that neither of the former village communities will give up its peculiar set of privileges, so that a twofold division of the community, as accentuated by these privileges, will persist. If we imagine this process to have occurred several times, we will gradually arrive at a community which is subdivided into several smaller units which we may call septs or bands, or perhaps even clans, each of which has its distinct stock of legendary traditions and privileges exercised by its titled representatives and whose former connection with a definite locality is still remembered. The growth of the village community does not need, of course, to have taken place only in this fashion. Many other factors may be at work. The group added to the original community may be the survivors of a conquered village who are given a subordinate place. Furthermore, a member of another tribe or community that has married into the community may, if he (or she) has sufficient prestige, be able to assert the higher rank that he (she) brings with him (her) and found a new line of descent which will take its place side by side with those already represented. We see, then, a number of ways in which the typical division of a tribe into clans, such as we find among the Haida, may be expected to originate. Such a clan, from the point of view of West Coast conditions,

may be defined as a group of kinsmen, real or supposed, who form one of the subdivisions of a village community and who inherit a common stock of traditions associated with a definite locality, the original home of the group.

Clans in this sense we have among the southern tribes that we have enumerated; but it is not until we reach the more northern tribes, such as the Tlingit, Haida, and Tsimshian, that the clan becomes a clearly defined and perfectly solidified unit. This is brought about primarily by the restriction of inheritance. Among the Nootka Indians, for instance, it is possible to inherit privileges in both the male and female lines, preference, where possible, being given to the former. This being the case, it is often hard to see exactly to which sept or clan a person properly belongs, and the decision is generally based on the character of the privileges that are transmitted to him, for, as we have seen, a privilege is always connected with a definite locality, sept, or original village community. In other words, a person steps into certain rights to which he has a claim by descent, and in the exercise of these becomes identified with the particular sept or clan with which they are associated. As the septs have their definite seating at feasts, it is easy to see how the identification of an individual with one sept rather than with another can be made visible. This will indicate also that there are certain natural limitations to the inheritance of all privileges that one has a theoretical claim to. This sort of clan division, however, for the reason that it is too ill-defined and vacillating, can hardly be considered as typical of what we ordinarily understand by clan organization. If, however, we once limit the inheritance of status and privileges to either the male or female line, to the absolute exclusion of the other, we obtain a series of septs or clans that are once and for all rigidly set off against each other. Among the more northern tribes, then, who inherit through the female line alone, there can never be the slightest doubt as to what clan a person is to be identified with.

Furthermore, among the more southern tribes intermarriage is prohibited only between such as are demonstrably related by blood, even if fairly remotely so. Owing to the structure of the village community, this would in many cases

mean that there are few persons in a village that one is legally entitled to marry; but it is important to note that the village community as such need not be exogamous, that is, does not specifically prohibit intermarriage among its members. The clan of the northern tribes, which is more rigidly defined by descent and which therefore gains in solidarity, is further accentuated by strict exogamy. Whether such exogamy is a primary feature of the clan itself or is only a necessary consequence of the exogamy of certain larger groups known as phratries, which we shall take up in a moment, is a question which I would not venture to decide and which need not occupy us here. We spoke before of the fact that the original village communities, before amalgamating, each had its peculiar privileges. Certain of these privileges, particularly the crest paintings and carvings, are emblematic of the communities and may be said to give the septs or clans a totemic character. Among the southern tribes, however, it would seem that the crests, which are generally animals or supernatural beings, are employed exclusively by the nobles and that a commoner, even though identified with a particular sept, cannot be said to be in any sense associated with the crest. To what extent the crests are characteristic of the clan generally in the north and to what extent they are more especially in the nature of privileges enjoyed by the nobles, has not been made perfectly clear. It would seem that certain crests, whose origin is particularly remote, have lost such individual value as they may have had and have become clan emblems properly speaking, whereas others are more restricted in their use and would seem to be the peculiar privilege of certain titled individuals or families.

We shall now briefly review the main facts of clan organization among the Tlingit, Haida, Tsimshian, and Kwakiutl, concerning whom our published information is fullest. The Tlingit are divided into two main divisions, known respectively as Ravens and Wolves, the latter being in some of the villages referred to also as Eagles. In at least one of the southern Tlingit tribes, the Sanya, there is a division which stands outside of the grouping into two phratries, and the members of which may intermarry with either the Ravens or the Wolves. The Ravens and Wolves are

respectively debarred from intermarriage within their own ranks. A Raven man must marry a Wolf woman, a Wolf man a Raven women, while the children of the pair belong to the phratry of the mother. It is important to bear in mind that this dual division of the Tlingit Indians is not associated with particular villages or even tribes, but applies to all the Tlingit tribes. A Raven, for instance, from Tongas, the southernmost Tlingit village, is as strictly debarred from marrying a Raven woman of Yakutat, in the extreme north, as a Raven woman of his own village. When we remember that he may never have been within miles of Yakutat and may know few or no Indians from that region, we see clearly that whether or not phratric exogamy is in origin an outgrowth of an interdict against marriage of those of close kin, an interdict which we find to be practically universal, it is certainly rather different from its psychologically. The leading crest or emblem of the Raven people is the raven, who is at the same time the most important mythological being in the beliefs of the Tlingit Indians. The main crest of the Wolf people is the wolf. The phratries stand to each other as opposites that do each other mutual services. Thus, the Wolves conduct the funeral ceremonies of the Ravens and, when they give a feast, distribute the property to the Ravens.

Each phratry is subdivided into a considerable number of clans, each with its own distinctive crest or crests, generally in addition to the general crest of the phratry to which it belongs. Unlike the two main phratries, the clans are not found in all the villages of the Tlingit, though many of them are found represented in more than one village. If we assume, as I believe to be the case, that the clans were originally nothing but village communities, it follows that the present distribution of clans is secondary and due to migrations or movements of part of the clansmen away from the main body of their kinsmen. Should a number of clansmen of the original clan village be induced for one reason or another to take up residence in another village, the home primarily of another clan, it is clear that they would, to begin with, be an intrusive element in their new home; but would in course of time be looked upon as forming an integral part of the village community, though of lesser importance than

the dominant clan. The legends of the Indians themselves clearly indicate that such whole or partial clan movements have frequently taken place. Many of the names of the clans themselves plainly indicate their local origin. Thus, the Kiksadi are a Raven clan that are found represented in several Tlingit tribes, such as the Sanya, the Stikine people, and the Sitka Indians. The name means nothing more than People-of-the-Island-Kiks and clearly implies that the clan was, to begin with, at home in a particular locality and gradually became distributed over a large area by various movements of population. The force of tradition would always be strong enough to keep up the old clan crests and other clan privileges, wherever the clansmen moved. In course of time the appearance is attained of a clan distribution which has nothing to do with local communities as such.

Very similar conditions prevail among the Haida Indians. Here again we have two main phratries, subdivided into a large number of clans. As among the Tlingit, the Haida phratries are exogamous and descent in them is reckoned through the female line. One of them is termed Raven, though curiously enough, the main crest of this phratry is not the raven but the killer-whale. The opposite phratry is termed Eagle, this animal being the chief crest of the phratry. Among the Haida, as among the Tlingit, the native legends indicate that the clans were originally confined to certain definite localities, but that in course of time the clansmen moved about in various ways until now, when they are represented in a number of villages. One concrete instance will serve to illustrate the actual state of affairs. In the town of Skidegate there were represented in earlier times three distinct Eagle clans, and three distinct Raven clans, each of these six clans occupying its own houses. Of the six clans the dominant one was an Eagle clan known as People-of-the-great-house, claiming as their crests the Raven (this in spite of the fact that they do not belong to the Raven phratry), a supernatural being known as *wāsgo*, the dog-fish, the weasel, the eagle, the sculpin, and the halibut. Presumably this clan formed the original nucleus of the present town of Skidegate about which the other clans in course of time clustered. The

Haida clan names are generally either local in character, like most of the Tlingit names, or of an honorific character, like the one that we have just quoted.

The Tsimshian are organized similarly to the Tlingit and Haida, except that their clans are grouped into four phratries: the Raven, Eagle, Wolf and Grizzly Bear.

Among the southern Kwakiutl also the single tribes are subdivided into a number of clans, each of which, there is reason to believe on legendary and other evidence, originally formed a separate village community. These have chiefly honorific titles, as "The-chiefs," "Those-who-receive-first," and "Having-a-great-name." Some of these names occur in more than one of the Kwakiutl tribes; but it seems more likely that these correspondences in name are due to imitations rather than to a genealogical connection between the clans of like name. The social structure of the Kwakiutl Indians differs from that of the Tlingit and Haida in that the clans are not grouped into phratries, and that they do not seem to be exogamous. As to descent, it seems that at least the most important privileges are regularly transmitted as a dowry to the son-in-law, who holds them in trust for his son. This method of inheritance has been explained as a peculiar Kwakiutl adaptation of an originally paternal system of inheritance to the maternal system in vogue among the more northern tribes, by whom the Kwakiutl were presumably influenced. There are, however, some difficulties in the way of this explanation, one of which is the fact that the Nootka Indians to the south are not organized on a purely paternal basis, but allow many privileges to descend through the female line. Among them also such privileges may be handed over as a dowry, though this system has not been standardized among them to the same extent as among the Kwakiutl.

There are two important peculiarities of the West Coast crests which make them contrast with the totems of such typical totemic communities as the Iroquois Indians of the east or the Pueblos of the southwest. Among these latter, who, like the Haida and Tlingit, are organized into exogamous clans of maternal descent, a clan has a single crest or totem after which it is named. Moreover, no other clan can use this totem. The West Coast clans differ in both these respects.

As we have already shown in the case of one of the Haida Eagle clans, a group of clansmen generally lay claim to more than one crest; further, only certain crests are confined to single clans, the more important ones being generally represented in several. Thus, the grizzly-bear is claimed as a crest by no less than twelve distinct Haida clans of the Raven phratry, the rainbow by eight, the sea-lion by five, the beaver by twelve Eagle clans, the whale by seven, the humming-bird by three, and so on. In some cases a clan even makes use of a crest which primarily belongs to the opposite phratry. Evidently there is not the same intimate and clear-cut association between totem and clan, as such, that is typical of the Iroquois and Pueblo Indians.

It is probable that the duplication of crests is to be explained chiefly on the theory that many clans arose as subdivisions of other clans. Such a clan offshoot would keep the old crest or crests, but might in time add one or more to its stock, without sharing them with the mother clan. The clan can, indeed, be arranged in the form of a genealogical tree and the crests stratified. The older the crest, the greater number of times is it found in the various clans; on the other hand, a crest found in only one clan may be suspected to be of recent origin, as it probably does not antedate the severance of its clan from the older group originally including it.

Whatever may have been its origin, the crest seems to have become, to a large extent, a symbol of greatness, and it became the desire of the chiefs to add to their prestige by the acquisition of new crests. They were not only obtained by inheritance, but could be secured as gifts, or even by forcible means in war. The fact that the name of the clan does not as a rule refer to a totem also seems to indicate that the clan may not, to begin with, be organically connected with a particular crest. That the clansmen are not conceived of as descended from one of their crest animals, and that there seem to be no taboos in force against the eating or killing of the crest animals, need not matter, for these are by no means constant features of even typical totemic societies.

There is another feature of the crests of the West Coast Indians which accentuates their difference from typical clan

totems. This is the tendency they have to be thought of in very concrete terms, as carvings or paintings. It would in many cases, for instance, be more correct to say that a certain chief uses a ceremonial hat representing the Beaver, or that he has the right to paint the Thunder-bird on the outside of his house, than that he possesses the Beaver or Thunder-bird crest or totem. His justification for the use of these would be a legend, telling of how one of his ancestors gained the privilege by contact with the crest animals – a type of legend which is told to account for the use of nearly all crests. We see more clearly now why earlier in this paper I referred to crests as a particular type of an inheritable privilege. Incidentally, it is interesting to note that the Kwakiutl term for crest seems to denote primarily a carving.

Crests are shown or utilized in different ways. They may be painted on movable boards used as screens or otherwise, painted on the outside of the house or along the bed platform, carved on the house-posts or beams, or on memorial columns, or on the outside house-posts popularly known as totem poles, tattooed on the body, painted on the face during feasts, represented in dance-hats, masks, staffs, or other ceremonial paraphernalia, woven in ceremonial robes, referred to in clan legends, dramatically represented at potlatches in performances based on such legends, referred to in songs owned by the clan or clan-chiefs, and in individual or house names. Not all house names, however, refer to a crest. The village and clan names are also, as a rule, unconnected with crests. So accustomed have the West Coast Indians, particularly those of the north, become to the representation of crest animals in carving and painting, that they introduce them even in objects that are not as a rule connected with the exercise of privileges. Among such objects the beautifully ornamented dishes, boxes, batons, spoons, rattles, clubbers, and gambling-sticks that are so often admired in ethnological museums. We see how the elaboration of the crest system has fostered among these Indians the development of plastic art. It has also been suggested, and I believe with justice, that the tendency to artistic and dramatic representation in turn reacted upon the development of the crest system, a development that was

strengthened by the ever-present desire for new privileges and for novel ways of exhibiting the old ones.

The origin of the crests need not have been the same in all cases. In some cases, for instance, it can be shown that they were obtained by marriage or as gifts in return for a service. These new crests would of course be handed down along with the old inherited ones. Such methods of obtaining crests, however, must be considered as purely secondary, and the real problem of accounting for their origin still remains. The most plausible explanation that has been offered is, on the whole, that which considers the clan crest as an extension of the personal manitou or tutelary being. Among practically all Indians we find the practice of seeking supernatural protection or power by fasting and dreaming of certain animals or objects that are believed to be endowed with such power. If we suppose that a personal guardian thus obtained is handed down by inheritance, we can readily understand how the manitou of an ancestor may gradually become transformed into a clan totem or crest. The main difficulty with this theory is that personal guardians or medicines do not normally seem to be inheritable. On the other hand, the legends related by the West Coast Indians to account for the origin of crests do bear an unmistaken resemblance to tales of the acquisition of supernatural guardians. It is not difficult to understand how the religious element, which must have been strongly emphasized in the manitou, gradually faded away as the manitou developed (or degenerated) into a crest. At any rate, the problem is far from satisfactorily solved.

Even more fundamental than the clans are, among the northern tribes, the phratries which include them. Their origin also is far from clear. Whether they resulted from the amalgamation of a number of clans into larger units, or whether, on the contrary, the clans within the phratry are to be considered as local off-shoots from it, is often difficult to decide. On the whole, however, the latter alternative seems the more typical one. This is indicated, first of all, by the fact that each of the two main phratries is represented in every village, though, on the other hand, the necessary intermarriages between the phratries might

soon bring about this state of affairs under any circumstances. More important is the fact that the phratric crest is shared by all or practically all the clans of the phratry; this seems to imply that the phratry with its crest is a fundamental unit antedating the rise of the separate clans. The fundamental importance of the two phratric divisions of the Haida is beautifully illustrated by their belief in the validity of this social arrangement in the supernatural world. Thus, every being of the sea was conceived of as belonging from the beginning of time to either the Raven or Eagle phratry. It is conceivable that the phratries are sociologically reinterpreted forms of originally distinct tribal units. Apropos of this possibility, it may be noted that in many tribal organizations certain clans, gentes, camp-circle units, or other social units are, either in fact or origin, a group of aliens incorporated into the main tribe. According to Tlingit legend, indeed, the Ravens were originally Coast people, the Wolves inland people. This may, however, be a mere rationalization of an obvious fact of zoological distribution, the raven being common on the coast while the wolf is chiefly confined to the woods.

So much for social organization according to rank and kinship. The third type of organization, the local, we have had to take up in connection with the other two. Local classifications as distinct from kin classifications arise only when the clan ceases to be confined to a single locality. When this happens, the kin and local groupings necessarily intercross and town administration arises, which provides for more than the needs of a clan or group of kinsmen.

The ritual organization which we have listed as a fourth type of social organization is best developed among the Kwakiutl Indians. Among these Indians the clan system which is operative during the greater part of the year, the so-called profane season, gives place during the winter to a ritualistic organization based on the right to the performance of religious dances. The dancers impersonate various supernatural beings from whom they are supposed to have received manitou power. In actual practice the performance of the dance is conditioned by the inherited right to them. Such rights are justified in legends accounting for the intro-

duction of the dance by an ancestor, supposed to have come in contact with the supernatural being himself and to have been instructed by him. In a sense all those who perform the same dance form a secret society, though this term, which has been often used, does not seem particularly appropriate to me. The dances are graded into two series – a lower and a higher one. The dancers of the lower series are collectively known as Sparrows[1], those of the higher as Seals. One may pass in successive seasons from one so-called society to another, up to the point allowed by his or her particular inheritance. The most important of the dance-societies are the Ghosts, the Fool-dancers, the Grizzly-bears, and the Cannibals. While there are certain external resemblances between the ritual and clan organizations of the Kwakiutl, I believe it would be erroneous to consider the former as specialized forms of the latter. I consider it far more likely that the ritualistic activities were simply patterned on the normal clan organization, the ever-present tendency to ranking finding expression in both. The other tribes of this region have borrowed much of the Kwakiutl rituals, but do not seem to share their elaborate ritual organization.

The space at our disposal will not permit us to go more deeply into the intricacies of West Coast social organization. It is difficult to render clear in a few strokes what seems an essentially involved set of social phenomena and I am not at all certain that I have succeeded in my object. The main points that I have tried to bring out are the fundamental importance of inherited privileges as such, the growth of the village community into a clan, the peculiar character of the crest system of these Indians when compared with typical totemism elsewhere, and the almost exaggerated development of the idea of grading of individuals and privileges.

[1] Or some other small bird.

Social Organization of the Haida

JOHN R. SWANTON

According to an estimate made about the year 1840 the whole number of people speaking Haida (or Skittagetan) was upwards of eight thousand. This estimate undoubtedly included the slaves. About six thousand Haida were then upon the Queen Charlotte Islands and the remainder upon the southern extremity of Prince of Wales Island, Alaska. These latter now number about three hundred, distributed in three towns; the former six hundred in two towns. All together the Haida thus count in the neighbourhood of nine hundred souls, little more than one-tenth of their former strength. For such an astonishing decrease smallpox and immorality are mainly responsible.

At Masset, on the northern coast of the Queen Charlotte Islands, the dialect spoken is almost identical with that of the Alaskan Haida, but the language of Skidegate presents many striking differences and appears to represent the oldest form of speech.

Like the other coast tribes of British Columbia and Alaska the Haida lived in houses built of cedar planks and huge cedar beams. They varied in size from mere "shacks" to huge buildings accommodating a hundred people or more. The Tlingit and Tsimshian houses were constructed in practically the same way, but those further south varied considerably. These three peoples – Haida, Tlingit and Tsimshian – were, indeed, very closely related to each other, especially the two former.

Source: *Proceedings of the International Congress of Americanists*, 13th Session, New York, 1902. (Easton, Pa.: Eschenbach Printing Co., 1905), pp. 327-334.

The Haida and Tlingit were both divided into two sides or clans. Among the Tlingit they were called Raven and Wolf, or Raven and Eagle. Among the Haida they were the Raven and the Eagle, or, as it was also called, the Gît'î'ns, a word of uncertain meaning. These have sometimes been denominated phratries, but that term would be inapplicable in the sense in which it is generally used, because there are no clans to group under them. Each clan was strictly exogamic, a regulation which applied to none of the minor divisions, and children always belonged to the mother's side. According to some writers, the people throughout this region sometimes transferred a child to its father's clan by giving it to his sister to bring up, and such a custom may have been known to the Haida, but I did not hear of it. Chief's sons were, however, sometimes adopted by other chiefs of the same side as their own fathers.

The distinction between these two sides was most rigid. Theoretically they could not have the same personal, house, or canoe names, or wear the same crests, and only in a very few cases was this rule infringed. A man was initiated into the secret-society by his opposites, and, when he died, they conducted the funeral. In the grave-houses Ravens lay with Ravens, Eagles with Eagles only. Thus husband and wife were never buried together. So deep was the fission between husband and wife that the latter sometimes betrayed her husband into the hands of her own people when they were at war with his family. A man spoke of the members of his own clan as "friends," "uncles," or "brothers"; of those of the opposite clan as "opposites," "cousins," "uncles' children," or "brothers-" and "sisters-in-law."

The terms of relationship were, indeed, directly dependent on this division in the state, and here is the best place in which to speak of them. With us they are governed by three considerations, sex, relative age and nearness in blood.

Thus our own system is as follows:

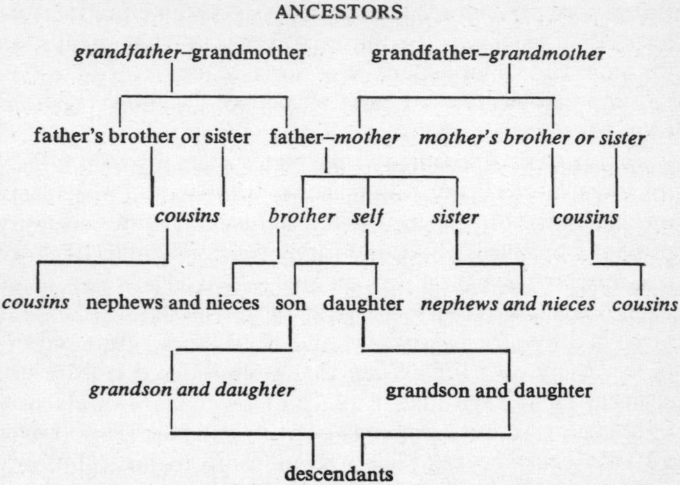

But terms of relationship, by their very name, are used to mark the relation in which those that bear them stand to self. And since to a Haida it is of the very greatest importance into which *clan* any man or woman falls, it is perfectly natural that the terms of relationship should be made to indicate that position. If, however, you should superpose this system upon the above a longer set of names would be required, and a very cumbersome system would result. Taking only the three generations of my parents, myself and my children, it would be necessary to add new names for my father's brother and my father's sister, for the children of my uncles on my mother's and my aunts on my father's side, and for the male and female children of my brothers. That is to say, there would be in those three generations at least fourteen different names instead of nine, to which would have to be added terms of relationship brought about by marriage and terms for more remote generations. It is hardly to be expected that tribes in the stage of culture of the Haida should develop such a lengthy system if an easier were possible.

In the above suppositious case I have maintained the

sacredness of the Aryan family, retaining separate names for father, mother, sister, brother, son, daughter, nephew, niece. But suppose the importance of one's immediate family were altogether secondary to the importance of that great clan division above indicated. We say that our closest blood relations should receive those terms, because their relations to us are the most important. With the Haida, however, that is not the case. According to the clan system my own father, my own mother, my father's own brother and sister, my mother's own brother and sister, my brother, my sister, my mother's brother's child, my father's sister's child, my own son, my own daughter, my own nephew and my own niece each belongs to a class, the relation of which towards me is governed by strict clan laws and is of the greatest importance in my own life. When that is considered it does not seem at all strange that in place of inventing entirely new ones each of these terms has been so extended as to cover all who bear the same clan relationship to me. Thus my fathers are all the men of the opposite clan of my father's generation, my mothers are all the women of my mother's clan and generation, my aunts all the women of my father's clan and generation, my uncles all the men of my mother's clan and generation. My brothers are all the men of my own clan and generation. They are further distinguished into elder and younger brothers. My sisters are all the women of my own clan and generation. My cousins male are all the men of the opposite clan and my generation. My cousins female are all the women of the opposite clan and my generation. All the men and women of the opposite clan and the generation succeeding mine are sons and daughters and all the men and women of my own clan and the following, nephews and nieces. Similarly in relationship through marriage there is one name for the men of the same clan and generation as my wife – or, more generally, for those of the same clan irrespective of age – and another for the women. I have not found, however, that the term for father-in-law or mother-in-law is applied to any one except the father and mother of one's own wife and husband, or the term son-in-law to any but the husband of one's own daughter. The terms for father-in-law and son-in-law are identical. The

terms of relationship used by a woman are almost identical with those for a man, involving a few obviously necessary changes and an independent term for father, the reason for the use of which I have not yet investigated.

At the same time it must not be assumed that the immediate relationships according to our own notions are not recognized or that there is the least doubt regarding them, any more than it can be assumed that *we* do not distinguish between the children of our uncles and aunts and more remote relations because we call them all cousins. In a Haida town every one is pretty well informed as to the exact relationship of everybody else in it, and it requires a very slight hint to let him know whether one is speaking of his own father or brother, or some one more remotely related. In the myths this difficulty is often met by telling about the hero's birth. Sometimes it is specified of brothers that "their father was one; their mother was one," or again it may not be thought of enough importance to specify the blood-relationship at all. As long as the relative clan standing is understood that is sufficient. Similarly in speaking to strangers who may not be supposed to be especially interested in their immediate family affairs, white people do not always take the trouble to specify whether they are talking about an own cousin, or about a second or third. I dwell upon this because I think too much importance has been laid upon the terms of relationship as used by such tribes as the Haida by some writers as proof of certain primitive conditions of the family, such as group-marriages. If such really existed, I do not think that Haida terms of relationship can be appealed to for any positive evidence. Indeed, the term uncle or aunt is often applied to one who lived centuries ago. It merely serves to mark that such and such a person did belong to such and such a clan. Not only so, but supernatural beings are called "father," if they are supposed to belong to the same clan as my own father; for it is a matter of peculiar interest that the supernatural beings are all supposed to be divided in the same way as are human beings. (Danger of identifying Haida kin as relationship with those to which they most nearly correspond among white people.)

In spite of the important part played by what I have called

clans, there was no such thing as a clan government or clan ownership. Each of the houses in a town was owned by one man, the I'lixagidas or House-chief. His wife had a high position in it from that fact and, usually also, as being a chief's daughter, but she had no right to the house itself. In one remarkable case a man was so fond of his wife as to let her own the house, but such occurrences were altogether exceptional. The wife, however, could hold property independently of her husband. Since she belonged to the opposite clan, it was through her that the chief treated with his opposites, and she sometimes presided when he called the people of her side in to a feast.

Since, however, descent was in the female line, the wife was very much like a stranger in a strange land. There were generally houses owned by both Ravens and Eagles in the same town, in which case her own people might live near her, but frequently she belonged to a different place, and, when hostilities occurred between the two, her position must have been somewhat awkward to say the least. Her children, too, had no claim upon the people among whom they lived, and the latter regarded them as strangers. Such being the case, and since one received no assistance in time of trouble, from members of any family besides his own, it was only natural that, in most cases, they preferred to return to their mother's town. This tendency was accentuated by the custom of taking a boy away to live with his uncle when he was quite young. It was thought he would be spoiled if he remained near his mother. This was more apt to happen if the boy was next in succession to a position in one of the houses of his mother's town. From his uncle he received all the instruction necessary to prepare him to take that place, and he acted as his uncle's right-hand man, or spokesman on all occasions. He was expected to marry his uncle's widow when he succeeded. Often he married the daughter of the chief he was to succeed.

Girls were often married in the same town where they were brought up without ever going back to their own people. When a house-chief died, the brother or nephew who succeeded was, as already stated, expected to marry the widow. When she died, however, there was no bond

connecting her unmarried children with that town and they usually returned to her place to live with their uncles.

Younger sons might continue to live with their elder brothers until the death of the former gave them the chieftainship, or they might accumulate property, potlatch and put up a house of their own. In this case they generally erected it in their mother's town. Sometimes, however, a man chose to put up a house in the town where he was brought up or the one into which he married. This would happen oftenest where two towns were near each other, or where two towns were in the habit of intermarrying so that there was always a large population from each in both places. So that it came about that in most towns there were houses belonging to both clans. Nevertheless, according to the stories, a town normally consisted of houses belonging to one family only.

Usually each household had its own camping-ground on a salmon creek, where its smoke-house stood, and whither the people went in the spring to dry salmon and halibut, trap bear, gather berries, dig roots and make canoes, returning to town in the fall.

Higher in order were the "families" (Gwai′ giagañ). A family embraced everywhere from one to a dozen houses. Nearly all of these families bear the name of some ancient town, some camping-place or some part of a town, so it is readily seen that they are nothing more than local groups. My investigations have shown the process of family formation in all stages. Certain families embraced subdivisions with no special name, although the members of each dressed somewhat differently at the potlatches; others included sections named from the part of the town they occupied or from some camping-place. Between still others there was simply a historical relationship, and only vague traditions indicate the connection between certain of the grander divisions. According to their own testimony all of the Ravens had one origin and all the Eagles one origin, but this is probably not quite true. The distinction between Ravens and Eagles was considered absolute and eternal.

The fact is each Haida household was so complete in itself that all it required was a name and a certain amount of

isolation to develop into an entirely independent family, and there was a constant tendency in that direction.

The largest body of people under one government among the Haida were those in the same town. Although one family might own two or more towns, there were more often several families in one town; and, although all had their own family chiefs, one of these was chief of the town, the Lä'na a'oga (Town-mother) or Lä'na l'e'igas (Town-master).

I have elsewhere hinted that elder nephews succeeded to a position before younger. That was, however, rather a natural than a legal condition of affairs. In choosing a successor to any position the first requisite appears to have been success in amassing property. So it happened that elder sons were sometimes passed over by younger ones, or nearer relatives for those more remote. In one case two succeeded to the same position. The position of town or family chief did not go with the same house, unless that happened to be the only great house in the family, for it must be stated that there were many low-class families or low divisions of families called "food-steamers," which usually had no chief at all and generally lived in mean houses or acted as servants in the houses of the higher classes.

A chief's power varied considerably, resting mainly, as has been said, on the amount of his property. With the possible exception of members of the low families, above referred to, any one might become chief of his family, and, if his family owned a town, chief of the town as well. Property was partly inherited; partly amassed in trade or war. War was, indeed, undertaken mainly to obtain slaves. That object and revenge went hand in hand. A chief's power also rested very largely with himself. Some might be called absolute monarchs and even tyrants, while others lost all influence and, if not deposed, were practically unrecognized and unhonored by their inferiors.

There were certain tendencies to combination between towns owned by the same clan or those that had much to do with each other in war-expeditions, but they did not result in the subordination of the canoes of one town to those of another.

An excellent sidelight is cast upon Haida social organiza-

tion by the order maintained by war parties. Each house generally outfitted one canoe, in which the house-chief or his representative occupied the stern and was called war-chief. The conduct of the canoe when in action was, however, entrusted to another man, the Sik la'dia, whose place was at the bow. He was always an experienced warrior and, in authority though not in name, was the real war-chief. While the warriors were away his wife led the dances which their wives kept up until their return. When a whole family went to war, the family-chief, himself was war-chief. If two or three families went, the heads of all were the war-chiefs.

TO SUMMARIZE

The essential points in Haida social organization were, firstly, the division into two great exogamous clans, a division which reflected itself, as we have seen, in the terms of relationship; and, second, the organization of each house under one house-chief. The organization of families and towns was simply a larger application of that of each household.

The Ancestral Family of the Bella Coola

T. F. MCILWRAITH

As in other communities, the social, religious, and economic aspects of Bella Coola life are interdependent, but there is an added complexity in the influence of mythological concepts. This not only complicates investigation in the field, but it also renders a logical description of their customs difficult. Some reference to practices recorded in detail in later chapters is unavoidable.

In many communities, ethnologists have been able to begin with the social organization of the people. Among the Bella Coola, this is impossible, since their religious beliefs colour every aspect of their life, and these must be understood by anyone who wishes to comprehend their culture as a whole. In this chapter, too, it is necessary to commence with a description of that aspect of mythology which serves as the cohesive bond to one of the social units, the ancestral family.

ANCESTRAL FAMILY

As recorded in the last chapter, it is believed that in the beginning of time Ałquntäm caused the first men and women to be created in his house above and sent them down to populate the earth. They came in groups of two, three, four, or more, brothers and sisters, or more rarely man and wife, to different parts of the Bella Coola valley. They brought with them tools, houses, clothing, even sustenance in the shape of fish and animals. More important, from the point of view of social organization, they brought with them names and ceremonial prerogatives. In fact, the Bella Coola

Source: T. F. McIlwraith, *The Bella Coola Indians*, 2 vols. (Toronto: The University of Toronto Press, 1948), I, 117-129. Reprinted by permission of the publisher. Title supplied by editor.

believe that their culture was created by Ałqụntäm in the distant past, and has not been the result of slow growth. It is true that there have been many changes. Raven, the culture hero, taught the early settlers many useful arts, and they were themselves so powerful that they were able to create ceremonial and other prerogatives in a manner impossible to their descendants. Moreover, the people realize that they have been influenced by neighbouring tribes since that time, but in spite of these additions, they believe that their life is patterned on that of their earliest forbears.

As a group, the Bella Coola are philosophers. They demand a reason for everything, though once a reason has been given, and accepted, they think no more about the matter. The elaboration of Bella Coola mythology may be due in part to their desire to explain their social organization; but without question these myths, now accepted as facts, have had a great influence on the lives of the people. In fact the social structure of the tribe has tended to conform to the myths.

It is believed that each group of first people formed a village community, and pre-empted hunting-grounds in the vicinity. These usually consisted of small valleys opening from the main Bella Coola River, tracts which could thus be easily defined. Each group also took possession of a suitable part of the river for a salmon-weir, or, if located on the coast, a convenient place for an ocean fish-trap. In course of time the first people married, of necessity with members of other villages. According to mythology, and equally according to modern practice, the women usually moved to the villages of their husbands. When a child was born, it naturally grew up to share in the hunting-grounds of its father's village. Moreover, the father was able to bestow on his child various ceremonial dances; the concepts of some he had brought with him from above, others he had formulated on this earth. It is assumed that all the first people were mighty chiefs, able to initiate rites in a way that few modern men have been able to equal. But the mothers of these children, the first born on this earth, did not surrender the privileges of their own villages at marriage. Consequently, their children were of almost as much interest to

the brothers and other relatives of their mothers as to their fathers. It was taken as a matter of course that a child had full rights in the village of his mother, and from her, as from her relatives, he likewise received various prerogatives. Thus each child was a member of a bilateral social group. From actual residence in his father's village he tended to be more intimately associated with him and his brothers than with his mother's relatives, but this did not prevent him from visiting at the home of the latter, where he was received as a member of that village. Through the bestowal of prerogatives by his mother and the members of her family, his relationship with them was further emphasized. Such a child was, in fact, a full member of two groups.

When the members of the second generation married and begot children, each of these could have been a member of four groups; that of his father's father, father's mother, mother's father, and mother's mother. The Bella Coola believe that there were approximately forty-five groups of first settlers, corresponding to the forty-five towns, and it is obvious that if the system of intermarriage had continued for a few generations, a man would have been a member of each of these first groups. They assume that their first ancestors came to this earth far more than a few generations ago, and yet at the present time no one claims to be a descendant of more than eight of these first groups, and most claim descent from only two or three. In part this can be explained by forgetfulness, though a Bella Coola would regard this statement as heresy. The residence of a man in the village of his father has tended to emphasize relationship with the ancestral group that first populated that village, and there is no doubt that actual relationship, through the mother, with the members of other groups must in many cases have been forgotten in the course of generations. The term *ancestral family*, *mınmınts*, is used in this monograph to designate those individuals who believe themselves to be descended from one of the first groups that populated this earth.

A man may claim descent from as many as eight of these groups, that is, he may be a member of eight ancestral families. Some restrictive means must have been employed

to limit the choice of marriage partners, otherwise a man's membership in ancestral families would have been far greater than it is. The explanation lies in the high regard with which the members of an ancestral family esteem the prerogatives they have received from their forbears. With the marriage of the first women, their brothers were called upon to share their rights, both practical in regard to hunting territory, and ceremonial with regard to dance prerogatives, with their sisters' children. Bella Coola mythology contains no references to unwillingness on the part of the first men to do this; in fact, their own children benefited equally from the marriages of their fathers with other women. But, say the Bella Coola, after these first marriages, necessarily exogamic, men realized that it would be foolish to allow their children to marry far afield and so diffuse valuable prerogatives. It was far wiser for a man to seek as future son-in-law a youth belonging to the same ancestral family as himself or his wife. Then any resultant children would come into this world provided by both parents with common relatives, so that the child would be, as they express it, "Held close and supported by a close circle of ancestors."

Bella Coola logic does not explain how marriages could have been arranged in the early generations without violating the laws of incest. The endogamic principle displayed at that time, however, has been carried out until the present day, so that a man endeavours to arrange marriages for his children with members of the same ancestral family. One of the strongest Bella Coola desires is to "make good the path" for his offspring, and this can best be done when they are born amply provided with relatives of common ancestry. There is no belief in the active participation of distant ancestors in the affairs of men, yet, though incapable of clear expression, the Bella Coola feel strongly that a child is born into the companionship of its deceased relatives back to the beginning of time. . . .

In recent years there has been a tendency for some men to marry foreign women in order that they, or their children, might obtain new prerogatives. Thus a trend towards exogamy has arisen from the same reason which is supposed to have caused endogamy. The offspring of such marriages

cannot enjoy the feeling of strength and comfort that comes from the membership of both parents in the same ancestral family, but some individuals have felt that this was offset by the gain of highly desirable foreign prerogatives. It is said that this practice was initiated by a certain Potłɛs, father of a man about sixty years old in 1923. White influence probably had nothing to do with this radical innovation, although its wide adoption has been made more easy by the establishment of peaceful conditions on the coast.

Strong as is the belief in a common ancestry, it is unlikely that this would have sufficed to hold together the members of the ancestral family, without some definite prerogatives. These are of two kinds: names and land.

NAMES

The fundamental principle governing Bella Coola nomenclature is that each name must have originated in connection with some event of comparative importance. It is unthinkable to apply a casual designation to a child. At a person's death his name, or names, may be transmitted to a relative, and it is proper that the owner of a name should know when, by whom, and for what reason, it was first created. Tradition affirms that, before coming to this earth, the first people were all given designations by Ałquntäm; these have been carefully handed down and are still in use. One name cannot be given to two individuals; instances occur of two people having the same one, but in such cases they have different origins. One person may have several names of different kinds, each carrying with it some definite prerogative of a dance or other function, but all are transmissible, and at the owner's death these may fall to different relatives. A name may pass from man to woman, or *vice versa*, in some cases with a minor alteration. The only non-inheritable appellations are those obtained by shamans as a result of their supernatural experiences.

Not only did each group of first settlers bring with them a number of designations from above, but they also created a number on this earth and bestowed them on their children, and on the children of their sisters or brothers, in whom

they felt an almost parental interest. To mark the dignity of the names, all present at the ceremony of bestowal received gifts from the creator of the name, the person who called them together for the rite. The importance of the individual depended largely upon the value of the goods distributed with respect to his name, a concept which will be elaborated in the following chapter. The descendants of these first people likewise created new designations and established their dignity by distributing presents, a practice which still continues. It follows that any complete origin myth should include a large number of names, those brought down from the land above[1] and also those created by the powerful first people on this earth itself.[2] Both types of cognomen will be referred to henceforth as "ancestral names," no distinction being made between those actually brought from above and those made on earth. This is in accordance with Bella Coola usage.

Soon after the birth of a child his father, uncle, or other near relative,[3] either on the paternal or maternal side, calls the members of the village together to bestow a name on the infant. The one selected must be embodied in the origin myth of one or other of the parents, and must be one not then in use by any other member of the ancestral family. A relative may give the child one of his own names, in which case the donor surrenders all claim to it. This designation is the obvious mark of the position of the child in the ancestral family. Without such a formal conferring of an ancestral name an infant would be without status in the community, but, as children are always welcome, some relative is invariably ready to confirm the bestowal by the necessary distribution of goods, a feature that is present in every Bella Coola ceremonial. On such occasions the guests are called by their ancestral names. An effort was made to learn what would happen if the number of children born into an ancestral family exceeded the number of ancestral names embodied in its origin myth, but no answer was forthcoming.

[1] Such a name is a smätläs skwatsta, or "Petrified Name."

[2] Such a name is a sxwanät·a skwatsta, or "Earth-Made Name."

[3] The most careful investigation failed to show that it was incumbent on any particular relative.

Established custom demands that a name be provided for every child, and one is always provided. Without question designations must be invented, usually from some event in the origin myth, but it is always claimed that such were used by a long-deceased ancestor. In fact, the social custom agrees with the requirements of the mythological concept. Since bestowal of names is a matter of pride, it follows that a child often receives several from the ancestral families of which he is a member; the possession of these is a source of gratification to the owner.

An ancestral name given to a child is spoken of as an ätsq̀tutł name, and the recipient as an ätsq̀tutł, which may be translated, "commoner." He may be given several names from one origin myth, or ones from diverse origin myths if his parents are members of different ancestral families. These designations may either be those brought down from above by the first people, those made on this earth by them, or those made at some important event by later persons. Irrespective of what combination of these possibilities a child may have, he is still a commoner, and his ability to rise to the position of chief depends on his own, or his parents', ability to give potlatches, as will be described in the next chapter. In such a case his ätsq̀tutł name is said to have been elevated to that of a stältımx̭ (chief's) name.

The ancestral family may, therefore, be defined as those whose ätsq̀tutł names are embodied in the same origin myth.

What is the stability of this group?

In consequence of the large number of names theoretically embodied in every myth, and of the necessity for validating the bestowal of any one of these by means of presents, it follows that there is always a large number of dormant names. The Bella Coola describe these as being, "In the burial ground." They are, in fact, dead. Any one of these may be resurrected by any member of the ancestral family. If a woman marries into a foreign tribe her relatives occasionally give her husband, outright, an ancestral name. In such a case that name is permanently alienated from the family to which it formerly belonged; this should happen only when the group is reduced to a few individuals, all of

whom agree to the transaction. But more often a woman takes as a wedding gift to her husband a name which it is understood cannot be transmitted to one of his relatives unless he has children. On the death of the childless husband, this designation reverts to his widow's ancestral family. If there are children, they cement the bond of friendship between the two families. The brother of a woman so married also bestows names on her children, as further mark of their incorporation into her ancestral family. It is customary and proper, however, for the ancestral family into which a woman is married and bears children to reciprocate the compliment a few generations later, and by the marriage of one of their women to restore such names to the ancestral family to which they originally belonged. According to the Bella Coola, this practice of "return-marriage" has been the rule since the first exogamic marriages of the first people, with the result that names usually return to the patrilineal descendants of the first people to use them.

If a woman marries outside her ancestral family, her children will belong to at least two distinct ancestral groups. It is difficult to say how long an individual remembers the different units with which he is connected, but the following is an instance of survival for several generations. Qwai·lits is an orphan about ten years of age, now living in Bella Coola; he is looked upon with considerable respect as being a member of ancestral families in Bella Coola, Kimsquit, Smith Inlet, Kitkatla, and Kitlobe. His pedigree, given below, explains his powers. The symbol = marks a marriage, and the male is shown on the left in each case.

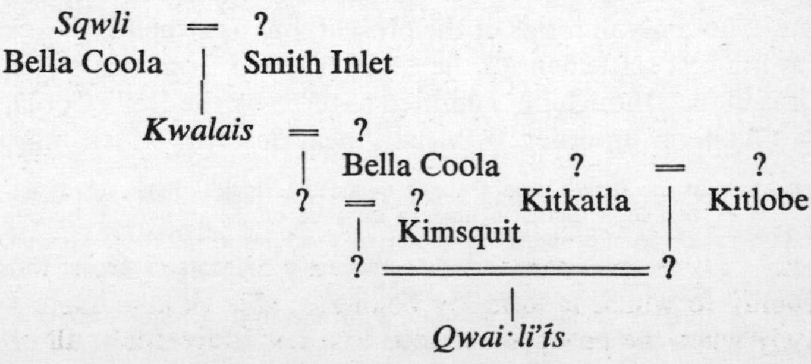

Theoretically, Qwai·lis̆ is as much a native of Smith Inlet as he is of Bella Coola where his father made his home. If he should visit Smith Inlet and make known his pedigree, he would be received by the members of the ancestral family of his great-great-grandmother.[4] His welcome would be more assured if he were the owner of a name from their origin myth. Difficulties of communication and frequent wars made it virtually impossible in the old days to keep in touch with relatives in distant tribes, except in the case of a mighty chief who was able to invite visitors from great distances to feasts. Thus names taken by women to foreign husbands were virtually lost to the members of her ancestral family. In the course of a few generations, such designations carried afield would be revived as if dormant by some member of the family, and all recollection of the foreign marriage forgotten.

The converse of this process of loss is the assimilation to an origin myth of names originally brought into the ancestral family by a woman from abroad. Unless intercourse and friendly relations were maintained by "return marriages," in a few generations no tradition would be remembered to account for the name, and this, if used at all, would be interwoven into the well-known ancestral myth. Hence a myth is not static with regard to the names embodied in it. These change from generation to generation; it is probable that elements of the story itself suffer like additions and alterations, even though the people do not consider this to be the case.

The Bella Coola regard the ancestral family as a social unit, not only in terms of the present, but as stretching back to the first settlement of the earth. Viewed from this angle, it is in fact, though not admitted to be so by the Bella Coola, a unilateral grouping with patrilineal descent, which may,

[4] As the Bella Coola are now living in a single village, it was impossible to obtain a modern instance of the ownership by one individual of rights in a number of localities within the tribal area. It appears certain, however, that the sentiments expressed with regard to Qwai·lits at Smith Inlet are identical with those formerly held for possessions in ancestral families located in different Bella Coola villages.

in both the most recent and most ancient generations, be marked by matrilineal descent instead. A man frequently uses prerogatives obtained through his mother, her mother, or even her mother's mother, but it is tacitly assumed that for many previous generations such rights passed in the patrilineal line. Sometimes this succession extended back to the beginning of time; in other cases, prerogatives were transmitted matrilineally for a considerable period after the settlement of the earth, before gradually becoming patrilineal.

It has been thus far assumed that the only prerogative wrapped up in an ancestral name is a knowledge of the myth in which it is embodied. But there are others. For example, several of the first inhabitants of the world are said to have erected totem-poles, each of which was displayed by its owner at the gathering when he took for himself a name. Thenceforth, the only person entitled to use that particular totem-pole design was the person with the legal right to the name in question. The same principle governs all dance names; each entitles its owner to perform a certain ceremonial. Thus it is possible to enlarge the previous definition by saying that:

The ancestral family consists of those whose ancestral names, embodying definite prerogatives, are embodied in a single origin myth.

A stranger finds it easier to understand why names are so carefully maintained within the ancestral family by thinking of them as symbols of prerogatives, but it must be emphasized that the Bella Coola preserve with equal jealousy those designations of which the only prerogative is the marking of this actual membership.

If, then, the ancestral family be regarded as a group possessing a large number of name-prerogatives, it may well be asked how these are distributed among the members. The first point to be emphasized is that the ancestral family is a unit held together without definite social mechanism. There is no accepted "head" of the family, nor are there any clearly formulated laws governing the transmission of the name-prerogatives. Before death a man usually calls together his

relatives and bequeaths,[5] according to his desire, his personal property in slaves and canoes, and his intangible property in names. Such a designation does not become the property of the new owner unless he is able to validate his ownership by a distribution of presents; meanwhile the name is "dead." If, during this period, some other member of the ancestral family should desire it for a child, or for himself, he can take possession of it by the customary distribution of presents. In doing so he would anger the legatee, but the latter cannot himself use the appellation since it is already in use. Even at the present time there are bitter quarrels over the assumption of names, and such have certainly occurred for many generations. If a man can validate fairly promptly a name willed to him, it is most unusual for anyone else to try to forestall him.

If a man dies intestate, his sons consider themselves his normal heirs, and the most respected of them validates for himself as many names as he desires or is able to assume. Disputes are not as common as might be expected since the influence of a chief is usually sufficient to settle claims as to which of his brothers shall receive which name. Even if none of them is a chief, some one of them is certain to have greater influence than the others. If a dead man has no sons, his daughters can assume his names, which they may transmit to their children. Failing both sons and daughters, a man's brothers and sisters are his heirs, as usual, the one of influence being the one who really arranges matters.[6] None the less, it must be emphasized that if the members of the immediate family are slow to validate a dead man's names, they may be taken by any member of the ancestral family.

In former days it was customary to create a "remembrancer" to preserve the ancestral myth. The older and more influential members of the ancestral family would choose an intelligent young relative to whom to relate the myth in great detail. One informant described how her mother, the last official "remembrancer," had been instructed by her grand-

[5] In case of sudden death or failure to make a will confusion sometimes occurs.

[6] At the present time the same principle governs the disposal of houses and gardens on the reserve.

father. The old man had been accustomed to take his granddaughter, a girl about twelve years of age, to bed with him, and whisper to her the myth, with his hand pressed over her anus to prevent escape of his words. At the conclusion of the recitation he always spat in her ears to make the words stick. The members of the ancestral family, recognizing that the "remembrancer" was the person best acquainted with the myth, were wont to consult him or her about it, and, of course, about the names embodied in it. A "remembrancer" had no authority to decree who should receive names, but appeals were often made to him, and a tactful individual was frequently able to settle disputes.

Considering the extreme fluidity of the whole system it is surprising that quarrels are not more common. These are limited by the system of wills, through which a man bequeaths his most valuable personal property, especially his intangible property in kusiut name-prerogatives. Ancestral names are also willed, but since their value depends on the goods expended to validate them, there is seldom bitterness about their allotment. Indeed, a chief who is the legal owner of a designation which came from above in the beginning of time, will in many cases choose to elevate his position with respect to a title of comparatively recent date. But if any person who is not a member of the ancestral family should dare to use an ancestral name, all the members rise to avenge the theft, for such they feel it to be. In recent years, however, this practice has become comparatively common. In such cases a man, eager to share in the glories of a myth and able to give a potlatch, has validated an ancestral name to which he has no right. The presence of the white man alone restrains the injured ancestral family. Names are sometimes lent or hired to those who are not members of the group for definite sums; the recipient recompenses the individual. If such names are not returned for several generations quarrels are apt to arise since the recipient claims to be the real owner and not the temporary possessor. During his tenancy of the name he is entitled to any prerogative attached to it, but he is not considered a *bona fide* member of the ancestral family.

Instances have occurred in which an old man or woman,

believing himself to be the last survivor of an ancestral family, has donated his names and myth to those who have befriended him, or these have been taken by those who buried him. Some individuals are constantly watching to conduct the funerals of friendless old people in the hope of so obtaining names. But in almost every case this leads to friction, since it is virtually impossible for an ancestral family to die out. Perhaps in the next generation, perhaps in the following one, some youth will claim descent from the first ancestors of the supposedly defunct family, and claim the myth and names embodied therein. This leads to a feud with the person, or his descendants, who has received the names through aid given to the "last" of the family.

Such instances of an ancestral family becoming practically extinct, are unusual; normally, the group is largely centred in one village, but with members scattered in other localities. There is no central organization. It is generally recognized that such a unit belongs in the village where its first ancestors settled, and the leading chief of that village is, therefore, an important person in the family, though without status of "head" of it. His advice may be appealed to in cases of disputes concerning names, but he lacks judicial authority. Theoretically, the descendants of the elder of two first people are considered as "elder brothers and elder sisters" of those descended from a younger brother or sister; but this is nothing more than an accepted fact; it plays no part in the social life of the community.

In addition to human names, the origin myths include those applied to dogs. The first ancestral group had dogs, and these animals had names, or were given them by their powerful masters. Ever since that time their descendants can apply these designations to their own dogs. It is unnecessary to validate such names, but no two canines can be given the same one at the same time, according to the rule which governs the bestowal of human names. This matter was not investigated in detail, and the only dog's name collected was one for which the origin myth is as follows:

When Täl-io was first settled in the beginning of time, the houses were built in parallel rows, one above the other, up the side of a steep knoll. At the very top was a toilet-house, built over such a steep incline that excrement rolled down the hillside. In consequence, one of the early chiefs living there gave to his dog the name, Nuliq̓wıwutł di mınk‘, "Rolling excrement," which has since been preserved in the ancestral family of his descendants.

PART THREE
THE POTLATCH

The Potlatch

FRANZ BOAS

Before proceeding any further it will be necessary to describe the method of acquiring rank. This is done by means of the potlatch, or the distribution of property. This custom has been described often, but it has been thoroughly misunderstood by most observers. The underlying principle is that of the interest-bearing investment of property.

The child when born is given the name of the place where it is born. This name (g·î′nʟaxʟē) it keeps until about a year old. Then his father, mother, or some other relative, gives a paddle or a mat to each member of the clan and the child receives his second name (nā′map'axʟēya). When the boy is about 10 or 12 years old, he obtains his third name (Sōmiatsᴇxʟä′yē). In order to obtain it, he must distribute a number of small presents, such as shirts or single blankets, among his own clan or tribe. When the youth thus starts out in life, he is liberally assisted by his elders, particularly by the nobility of the tribe.

I must say here that the unit of value is the single blanket, nowadays a cheap white woollen blanket, which is valued at 50 cents. The double blanket is valued at three single

---

Source: Franz Boas, *The Social Organization and Secret Societies of the Kwakiutl Indians*. Reports of the United States National Museum (Washington, D.C., 1895), pp. 341-355. Reprinted by permission of the Smithsonian Institution. The original text contained three illustrations of coppers which have been omitted in this reprint.–[ed.]

blankets. These blankets form the means of exchange of the Indians, and everything is paid for in blankets or in objects the value of which is measured by blankets. When a native has to pay debts and has not a sufficient number of blankets, he borrows them from his friends and has to pay the following rates of interest:

For a period of a few months, for 5 borrowed blankets 6 must be returned (Lē'k·ō); for a period of six months, for 5 borrowed blankets 7 must be returned (mā''Laxsa Lē'k·ōyō); for a period of twelve months or longer, for 5 borrowed blankets 10 must be returned (dē'ida or g·ē'La).

When a person has a poor credit, he may pawn his name for a year. Then the name must not be used during that period, and for 30 blankets which he has borrowed he must pay 100 in order to redeem his name. This is called q'ā'q'oaxō (selling a slave).

The rate of interest of the Lē'k·ō varies somewhat around 25 per cent, according to the kindness of the loaner and the credit of the borrower. For a very short time blankets may be loaned without interest. This is designated by the same term.

When the boy is about to take his third name, he will borrow blankets from the other members of the tribe, who all assist him. He must repay them after a year, or later, with 100 per cent interest. Thus he may have gathered 100 blankets. In June, the time set for this act, the boy will distribute these blankets among his own tribe, giving proportionately to every member of the tribe, but a few more to the chief. This is called Lā'X'uit. When after this time any member of the tribe distributes blankets, the boy receives treble the amount he has given. The people make it a point to repay him inside of a month. Thus he owns 300 blankets, of which, however, he must repay 200 after the lapse of a year. He loans the blankets out among his friends, and thus at the close of the year he may possess about 400 blankets.

The next June he pays his debts (qoana') in a festival, at which all the clans from whom he borrowed blankets are present. The festival is generally held on the street or on an open place near the village. Up to this time he is not allowed to take part in feasts. But now he may distribute property

in order to obtain a potlatch name (p'ā'tsaxLäyē). This is also called Lā'X'uit.

At this time the father gives up his seat (Lā'Xoē) in favour of his son. After the boy has paid his debts, the chief calls all the older members of the tribe to a council, in which it is resolved that the boy is to receive his father's seat. The chief sends his speaker to call the boy, and his clan go out in company with the speaker. The young man – for henceforth he will be counted among the men – dresses with a black headband and paints long vertical stripes, one on each side of his face, running down from the outer corners of the eyes. The stripes represent tears. He gives a number of blankets to his friends, who carry them into the house where the council is being held. The speaker enters first and announces his arrival. The young man follows, and after him enter his friends, carrying blankets. He remains standing in front of the fire, and the chief announces to him that he is to take his father's seat. Then the boy distributes his blankets among the other clans and sells some for food, with which a feast is prepared. His father gives up his seat and takes his place among the old men (Nō'matsēiL). The blankets given away at this feast are repaid with 100 per cent interest. In this manner the young man continues to loan and to distribute blankets, and thus is able, with due circumspection and foresight, to amass a fortune. Sometimes it happens that the successor to a man's name (Lawu'lqame) already has a name of his own. In all such cases (also when the name is acquired by inheritance) the successor gives up his name and his property to his own successor.

Possession of wealth is considered honourable, and it is the endeavour of each Indian to acquire a fortune. But it is not as much the possession of wealth as the ability to give great festivals which makes wealth a desirable object to the Indian. As the boy acquires his second name and man's estate by means of a distribution of property, which in course of time will revert to him with interest, the man's name acquires greater weight in the councils of the tribe and greater renown among the whole people, as he is able to distribute more and more property at each subsequent festival. Therefore boys and men are vying with each other

in the arrangement of great distributions of property. Boys of different clans are pitted against each other by their elders, and each is exhorted to do his utmost to outdo his rival. And as the boys strive against each other, so do the chiefs and the whole clans, and the one object of the Indian is to outdo his rival. Formerly feats of bravery counted as well as distributions of property, but nowadays, as the Indians say, "rivals fight with property only." The clans are thus perpetually pitted against each other according to their rank. The Kwakiutl tribes are counted as the highest in the order given in the above list. In intertribal rivalry they do not strive against each other, but the

Guē′tEla against the Ma′malēleqala.
Q'ō′moyuē against the Qoē′xsōt'ēnôx.
Q'ō′mk·ūtis against the NE′mqîc or Laō′koatx.
Wā′las Kwakiutl against the Lau′itsîs or Ts'ā′mas.

I referred several times to the distribution of blankets. The recipient in such a distribution is not at liberty to refuse the gift, although according to what I have said it is nothing but an interest-bearing loan that must be refunded at some future time with 100 per cent interest. This festival is called p'a′sa, literally, flattening something (for instance, a basket). This means that by the amount of property given the name of the rival is flattened.

There is still another method of rising in the social scale, namely, by showing one's self superior to the rival. This may be done by inviting the rival and his clan or tribe to a festival and giving him a considerable number of blankets. He is compelled to accept these, but is not allowed to do so until after he has placed an equal number of blankets on top of the pile offered to him. This is called dāpEntg·ala and the blankets placed on top of the first pile are called dā′pEnō. Then he receives the whole pile and becomes debtor to that amount, i.e., he must repay the gift with 100 per cent interest.

A similar proceeding takes place when a canoe is given to a rival. The latter, when the gift is offered to him, must put blankets to the amount of half the value of the canoe on to it. This is called dā′g·ōt, taking hold of the bow of the

canoe. These blankets are kept by the first owner of the canoe. Later on, the recipient of the canoe must return another canoe, together with an adequate number of blankets, as an "anchor line" for the canoe. This giving of a canoe is called sā′k·a.

Still more complicated is the purchase of the gift, however one chooses to term it, of a "copper." All along the North Pacific Coast, from Yakutat to Comox, curiously shaped copper plates are in use, which in olden times were made of native copper, which is found in Alaska and probably also on Nass River, but which nowadays are worked out of imported copper. . . . The front of the copper is covered with black lead, in which a face, representing the crest animal of the owner, is graven. These coppers have the same function which bank notes of high denominations have with us. The actual value of the piece of copper is small, but it is made to represent a large number of blankets and can always be sold for blankets. The value is not arbitrarily set, but depends upon the amount of property given away in the festival at which the copper is sold. On the whole, the oftener a copper is sold the higher its value, as every new buyer tries to invest more blankets in it. Therefore the purchase of a copper also brings distinction, because it proves that the buyer is able to bring together a vast amount of property.

Each copper has a name of its own, and from the following list of coppers, which were in Fort Rupert in 1893, the values attached to some of them may be seen:

Mā′xts'ōlEm (= all other coppers are ashamed to look at it), 7,500 blankets.[1]

L'ā′xolamas (= steel-head salmon, i.e., it glides out of one's hands like a salmon), 6,000 blankets.

Lō′pēLila (= making the house empty of blankets), 5,000 blankets.

DE′nt'alayō (= about whose possession all are quarrelling).

Mau′ak·'a (= sea lion).

Qau'lō′ma (= beaver face).

[1] This copper has two crosspieces.

Lē'ita (=looking below; namely, in order to find blankets with which to buy it).

Nū'sē (=moon; its engraving represents the half moon, in which a man is sitting).

G·ā'waqa (=a spirit. Hē'iltsuq dialect, corresponding to the Kwakiutl Ts'ō'nōqoa).

NE'lqEmāla (=day face).

NE'nqEmāla (=bear face).

K·'ā'na (=crow; Hē'iltsuq dialect).

Qoayî'm (=whale).

Mā'x'ēnôx (=killer whale).

Qoayî'mk·in (=too great a whale).

Wī'na (=war, against the blankets of the purchaser).

. . . It was described above how a boy is introduced into the distributions of property going on among the tribe. It remains to state how he acquires his first copper. When the young man has acquired a certain number of blankets, one of his older friends invites him to take a share in the purchase of one of the cheaper coppers, which may have a value of, say, 500 blankets. The boy contributes 200 blankets as his share and the other man purchases it, announcing the young man as his partner in the transaction. The copper is delivered to the young man, who becomes a debtor to his partner for the amount of blankets contributed by the latter. He announces at once that he will sell the copper the following year, but that he is willing to deliver the copper on the spot. With these words he lays it down before the tribe. One of the chiefs of a rival tribe takes the copper and pays as a first installment 100 blankets. Then the boy promises a distribution of blankets (tsō'Xua) for the following year and loans out the 100 blankets which he has received. The next year he calls in his outstanding debts and invites all the neighbouring tribes to a feast, to which his own tribe contributes food and fuel. In the course of the festival he pays the chief who took his copper 200 blankets, being the value of the 100 blankets received the previous year, together with 100 per cent interest (see p. 73). Then the purchaser pays the sum of 750 blankets for the copper, including boxes and belt, as described above. Of this amount 700 are dis-

tributed on the following day in the prescribed fashion among the neighbouring tribes. Now the young man proceeds to loan out his blankets until within a few years he is able to repay the share of his partner who first helped him to buy the copper. When the time has come for this transaction, his partner pays him double the amount of what he (the partner) has contributed, and the young man returns to him double of this amount.

The rivalry between chiefs and clans finds its strongest expression in the destruction of property. A chief will burn blankets, a canoe, or break a copper, thus indicating his disregard of the amount of property destroyed and showing that his mind is stronger, his power greater, than that of his rival. If the latter is not able to destroy an equal amount of property without much delay, his name is "broken." He is vanquished by his rival and his influence with his tribe is lost, while the name of the other chief gains correspondingly in renown.

Feasts may also be counted as destruction of property, because the food given can not be returned except by giving another feast. The most expensive sort of feast is the one at which enormous quantities of fish oil (made of the oulachon) are consumed and burnt, the so-called "grease feast." Therefore it also raises the name of the person who can afford to give it, and the neglect to speedily return it entails a severe loss of prestige. Still more feared is the breaking of a valuable copper. A chief may break his copper and give the broken parts to his rival. If the latter wants to keep his prestige, he must break a copper of equal or higher value, and then return both his own broken copper and the fragments which he has received to his rival. The latter may then pay for the copper which he has thus received. The chief to whom the fragments of the first copper are given may, however, also break his copper and throw both into the sea. The Indians consider that by this act the attacked rival has shown himself superior to his aggressor, because the latter may have expected to receive the broken copper of his rival in return so that an actual loss would have been prevented.

In by far the greater number of cases where coppers are broken the copper is preserved. The owner breaks or cuts

off one part after the other until finally only the T-shaped ridge remains. This is valued at two-thirds of the total value of the copper and is the last part to be given away. . . . The rival to whom the piece that has been broken off is given, breaks off a similar piece, and returns both to the owner. Thus a copper may be broken up in contests with different rivals. Finally, somebody succeeds in buying up all the broken fragments, which are riveted together, and the copper has attained an increased value. Since the broken copper indicates the fact that the owner has destroyed property, the Indians pride themselves upon their possession.

The rivalry between chiefs, when carried so far that coppers are destroyed and that grease feasts are given in order to destroy the prestige of the rival, often develop into open enmity. When a person gives a grease feast, a great fire is lighted in the centre of the house. The flames leap up to the roof and the guests are almost scorched by the heat. Still the etiquette demands that they do not stir, else the host's fire has conquered them. Even when the roof begins to burn and the fire attacks the rafters, they must appear unconcerned. The hos alone has the right to send a man up to the roof to put out the fire. While the feast is in progress the host sings a scathing song ridiculing his rival and praising his own clan, the feats of his forefathers and his own. Then the grease is filled in large spoons and passed to the rival chief first. If a person thinks he has given a greater grease feast than that offered by the host, he refuses the spoon. Then he runs out of the house (g·ē′qEmx'it=chief rises against his face) to fetch his copper "to squelch with it the fire." The host proceeds at once to tie a copper to each of his house posts. If he should not do so, the person who refused the spoon would on returning strike the posts with the copper, which is considered equal to striking the chief's face (k·î′lxa). Then the man who went to fetch his copper breaks it and gives it to the host. This is called "squelching the host's fire." The host retaliates as described above.

The following songs show the manner in which rivals scathe each other.

First NEqā'pEnk·Em(=ten fathom face) let his clan sing the following song at a feast which he gave:

1. Our great famous chief is known even outside of our world, oh! he is the highest chief of all. [Then he sang:] *The chiefs of all the tribes are my servants, the chiefs of all the tribes are my speakers. They are pieces of copper which I have broken.*

[The people:] *Do not let our chief rise too high. Do not let him destroy too much property, else we shall be made like broken pieces of copper by the great breakers of coppers, the great splitter of coppers, the great chief who throws coppers into the water, the great one who can not be surpassed by anybody, the one surmounting all the chiefs. Long ago you went and burnt all the tribes to ashes. You went and defeated the chief of all the tribes; you made his people run away and look for their relatives whom you had slain. You went and the fame of your power was heard among the northern tribes. You went and gave blankets to everybody, chief of all tribes.*

2. Do not let us stand in front of him, of whom we are always hearing, even at the outermost limits of this world. Do not let us steal from our chief, tribes! else he will become enraged and will tie our hands. He will hang us, the chief of the tribes.

[Neqā'pEnk·Em sings:] *Do not mind my greatness. My tribe alone is as great as four tribes. I am standing on our fortress; I am standing on top of the chiefs of the tribes. I am Copper Face, Great Mountain, Supporter, Obstacle; my tribes are my servants.*

The Nature of the Potlatch

H. G. BARNETT

So much has been written about the potlatch of the Northwest Coast tribes that almost everyone has some ideas about it. Generally, however, these ideas are not clear or consistent. As with every other complex institution, its various aspects and interrelationships have invited treatment from several different angles and points of reference. The result has been confusion in the minds of most students who have tried to reconcile the different emphases one with another and each with its cultural context. As Murdock says, too often it has appeared as an "excrescence." It seems justifiable, therefore, to attempt an evaluation of the essential facts, mainly with a view toward adjusting certain misunderstandings. It should be stated that access to unpublished data from the Tlingit, Nootka, and Coast Salish, lately collected by Olson, Drucker, and myself, has stimulated this attempt.

In its formal aspects the potlatch is a congregation of people, ceremoniously and often individually invited to witness a demonstration of family prerogative. Nominally, the entire kin or local group acts as host to the visitors. The composition of this body in terms of social units varies from time to time depending upon the character of the occasion and the importance of the principal in whose honour the celebration is held. The upper limit to the number of units which might thus act as host is conditioned mainly by the practical requirements of effective cooperation. The important fact, however, and one which has not heretofore received due attention, is that there is always a minimum unit which may undertake to entertain potlatch guests. This

Source: *American Anthropologist*, n.s., 40 (July-September, 1938), 349-57. Reprinted by permission of the publisher.

among the Kwakiutl is the so-called *numaym* or patrilineal kinship group which is united by a belief in descent from a common ancestor and by particular localized traditions and associations. The same situation exists among the Nootka and Salish. To the north the corresponding irreducible unit is the clan, or more exactly, the local segment thereof. In no case do members of these localized kinship groups receive at a potlatch given by any co-member. They unite in pledging support to the donor, preparing for the reception, and assisting at the formalities upon the appointed day. Conceptually and potentially all are donors and as such they do not share in the distribution.

This introduces the question of participation and provides a clue for a better understanding of it with reference to the categories of age, class, and sex. Since the potlatch is by nature a mechanism serving restricted family and individual interests, one person (or at most a few who are closely related) declares his intentions, invites the guests, and assumes the role of host. He is, in consequence, to be regarded as the donor. A potlatch, however, is by no means always a simple affair with one donor. Actually, in most cases it is either a series of minor individual distributions clustering about and taking advantage of the congregation occasioned by the major event; or it is a conjoint enterprise with any number of lesser contributors who publicize and retain their personal connections with their contributions and benefit accordingly. Thus it affords an opportunity for participation by all classes and degrees of property owners according to their means. These possibilities are open to any member of the society who has the least pretension to social prominence; and all parties, of high or low status, profit by the wider publicity and acclaim deriving from the cooperative character of the undertaking. The participation is direct and the return in prestige is immediate. Obviously the system allows for any degree of participation and it must not be supposed that those called commoners are excluded from it. They as well as the upper class members contribute through their chief and receive directly at potlatches. References to this fact are too numerous to be disregarded. That they participate indirectly, though none the less posi-

tively, there can be no doubt, for the common man is bound to be drawn into the system in some measure and to expend his energies in the interests of it. Nor is this sheer conscription; for the common man, the poor relative, and the skilled artisan all voluntarily trade their loyalty and their services for the patronage of a chief and the social favours he is able to bestow at a potlatch. None but slaves are excluded on any other basis than their own lack of industry or ambition. Even women and children participate freely, though the former usually have potlatches of their own separate from those of the men. Doubtless the number of people with an *active* interest in the requirements and the end results of potlatching is greater than has been supposed. Not only both sexes, but those of all ages and free classes are brought into an intimate relation with it. It is not an obsession, nor even an unremitting preoccupation, but it is a persistent incentive and a goal to be striven for.

One advantage of such an institution to the individual in a pre-literate, geographically extended society is obvious. As it operates on the Northwest Coast, this institution, the potlatch, enables the individual to assemble an appreciative and purposeful audience outside his immediate localized kinship group. He and his heirs benefit directly from the publicity inherent in the situation. They speak, sing, dance, or otherwise put themselves before the public eye at the same time that some claim to social distinction is expressed or implied with reference to them. Claims are commonly embodied in family names, so that the assumption of the latter customarily signifies a claim to certain distinctions and privileges. The announcement or reassertion of these claims is in all cases the reason for the potlatch, and no potlatch is devoid of them, despite the fact that in some accounts they appear as incidental to, rather than provocative of, the occasion. Conversely, so firm is the association that no claim whatever can be made without a distribution of goods to formally invited guests. This is the concluding feature of the celebration and the signal for the unceremonious departure of the visitors.

The goods distributed consist almost entirely of treasure items. They have an arbitrary value unrelated for the most

part to physical human needs. Their consumption utility, especially in recent times, has been negligible; they consist of cloth, blankets, and other surplus wealth which is manipulated solely upon the prestige level. Food, it is true, is consumed upon occasions which count in every way as potlatches; but the kinds and the quantities of food proper to such feasts preclude them from the category of subsistence economy. This becomes more certain when we realize that the materials of the potlatch are not intended to satisfy the hunger and comfort wants of the guests, but first and foremost to satisfy the prestige demands of the host, and secondarily that of the individual guests. Clocks, sewing machines, tables, and shawls are bestowed in quantities out of all proportion to their practical utility. The economic loss suffered upon occasions when slaves are murdered or emancipated is not great; in bondage they are as much of a liability as an asset and are useful primarily as an overt demonstration of the ability to possess them. The prestige value of potlatch goods was characteristic of them even in the days when they consisted mainly of such directly consumable commodities as meat, fat, and skins. A surplus in excess of need then, as later, was requisite for achieving social distinction. These facts have an important bearing upon the conclusions to follow, for it seems certain that the transfer of property at a potlatch bears but a remote resemblance to those exchanges which we ordinarily class as economic.[1]

In the first place, the goods are bestowed upon the assembled persons in their capacity as witnesses to the ceremony and the claims advanced. This is consonant with the public character of the proceedings and native statements leave no doubt about this aspect of the distribution. To that extent, therefore, it may be said to be a payment for services rendered.

It could further be argued perhaps that potlatch goods are given in return for the more tangible benefits of labour and ceremonial prerogative. Beyond question, compensation

[1] It will be noted that this statement has nothing to do with the economic aspects of wealth production. It is an assertion about the transfer of property at a potlatch which the following paragraphs are intended to explain.

for services is a concomitant of the distribution everywhere. Houses are built, posts carved and raised, and ceremonial offices performed by guest members of the congregation over all the area. This appears most clearly in the north where the notion of reciprocating groups is prominent; but it is just as true of the Kwakiutl and the Salish. None of the latter would think of building his own house or asking his family to do it. That would be degrading. In theory at least, only guests may do the work, and here as elsewhere they are paid for their services. But the character of both payment and service is worthy of attention. Sometimes members of the host group do more real labour than those who are paid for it. Again, imaginary services are paid for so that no one will be overlooked. Regularly, those who have given potlatches receive more than others. Chiefs always get more for their "services" than do common men – and very often do nothing. It is usual for them to delegate the performance of their duties to others. The truth is that their services are nominal and their pay is honorific. It is in recognition of an hereditary privilege and is not determined by the energy value, the necessity, or the intrinsic quality of the service. Finally, and conclusively, we have explicit statements as well as suggestive evidence that a man receives potlatch goods over and above his compensation. All this makes it appear that we must interpret the distribution as something more than a means of getting work done. That assuredly could be accomplished without the prodigality which is the keynote of the day.

It is also clear that the sums given to guests are not loans. Some confusion has arisen over this point, for the institution of the loan with interest, quite comparable to our own, flourished among the Kwakiutl and is known, at least, to some Salish, Haida, and Tsimshian. The significant fact is that lending and repayment form no part of the potlatch distribution. They are preliminary to it, and are engaged in for the purpose of accumulating the amounts necessary for the distribution. Dawson recognized this, and more recently Curtis and Murdock have verified it in print.

It follows, therefore, that potlatch presents are not capital investments, or are such in a secondary and derivative sense

only. They may be considered as prestige investments; but their more immediate character is that of a gift, a favour unconditionally bestowed. This soon becomes apparent to anyone attempting an inventory of a series of reciprocating potlatches, and finds warrant moreover in native attitudes. It is in complete harmony with the emphasis upon liberality and generosity (or their simulation) in evidence throughout the area. Virtue rests in publicly disposing of wealth, not in its mere acquisition and accumulation. Accumulation in any quantity by borrowing or otherwise is, in fact, unthinkable unless it be for the purpose of an immediate re-distribution.

Informal gifts expressive of friendship and good will are a well-known feature of this region. As an aggregate of formal gifts the potlatch achieves the same end, but the situation is complicated by its public character and by the unequal distribution factor. Representing as it does a convention of witnesses, the potlatch provides the means by which the individual may gain the desired publicity outside his own group. But publicity alone is not enough. He demands an active concern on the part of others with his worth. To achieve this he aims, by exploiting and virtue of liberality, to establish a basis of reputability in his associates' opinion. Until he has done this he has no social standing whatever; he has no name, no means of being recognized as a member of the society. Naturally, the basis which he aims to establish will be as favourable to himself as he can make it. He therefore makes an expenditure of wealth in accordance with the esteem in which he is held or wishes to be held; that is to say, in accordance with the status he holds or presumes to acquire. This is rather a close measure of his own self-esteem, or will tend to become so, for he cannot long support his own self-esteem in the face of the disesteem of his fellows, nor will it in the long run be less than that generally accorded to him by them. As a result, the totality of a man's potlatches, given by him or for him, is an acceptable gauge of the esteem in which he holds himself. At the same time it posits a formal basis for recognition by others. Furthermore, any one of a man's potlatches is a fair, but not certain, indication of his self-esteem since he constantly strives to outdo himself and those

who have done for him. The stimulus to excel in this sense is everywhere active, even when other comparisons are not impelling. As Drucker phrases it, the conscious effort to improve upon one's heritage is the only kind of "rivalry" known to the Nootkans.

The factor of unequal distribution has important consequences too. Any gift expresses some esteem, some recognition of the recipient's worth; but in order to know how much, there must be some basis for a comparison. This standard of reference is what other people get. Gifts are distributed at a potlatch according to the rank of the receiver. Thus the donor gives expression to the esteem in which he holds each recipient with respect to every other recipient. The inequality in the gifts reflects a judgment of comparative social worth from the particular donor's point of view.

That this is not a philosophic construction to explain the nature of the potlatch gift can be shown by a number of facts. The selective character of the gift, for one thing, is indicative of esteem. Not everyone is so honoured, nor in the same degree. There are many instances of gifts which discriminate between those who have given a certain kind of feast or entertainment and those who have not. The Salish "feel good" when they receive a dollar, but "cheap" if the gift is a quarter while others get a dollar. The Tlingit always give potlatches to the other moiety to "show them respect." The verbal responses of recipients are most significant. The most common ones are expressions of gratitude. Indeed, the whole potlatching complex is not so alien to our own conceptions that it cannot be readily understood with a little reflection upon the real character of our Christmas gifts, our reciprocal entertainments, and our custom of "treating."

The expression of esteem, both for self and for others, inherent in potlatch gifts are conventional *formal* expressions. They are customary and culturally approved modes of declaring estimability. There is no maintaining that every individual donor is prompted by the same emotions, nor even that a necessary ingredient of his emotional complex is esteem for his guests. He may be motivated by nothing more positive than the desire to conform to custom as he makes an unequal division of his goods. Nevertheless they

are acceptable vehicles for signifying regard and this use of them is immediately comprehensible to everyone.

As tokens of esteem they are productive of good will. They compliment and gratify the recipient. They flatter him by recognizing his social worth and gratify his wishes in establishing a basis for it. The result is necessarily a good-will institution since its aim (recognition for the individual) could not be achieved otherwise than by voluntary concurrence. There is abundant evidence to show that the potlatch is fundamentally of this character and it is important in view of widespread notions to the contrary. In spite of the inimical demonstrations connected with it at times (see below), guests are always thanked for coming, watching, and making complimentary speeches. It must be remembered too that it is the guests who labour and, in the north, perform the reciprocal ceremonial duties, all in a spirit of cooperation and good will.

It is apparent that the two factors (potlatching to establish position and receiving according to status) are complementary aspects of one fact. The second is but the fruition of the first. That is why the giving of a potlatch does not validate the status claims of the donor. He can only make a claim. Under ordinary circumstances such prestige claims are beyond question; they simply confirm publicly facts already conceded by everyone. Nevertheless, a closer analysis will reveal that validation of status must come from the other members of society – the potlatching members in fact – and it depends upon the good will which the claimant is able to establish among them.

As a set of gifts, by an acceptable assignment, are capable of expressing esteem (i.e., recognizing status) for the individual recipients, so they can be effective, by a contrary use, in expressing disesteem. As a device for precipitating insult situations the deliberate use of this is confined almost exclusively to the Kwakiutl. The characteristic response is an immediate reassertion of status by the affronted party. This takes the form of a significant gift to the offender, or a more general distribution or destruction of property. If the slight happens to be accidental, as is usually the case elsewhere than with the Kwakiutl, the offender atones with

a gift in excess of what would otherwise have been given. If not, the challenge is accepted and an extravagant contest with property develops. The so-called "face-saving" potlatch belongs to this same category since it is also effective in restoring esteem and reconstituting the ego. By means of it a person of consequence who has suffered a bodily injury or an indignity can "cover his shame" and prevent future reference to the matter by a distribution of property. This reaction to a shameful situation is known from the Tlingit to the Salish, with perhaps an over-development among the Kwakiutl.

It should be borne in mind that the recipient at a potlatch is not primarily concerned with getting back the amount he has previously given to his host. Receiving less is not prejudicial to his standing, and to assist upon an equivalence is contrary to the code of liberality. The expressions of esteem and counter esteem (for the recipient in each case) need not stand in a one-to-one relationship. Each is a purely relative statement of the recipients' rating with respect to one another upon a particular occasion. The individual is interested above all in the amount he receives as it compares with that of the other guests. That is his recognition. The sum total of the gifts is the concern of the donor; that indicates his status. Attention to the matter of the return, whether it should be greater or less, is also the concern of the host, for it establishes his rating with respect to the particular guest. It is a matter of self esteem to return as much as or more than one has received; failure to do so reflects upon no one but the defaulter. This is the motivation at work in the spectacular rivalry potlatches.

Such contests are therefore latent in any potlatch, but as a patterned response their elaboration is abnormal from an areal standpoint. Their development is understandable in the light of what has already been said plus certain historic factors; but that they are the essence of potlatching, or even its most frequent manifestations, is a fallacy which can easily be demonstrated. As with the loan, its chief exponents are the Kwakiutl, mainly those about Fort Rupert. Some Salish, Haida, and Tsimshian are at least acquainted with this manner of reckoning with opponents.

The Tlingit and Nootka know of it, but for the most part it is foreign to their conceptions of potlatching. As an outgrowth of an invidious comparison between donor and recipient it is almost wholly a contest of self appraisal. The factor of recipient esteem spoken of in connection with the ordinary potlatch and its multiple recipients does not enter. The motivation is quite different; the participants are often embittered and exert themselves to humiliate each other. Indeed, in the descriptions of the famous Kwakiutl contests attention is so completely centred upon the antagonistic attitudes of the two rivals that an important fact is lost sight of; namely, that they are only the principals in a drama, which like all dramas, is for the benefit of spectators. The spectators in this case are witnesses. Not only that, they are really judges. They, in the last analysis, choose the "winner" and make the final award which is formal recognition of the claims of one or the other of the rivals. This is the ultimate aim of all potlatching as has been shown before, and the present instance is no exception. Conquering a rival would be an empty victory – as it has been – without formal recognition of the fact by the other members of society. Their good will is essential for this, since each of them is a free agent under no compulsion beyond the dictates of his own conscience. Their majority decision is informally arrived at, and often one influential person can turn the tide of acceptance or rejection by being the first to acknowledge, at his potlatch, the right of one of the rivals to receive more, or in advance of the other. This, of course, is what is meant by formal recognition. Its expression, through the only possible medium of the potlatch, makes the latter an effective instrument of public opinion.

It is impossible to do justice to a subject so complex in a few pages, but it is hoped, at least, that sufficient evidence in its proper perspective has been offered to contribute to a better understanding of the potlatch. More is at hand and much of it is available to the patient reader of the published literature. Above all, the present summary points to a more refined and definitive concept, and consequently to a more circumspect use of the term. It signifies not simply an

exchange of gifts, for that custom is too widespread and diversely associated to be the criterion of the potlatch. Neither is the latter fundamentally competitive. It is characterized by certain formal requirements, by an implied equation of social worth with institutionalized liberality, and by its function as a vehicle for publicizing social status.

Fighting With Property

HELEN CODERE

"Fighting with property" instead of "with weapons," "wars of property" instead of "wars of blood," are Kwakiutl phrases expressing what has proved to be a fundamental historical change in Kwakiutl life occurring within the period known to history. It has been the purpose of this investigation to trace the various tendencies in Kwakiutl life as they were furthered or inhibited by the pressures of the contact culture and to determine both the binding force and the dynamics of this historical process. The general conclusion is that the binding force in Kwakiutl history was their limitless pursuit of a kind of social prestige which required continual proving to be established or maintained against rivals, and that the main shift in Kwakiutl history was from a time when success in warfare and head hunting was significant to the time when nothing counted but successful potlatching.

This conclusion about Kwakiutl history has emerged from the data and can be explained by them. That some of the Kwakiutl were aware of the historical change in their way of life gives additional confirmation as well as additional insight into the character of these people. Most of the Kwakiutl statements indicating this awareness were made within the period of the eighteen-day winter dance ceremonial given at Fort Rupert in 1895. The statements themselves are very explicit:

This song which we just sang was given by the wolves

Source: Helen Codere, *Fighting with Property: A Study of Kwakiutl Potlatching and Warfare, 1792-1930*. Monographs of the American Ethnological Society, vol. XVIII (New York: J. J. Augustin, 1950), 118-25. Reprinted by permission of the University of Washington Press, Seattle.

to Ya'xstaL . . . when he received the death bringer with which he was to burn his enemies or to transform them into stone or ashes. We are of Ya'xstaL's blood. But instead of fighting our enemies with his death bringer, we fight with these blankets and other kinds of property.

We are the Koskimo, who have never been vanquished by any tribe, neither in wars of blood nor in wars of property . . . Of olden times the Kwakiutl ill treated my forefathers and fought them so that the blood ran over the ground. Now we fight with button blankets and other kinds of property, smiling at each other. Oh, how good is the new time!

We used to fight with bows and arrows, with spears and guns. We robbed each other's blood. But now we fight with this here (pointing at the copper which he was holding in his hand), and if we have no coppers, we fight with canoes or blankets.

True is your word, . . . When I was young I have seen streams of blood shed in war. But since that time the white man came and stopped up that stream of blood with wealth. Now we are fighting with our wealth.

The time of fighting has passed. The fool dancer represents the warriors but we do not fight now with weapons: we fight with property.[1]

THE POTLATCH AS A KIND OF FIGHTING

Along with these statements goes a wealth of evidence demonstrating that the potlatch was considered to be a kind of fighting. The description of the potlatch given above included materials which indicated that potlatching was a metaphorical warfare, but it is necessary to show how much this was the case. Potlatches were planned like campaigns against an enemy. Although they were given by individuals, it must be remembered that the *numayn* and even the tribe to which the individual belonged had their prestige and rank at stake in every potlatch. Before and during a series of potlatches given in connection with the 1895 winter

[1] This statement was made with reference to a dancer whose predecessor in the ceremonial position had actually killed many men in war and head hunting.

dances, two of the Kwakiutl groups involved, the Koskimo and the Kwakiutl of Fort Rupert, had separate meetings in the course of which strategy was planned and they were exhorted to make the most intensive efforts to win out over their rivals, or "friends on the other side." The Kwakiutl of Fort Rupert were appealed to in the following fashion:

Friends, I ask you to keep yourselves in readiness, for the Koskimo are like to a vast mountain of wealth, from which rocks are rolling down all the time. If we do not defend ourselves, we shall be buried by their property. Behold, friends! They are dancing and making merry day after day. But we are not doing so. Remember this is our village and our battlefield. If we do not open our eyes and awake, we shall lose our high rank. Remember, Kwakiutl, we have never been vanquished by another tribe.

On each of the two days following, the Kwakiutl held secret meetings again. At the first they were told . . . "the Koskimo are likely to beat us in our war with property. Therefore I ask you not be to asleep, else the Koskimo will surely walk right over us, friends!" At the second, two speakers set forth reasons why they should be anxious about their potlatches with the Koskimo and should exert themselves:

. . . O friends! Let me ask you chiefs and new chiefs of my tribe, do you wish to be laughed at by our rivals? We are almost beaten by the Koskimo. We are only one potlatch ahead of them. After this pile has been distributed, we shall only be two potlatches ahead of them, instead of four as our fathers used to be. Take care friends! Our friends the Koskimo are strong in rivalling us in distribution of property . . .

. . . He spoke about our rivalry with the Koskimo, and said that we were beaten by them. This is true, although we are two potlatches ahead of them. You know that every time when the tribes come to our rich village, we always have four or five persons more to give blankets away than they have. Therefore, take care, young chiefs! else you will lose your high and lofty name; for our grandfathers were

never beaten, neither in war of blood nor in war of wealth, and therefore all the tribes are below us Kwakiutl in rank.

The speech made at a meeting of the Koskimo the next day shows that the Kwakiutl of Fort Rupert were correct in their estimate of the situation. The Koskimo were aware of their numerical advantage in potlatching but did not underestimate their potlatch enemies:

We have two chiefs in our tribe and therefore we cannot be vanquished in our strife with property. Look out! Do not let the Kwakiutl vanquish you, for they are a few only. See how many you are! There are enough Koskimo to fill the seats all round the walls. The Kwakiutl could not fill one half the seats in this house. Therefore they cannot vanquish us. Take care friends!

The element of contest and the evocation of an almost patriotic fervour, both warlike features absent in their actual warfare, are present in these speeches. The strategic planning of potlatches in order to challenge or to maintain positions is present in the full account from which the quoted speeches were taken.

It would be difficult to exaggerate the degree to which the talk, the songs and the ceremonies of potlatching borrowed the metaphor of war and even developed it to the point where the metaphorical war had more meaning and thoroughness than their one time "fighting with weapons." The usual word for potlatch was "p!Esa," to flatten, and it came to mean to flatten a rival under a pile of blankets or "means of flattening," for the word for "potlatch blanket" took its origin from the same root and had this literal meaning. The names of coppers often indicated that they were indeed the weapons of the new kind of warfare, potlatching: "War," "About whose possession all are quarrelling," "Cause of Fear," "Means of Strife." A great copper belonging to a chief was spoken of as his acropolis or fort on which he and his tribe could stand in safety and greatness. A broken copper was spoken of by its owners as "lying dead in the water off our beach" meaning that the breaking of it was as successful an attack against the rival as a killing would have been.

The songs sung at potlatches call upon all the imagery of war and apply it to the distribution of property. In the last song given below, the text speaks only of war, yet Boas was informed that every reference to war meant only the distribution of property in potlatches; that every image of war given here had its potlatch equivalent in meaning; and that the song actually commemorated a victory in potlatching by the Fort Rupert Kwakiutl over the Nimkish.

The great Ia'k·îm will rise from below.
He makes the sea boil, the great Ia'k·îm. We are afraid.
He will upheave the seas, the great Ia'k·îm. We shall be afraid.
He will throw blankets from out of the sea, the great Ia'k·îm.
He will distribute blankets among all the tribes, the great Ia'k·îm.
We fear him, the great Ia'k·îm.

What is on the enemies' blanket? Wiēē.
War is on the enemies' blanket. Wiēē.

Food will be given to me, food will be given to me, because I obtained this magic treasure.
I am swallowing food alive; I eat living men
I swallow wealth; I swallow the wealth my father is giving away.

Let us show what we gained by war!
. . . I did not turn my face backward to look at those who were bothering me when I went to make war on you friend.
Throw your power that is killing everybody, throw your fire of death, throw what makes them turn their faces downward, throw it against them who went to make war upon you.
I surpass them, they are the lowest of the whole world.
I pulled them into my canoe to be my slaves, that they bail out the war canoe.

The ceremonial, like the songs, not only takes much of its imagery from warfare but also substitutes in many cases the symbols of successful potlatches for what at an earlier

time was evidence of success in real war. For instance, in the description of the Koskimo winter ceremonial of 1895 there are many such details:

Each man carries as many hemlock wreaths as he had killed enemies during war expeditions. They also carry bows and arrows. Then they step up to the middle of the house and throw one wreath after the other into the fire, calling the name of the enemy whom it represents. As soon as a wreath is thrown into the fire they call "yē," and all repeat this cry. At the same time they shoot arrows into the fire. This ceremony is called yî'lxoa, which means placing the head of an enemy on a pole. The fire is called XusE'la which means fighting place. The whole ceremony is called al'Xts'āliL wā'lastEm (carrying blood into the house and giving away much property) or k·'ā'g·euLaxstā'la (sharp edge of a knife). At present the wreathes represent the number of coppers which a man has given away. They have taken the place of heads, because according to the usages of the Kwakiutl, a man who has given away a copper by doing so becomes a victor over his rival.

RIVALRY IN WHICH FIGHTING AND POTLATCHING WERE COMBINED

Although the imagery of warfare as it was applied to potlatching seems to have more force than the actual practices of war to which it refers, there seems to have been a time when fighting with weapons and fighting with property were more or less equal and interchangeable means of gaining prestige. The use of such imagery suggests a carry-over from an earlier situation of this sort and there is additional evidence to support this view. This evidence consists of three stories of rivalry between Kwakiutl chiefs. The dating of the stories is uncertain, but they have in common a mixture of potlatching and physical violence which is not characteristic of the potlatch as it is known and described in the latter part of the nineteenth century. In spite of the fact that the stories are undated and of a traditional character, the claim made for one of them by George Hunt that "this

is the true story of two chiefs" might be made with full justification for his story and the other two as well.

The first story is about the origin of the Kweka group of the Kwakiutl in the violent rivalry of two brothers; the victor and survivor established the new group. Charles Nowell repeats the story his father had once told him and introduces it by saying that the Kwakiutl did not like to be reminded that the Kweka or "murderers" had once worsted them and that they were the descendants of the brother who had been killed. He adds that the Kweka only made reference to this matter "when we are fighting them with potlatches." According to the story, the rivalry began when the two chiefs, Maxwa and Yakodlas, bet heavily against one another on the outcome of a throwing game their young men were playing. Yakdolas won and gave a potlatch to the tribe of Maxwa with his winnings. The story then reads ". . . Maxwa also gave a potlatch, and so they went on in that way. When the one give a feast, the other give a feast; when the one give a potlatch, the other give a potlatch. They begin to have hatred between them." Then Maxwa gave a feast and Yakodlas and his group noticed that one by one the men of Maxwa's group had slipped out of the house. They suspected trouble and left the house themselves holding a heavy cedar plank over the head of their chief, a wise precaution when it was seen that Maxwa had indeed posted one of his men on the roof with a great rock to throw down on Yakodlas. This open enmity continued and finally Maxwa was killed.

The second is the famous story of the two rival chiefs, Fast Runner and Throw Away, both chiefs of the same village of the Kwakiutl but of different *numayms*. The two chiefs "who were true friends in the beginning" became involved in deadly potlatch rivalry in which Throw Away was beaten when he was unable to equal the feats of Fast Runner in destroying a second copper, in breaking up and burning four canoes and in burning two slaves alive in connection with the winter ceremonial. Throw Away seems to have had no choice but to make a suicidal war against the Nootka. One man escaped to tell the Kwakiutl that Throw Away and the rest of his party had all been killed and the account ends: "Well, then was beaten Throw Away after that."

The last of the accounts is a tradition of the Nimkish, the Kwakiutl group living at what is now called Alert Bay. It concerns the violences committed out of the desire to possess the large copper, "Causing Destitution," that was obtained originally from the Bella Bella. The fathom and a half long copper was highly prized and soon after its second owner had bought it, for ten slaves and ten canoes and ten lynx blankets, he was pursued because of it but managed to hide it in the ground before he was killed. Two orphans found it and gave it to Wa′xwid, the successor of the man who had been killed, rather than to their own uncle who had not been treating them kindly. The two men quarrelled and the jealous uncle and his followers killed Wa′xwid and robbed him of all he possessed including the great copper, which was by this time worth a fabulous amount:

. . . there was nothing that was not paid for it. It made the house empty. Twenty canoes was its price; and twenty slaves was its price; and also ten coppers tied to the end was its price, and twenty lynx skins, and twenty marmot skins, and twenty sewed blankets, was its price; and twenty mink blankets was its price; and one hundred boards was its price; and forty wide planks was its price; and twenty boxes of dried berries added to it, and twenty boxes of clover, and also ten boxes of hemlock-bark, was its price; and forty boxes of grease was its price; and one hundred painted boxes was its price; and dried salmon not to be counted was its price; and two hundred cedar blankets was its price; and two hundred dishes was its price.

This valuable copper which would cost even more at its next potlatch sale, was then "obtained by killing" along with other property and the names and crests of the dead owner.

There is no certainty that these traditional accounts describe early conditions accurately but the suggestion they make of the existence of a period when physical violence and potlatching were equal means of winning over rivals is consistent with the views of the Kwakiutl as to the course of their history, the great extent to which potlatching retained the phraseology and symbol of war and violence, and the actual record of historical events and developments.

THE SHIFT FROM PHYSICAL VIOLENCE TO POTLATCHING

The historical materials have clearly detailed the continuous vigour and even growth of the potlatch until recent years, in contrast to the extinction of warfare and winter dancing in Kwakiutl life. The record of potlatching continues until about 1930 when the data become sparse and there is a doubt about its presence which can only be resolved by a field trip into the area. One of the most marked features of the historical record of the potlatch is the contrast in the size of the potlatches given before the approximate date of 1849 when a relatively small amount of property was distributed and after that date when the amount increased sharply. The winter dance ceremonial which was one of the many occasions for potlatching and which was associated with warfare in spirit and origin became extinct around the turn of the century. The last descriptions of the winter dance are dated 1895. The last war occurred in 1865 and this date must be used in connection with the facts that there is no record of any disturbance of the peace between the years 1837 and 1850, and that after 1850 the only notable breaches of the peace occurred in 1860. The date 1865, therefore, represents an extreme limit.

These dates give the rough outline of the historical change in Kwakiutl life. When the outline is filled in with a description of the character of the Kwakiutl potlatch and Kwakiutl warfare, and especially, when it is understood that the increased vigour of potlatching and the extinction of warfare were related and simultaneous occurrences, the picture becomes well-defined. When the rivalrous character of the Kwakiutl potlatch is kept in mind, the historical shift in Kwakiutl life is tellingly expressed by their own phrases, "wars of property" instead of "wars of blood" and "fighting with wealth" instead of "with weapons."

There is an interesting question as to the possibility of dating this shift more precisely. The period within which it occurred is between the time when the white men built Fort Rupert in 1849, and the attendant increase in the size of potlatches, and the time when warfare ceased in 1865. All the materials suggest that the shift should be placed early in

this period. Interest and activity in warfare seem to have been attenuated even before 1849. In one case, the end of "trouble" and the beginning of a peaceful era is definitely placed close to the year 1849. In 1895 an old man told George Hunt, "Your days, young men, are good. But our past ways were evil when we were all at war against each other. I mean you have no trouble nowadays. I was three times pursued by northern Indians at the time when we were still naked." The establishment of the trading post at Fort Rupert would have brought an end to the time when the Kwakiutl "were still naked." The Kwakiutl also said that "the white man came and stopped up [the] stream of blood with wealth" and, while it is not possible to know exactly how soon significant quantities of the white man's wealth came into Kwakiutl hands, the number of woollen trade blankets distributed at potlatches very shortly after 1849 indicates that it was early. Making due allowance for the fact that the data are not full and that there is an inherent difficulty in assigning a definite date to a cultural historical change which is essentially a development or a shift in emphasis rather than a discontinuity, this shift in Kwakiutl life seems to have occurred not long after 1849.

Some Variations on the Potlatch

PHILIP DRUCKER

The Tlingit viewed the potlatch as a cycle of rituals to mourn the death of a chief. It was not a single performance, but one that might take several years to carry to completion. It began with the reward to the group who had conducted the mortuary rites for the chief. These people always had to be of the opposite moiety from that of the deceased, that is, if the chief had been a Raven, a group from the Wolf side would take care of the body and bury it. In theory at least, this group should belong to the same lineage as the dead chief's father. In any case they were formally invited to a potlatch at which the new chief, the heir to the deceased, was presented. His rights to the position were explained and the origins of the various proper ties were recounted. For serving as witnesses, and for coming, as they said, "to console the [new] chief for his loss," they were given presents. At the same time, the chief who had been designated to take charge of the funerary proceedings was "paid." Subsequently, until the cycle was completed, the same people were summoned on various occasions: to rebuild the house of the new chief, and to raise a mortuary column in memory of his predecessor. Specifically, they were called upon to perform these tasks: to carve the mortuary column, to cut and carve the house posts, etc., so that some of the gifts were given to them in payment for their efforts, and some were given them simply as gifts.

The Tsimshian potlatch was essentially the same, although the overt expression of its purpose is sometimes

---

Source: Philip Drucker, *Indians of the Northwest Coast* (New York: McGraw-Hill Book Company, 1955), pp. 125-29. Title supplied by editor.

stated as being that of inheritance – that is, the announcement of and validation of the position of the new chief – rather than to stress the mourning function as did the Tlingit. Actually the potlatches of both peoples were essentially the same, serving at the same time to honour and commemorate the departed chief and to establish his heir officially in his place. The Haida, as will be brought out, likewise staged such affairs.

The Haida, according to available published sources, seem to have given potlatches most frequently to establish the position of a younger person as the heir presumptive. That is to say, a potlatch might be given in a child's honour by his parents before he went to live with his maternal uncle, whose status and rights he would eventually inherit. Although the child's father appeared to function as a host, the actual hosts were the mother and her lineage, who provided the property – both the ritual prerogatives bestowed and displayed and the material goods distributed as gifts. The father's lineage were the guests. Eventually, on the death of the maternal uncle, the heir gave a potlatch in the house which he was entitled to inherit, using the prerogatives and wealth of his own lineage. These combination memorial–status-assuming affairs were probably the major ones given by the Haida, as they were amongst their Tlingit and Tsimshian neighbours.

Among the Kwakiutl, Bella Coola, and Nootka, potlatches were often given, like those of the Haida, to establish a child or youth as the heir presumptive. In addition, these three peoples very often combined the potlatch with performances by the dancing societies. The latter were elaborate dramas representing the abduction of certain individuals (with inherited rights to the performances) by supernatural beings who returned them, endowed with varied and often spectacular ceremonial prerogatives.

The Salish groups, who had fewer ceremonial prerogatives to announce and validate, gave potlatches to confirm the status of their chiefs. To demonstrate that he was worthy of the post, and thereby validate his status, the headman of a Salish lineage might stage such a performance years after

he had nominally attained his position as leader of his extended family.

Too many years have passed since the last Chinook potlatch was given for us to have any detailed information on such variations as may have been made on the pattern along the lower Columbia. It seems most plausible to assume, however, that there was relatively little difference between their procedures and aims and those of their Salish neighbours.

The northernmost groups gave a minor variety that has been called a "face-saving" potlatch. When some misadventure befell a chief, or the heir to a chieftaincy – for example, if he stumbled and fell on some public occasion, or suffered any other public indignity – the damage to his honour could be repaired only by the formal distribution of gifts and the reaffirmation of his honourable status. The elaborateness of this performance depended to a large extent on the nature of the accident. If it was considered to have been a true accident and not the result of malicious human intent to demean him, a few small gifts sufficed to erase the damage to his dignity. If, however, there was any reason to believe that the affront had been deliberate, either through physical or magical means, a large and elaborate potlatch was called for. Among such groups as the Nootka and many of the Kwakiutl, where the function of the potlatch and its role in social integration was overtly recognized, a high-ranking guest at another chief's potlatch, when conducted to the wrong seat by the ushers, satisfied his honour by giving a single blanket to one of the hosts. In such a situation the host chief repaid this gift later on in the proceedings.

Competitive potlatches have received considerable attention in ethnographic literature because of their very spectacular nature. Two powerful rivals might give away and destroy thousands of dollars' worth of trade goods and money in the course of the contest. The destruction of property, of course, was to demonstrate that the chief was so powerful and so rich that the blankets or money he threw on the fire, or the "coppers" he broke, were of no moment at all to him. While such contests were held occasionally among many of the northern groups, they reached their highest de-

velopment – or perhaps one should say their peak of bitterest rivalry – in two places: Fort Rupert and Port Simpson. It appears fairly clear that nearly identical factors led to this development in the two localities. It will be recalled that several neighbouring Kwakiutl tribes moved into Fort Rupert when the Hudson's Bay Company post was established there, forming a loose confederation. Each of these tribes consisted of several local groups who, long ago, had formed fairly stable political entities, even though the local groups retained a certain independence of action as well as their individual property rights. Once the tribes occupied the common site, close to the trading post, they were faced with a very acute problem. It was inevitable that each tribe should sooner or later invite the others to potlatches. It is necessary to explain here that while the ranking of the individuals within each local group was well known, and in each tribe the lineages, and their respective chiefs, were graded in a well-established order of precedence from highest to lowest, there were no precise verbal designations for these sequences – that is to say, there were no native terms directly translatable as "first chief," "second chief," "third chief," etc. The crucial point, and the public recognition of a chief's claim to precedence, occurred at the time of the distribution of gifts to the guests. The highest-ranking chief was given the first gift – and ordinarily, to show respect for his rank, the largest single gift. The chief second in rank among the assembled guests was the recipient of the second gift, and so on in descending sequence. The chiefs of the newly organized Fort Rupert Confederacy had no precedents on which to base the relative rankings of the chiefs of the several tribes. This fact led them to initiate a series of potlatches in which certain of them asserted their claims to particular places – first, second, third, or fourth, and so on – in the consolidated precedence list. When two chiefs claimed the same place, the first one would give a potlatch, stating his claim; then the second would try to outdo him. Finally, one or the other gave away or destroyed more property than his opponent could possibly equal. The one who had been surpassed had no recourse. He could no longer contest his claim, for, in the native mind, it came to be regarded as

ridiculous that an individual of few resources (and of course this involved not only the man, but his entire local group) should attempt to make a claim against someone who had demonstrated power and wealth.

The extremes to which these competitions were carried and the attitude that developed in Fort Rupert – that great expenditures were sufficient to validate any sort of a claim – are exemplified by the unique institution which those people created. This was the title of "Eagle." An Eagle was a person who had the special right to receive his gift before the highest-ranking chief was presented with his. At one time there were twelve Eagle titles at Fort Rupert. Investigation has revealed that most of these Eagles were not chiefs at all, but were men of intermediate or even common status who through industry and clever trading amassed great quantities of material wealth. Some of them, in addition, were backed by certain chiefs who recognized them as potential tools to assist in the downfall of some high-ranking rival. It is interesting to note that the Eagles made no pretences at claiming tradition-hallowed names or crests, but assumed or tried to assume invented names that referred in some way to the privilege that they hoped to acquire – that of precedence in receiving gifts before the real nobles. There was even one individual who, in the early part of the last century, presumed to claim the right to receive his gift on the day *prior* to the potlatch. The chiefs would not tolerate this effrontery; when he insisted on his claim, they had him killed. Others of this *nouveau riche* contingent, however, managed to keep in the good graces of the chiefs and maintained their anomalous positions for many years.

After the nine Tsimshian tribes assembled at Port Simpson, they were faced with almost the identical problem regarding potlatch protocol. The order of precedence of the clan chiefs within each tribe had been established for a long time and was not subject to question. The intertribal rankings were not definite. Competitive potlatches, very similar to and quite as bitterly contested as those of the Fort Rupert Kwakiutl, became common. It is entirely possible that such contests occurred occasionally among various groups in the remote past when certain local groups assembled at common

winter villages in the process of tribal amalgamation. These prehistoric competitions never were so frequent or involved such quantities of valuables as at Fort Rupert and Port Simpson. An interesting sidelight on these specialized potlatches is afforded by the fact that among the Haida at Masset, fictitious competitions were staged solely to add a little spice to the occasion. The putative rivals agreed, in private, to expend identical amounts so that the affair would come out a draw. Some Southern Kwakiutl chiefs are known to have done this also.

Black Market in Prerogatives Among the Northern Kwakiutl

RONALD L. OLSON

The data in this paper refer primarily to the Owikeno or Rivers Inlet Kwakiutl and concern the illegal or surreptitious transfer of ceremonial prerogatives to alien tribes, chiefly to those groups of the same stock living to the south. The Owikeno were at one time perhaps the most numerous of the Kwakiutl-speaking tribes. Their prosperity resulted largely from the fact that theirs was the greatest salmon stream between the Fraser and the Skeena rivers. Owikeno wives were much sought after by neighbouring tribes for the Owikeno were extremely rich in the vast array of names, legends, songs, dances and all other items of the complex system of rank, privileges and prerogatives of the area, and these were normally acquired by advantageous marriages.

But the disasters attending contact with the whites struck the Owikeno with exceptional force. Their villages were not easily accessible and the restraining arm of the missionary and Indian Agent was scarcely ever felt. Neither mission nor school was ever established in their territory, nor did the Owikeno follow the example of many of their neighbours and attach themselves to a trading post or mission. Tribal morale fell to a low point. In 1935 a potlatch ended only with the burning of the entire village where the survivors had isolated themselves. Worse, all the ceremonial regalia were destroyed as well. Today only about twenty adults survive, but they and their children still retain the rights to all the names and the attendant prerogatives of their ancestors for these intan-

Source: *Kroeber Anthropological Society Papers*, Number 1 (Berkeley, California, 1950), pp. 78-80. Mimeograph. Reprinted by permission of the publisher.

gibles are in native theory eternal and indestructible. They may be in abeyance but they are not extinct. Those not in use lie dormant, so to speak, and may be revived at any time by an heir giving a potlatch and assuming the title in question.

Since the rights to literally hundreds of prerogatives now reside in the handful of survivors, each of these survivors holds at least potential or partial rights to more names and the attached prerogatives than he can possibly assume for no name may be assumed without giving a public festival (or potlatch) costing from a hundred to several thousand dollars. Furthermore, there is an elaborate but obscure code regarding the ethics and rights of potlatching. Much of this in turn revolves around concepts of social status, which again rests on intangible but elaborate standards. There are definite limits to which a man may aspire, however great his ambition or his willingness and ability to potlatch. Attempts to go beyond these limits would entail a loss of "face" as devastating as loss of "face" in China or Japan. The result is that a large number of titles heavy with prestige go begging for want of a candidate who is at once willing, able and worthy of assuming them.

Through centuries of intertribal marriage it has come to pass that almost all the natives from Seymour Narrows to Prince Rupert are in some way related, or claim to be. Accordingly, each has a potential or remote fractional share in many of the prerogatives not only of his own tribe but of other tribes. But there exists a fairly definite scheme of priorities which usually prevents indiscriminate assumption of titles by unworthy, unjust, or alien claimants.

Among the Owikeno these titles and the associated prerogatives are called *suyaema*, which translates as, "things which one may lay hold of," or almost, "things that men live by." Each adult among the survivors holds undisputed claim to one or several titles and a few persons of high rank could lay claim to many. As one man phrased it, "My *suyaema* are without number and beyond counting," – meaning that he had prior or secondary or other rights to a great many titles and prerogatives both active and dormant.

No right-thinking Owikeno would consider *selling* his

prerogatives. They may be given in a marriage, lent, given away in a potlatch, or disposed of to settle a financial or even a moral obligation, – but sold, never! "We Owikeno do not *sell* our *suyaema,*" they say, referring with contempt to that practice among some neighbouring tribes.

The aspirant to a name should make sure that there are no objections to his assumption of the dormant title. If there are none he proceeds to lay his plans. The attendant ceremonies are called "bringing out" or "showing." This clinches the right to the title since its assumption is done at a public festival, i.e., there are witnesses. A title not thus validated is worthless or, in effect, still dormant. Proof of just claim also involves a statement publicly made by the claimant or his "speaker" as to how the claimant came to inherit the right to the title. The usual mechanism or form includes the telling of a legend concerning an ancestor and how this ancestor came by the things in question. Usually a supernatural experience of this ancestor is related. These legends (and here is the crux of the matter) contain much detail such as names, descriptions and events which supposedly only a rightful heir could know. Above all they contain detailed references to local places which no alien or false claimant could conceivably duplicate. The distribution of gifts is in part a payment to the guests for honouring the host by listening to all this and witnessing the ritual.

In recent years some members of the tribe reputedly have sold several dormant Owikeno titles to aliens. These have not been the names of highest rank but names which nevertheless are decidedly worth owning. What they really sell are the legends which authenticate the titles, and which could not possibly carry thc mark of authenticity without the attendant details. Those who thus acquire the treasured prerogatives have only to "bring them out" by means of a potlatch. The price is usually several hundred dollars. This may be used by the black marketeer to finance a potlatch at which he or members of his family assume other dormant titles or add to the "heaviness" of those already held.

There is neither kin-group nor tribal mechanism for preventing the unscrupulous from thus disposing of the treasured items; neither is there a means of punishing them.

Public opinion has lost its force. Those who may have had equal or even greater claim to the title can do nothing beyond spreading gossip about the supposed transaction. The illegal trader in prerogatives may be called a "grabber of *suyaema*" with the connotation of "stinker"; but accomplishes nothing. In former times a feud of an intertribal war could have resulted. But now gossip is soon forgotten by all but those directly concerned. The unprincipled seller had at least a fractional claim to the things in question – as is proved by his knowledge of esoteric details. The buyer learns the details well enough to sound convincing when he assumes the title. The false claim becomes in time a true claim. The falsity is forgotten or ignored. An Owikeno title has been lost and no one can prove that it was a "black market" operation.

Gɪt-la′n Chief's Potlatch

VIOLA GARFIELD

A man may be forced into giving a potlatch by the taunts directed at his lineage during the feasts of others, or by untoward events which reflect upon the dignity of the lineage. Such was the position in which the present Gɪt-la′n chief, Gusgai'in, found himself.

When his uncle died in Port Simpson twenty years ago, he returned to the village from Victoria, where he had lived with his mother, to take part in the funeral. There he announced his intention to assume the name and position at a later date. Due to the fact that he is a Canadian citizen there was some opposition to his taking the name. However, he married in the village and signified, by participation in native affairs, his serious intention of making it his home. Another obstacle was the fact that there were less than twenty-five Gɪt-la′n in the village and he would have a very small number to aid him in giving the necessary potlatch.

Sometime after his uncle's death he was addressed by the chief's name (Gus-gai'in) at a potlatch given by one of the other chiefs. It is very improper to address a man by a name which he has not publicly taken and the chief and his tribesmen resented the slur, though they could not be sure that it had been intentional. It was also resented by the members of the Wolf clan, to which he belonged. As neither they nor the Gɪt-la′n were in a position to finance a feast then nothing was done.

Later another situation arose which they could not ignore. One day Gusgai'in and a Wolf clansman were going under

---

Source: Viola Garfield, *Tsimshian Clan and Society*. University of Washington Publications in Anthropology, vol. 7 (Seattle: University of Washington Press, 1939), pp. 204-206. Reprinted by permission of the publisher. Title supplied by editor.

the bridge with their gasboat, which was too wide for the opening and they were stuck between the piles. While they were struggling to push the boat free the tide fell away beneath them, adding further to their predicament. The remark was made in the hearing of the Wolves, "We saw a wolf hanging up under the bridge." The chief was approached by the leading Wolf clansmen of the village to consider some means of wiping out their humiliation.

He then called the Wolves to a feast, together with their wives and husbands, explained the situation to them and asked their advice. It was early fall and near the recognized time for festivities. The Wolves have a traditional feast[1] that is exclusive to the royal house of Niəs-łaganu·ʼs of the Tsimshian proper and Gusgai'in of the Nɪsqa, from whom the Gɪt-la'n chief traces his descent. This feast they decided to give.

Gusgai'in stated the amount that he had to spend and the Wolves and those married into the clan made contributions. As the giver of the feast, Gusgai'in was responsible for the return of contributions made by non-clan members. For instance, a clan sister contributed as a Wolf while her husband gave as an investment, the amount of which Gusgai'in would have to return at some future date. A clan sister of Gusgai'in took advantage of the occasion to give her son a name. This was a boy's name by which he is still generally known, though a potlatch was given for him the following year at which he assumed a man's name. At the feast his mother presented three dollars for him, announcing the new name. This sum was not returnable. Twenty-six people con-

[1] This feast is called the Feast of Early Snow (hai-mɔks, hai-, "early"; mɔks, "snow"). The feast commemorated the escape of the ancestors of the Wolf clansmen from their Tahltan relatives. The Tahltans had a war in which two of their chiefs, one of whom was Gusgai'in, were killed. Their brothers and nephews fled, part of them reaching the Nass River where they were adopted and where their descendants have since lived. The descendants of the others ultimately reached the coast Tsimshian. One of the incidents in the adventures of the escaping Tahltans was the safe passage of four brothers under a glacier on the Stikine River. The traditional dish for this feast, which the Gɪt-la'n Wolves decided to give, was snow and olachen grease, mixed with crabapples and berries. Various adventures of the Wolf clansmen in their migrations were dramatized.

tributed money, food and handkerchiefs for the forthcoming affair. One hundred and seventy dollars were raised, about half of which came from the chief. His father-in-law, who was also a Wolf, made a substantial contribution.

Before dawn on the morning of the feast day several men of the clan went howling through the village giving the wolf call. They kept this up for an hour or more until they had covered the whole village. They were followed later in the day by messengers who invited the villagers to the feast.

When the guests had assembled in the community hall, where the affair was given, the food was served. Ice cream was substituted for the traditional feast dish and especially large bowls of it were served to all those who had cast any aspersions on the Wolves in the past. A few guests had not come to the feast since the Wolf women had let it be known that they intended to retaliate for taunting remarks these guests had made about the Wolves. The Wolf clanswomen, dressed in wolf skins and headdresses, went after the absent guests in a body and brought each of them into the hall. During their "raid" the women howled like wolves. Before each person who had taunted them was set such a large dish of ice cream that he could not possibly eat it. Gorging a guest and then making fun of him was a favourite form of ridicule and provided much amusement for the guests. The women also entertained with humorous songs which they had composed for the occasion. In these they commented on the failings of the guests.

When the feast and hilarity were over the chief arose and explained the mythological background for the feast they were giving. He thanked the guests for coming and announced that, in so far as he was able, he would fill the position of his late uncle. Then La'is, the senior Wolf of the Gɩlutsa'u tribe, arose as the chief's spokesman and said that, as the chief had been publicly addressed as Gusgai'in, the latter was hereby acknowledging the name and assuming the position. He also stated that the bridge incident was now wiped out, and should not be remembered, much less mentioned, hereafter. The second spokesman was Niʋks, the eldest man in the Gɩt-la'n tribe, who praised the new chief and commented that, under him, the tribe could expect a

great future. Spokesmen for each guest chief affirmed Gusgai'in's right to the name and position and welcomed the new chief as a brother. They also acknowledged that the bridge incident and the other slurs would be forgotten. Much of tribal history was narrated during the speeches and many compliments were paid the host and his lineage. After the conclusion of the speeches gifts of food and handkerchiefs were distributed to the guest chiefs and to all the adult men and women. Dancing ended the festivities.

Daniel Cranmer's Potlatch

HELEN CODERE

Kwakiutl ethnography contains many accounts of actual potlatches. The procedures used and the nature of the potlatch as a great social occasion are fully revealed (Boas 1897).* Because Daniel Cranmer's 1921 potlatch at Village Island shows the same general features that are shown in these earlier accounts, but also the greater size, scope, and complexity of potlatching characteristic of the later years of the Potlatch Period, some details are in order. The following is his summary of the main events of this potlatch:

The potlatch was at Village Island, because that was away from the agent and that is where my wife's relatives were. People came from all over, from Lekwiltok to Smith's Inlet. The invitation was given to all the chiefs of all the tribes. Only a few Nimpkish went, however, because they were afraid of the agent there. Three to four hundred men, women and children turned up.

The first thing that was done, was that all the things I gave were transferred over to me from my wife's side. The chiefs of her tribe made speeches. Those who made the speeches, my wife and her relatives and I were in button blankets.

That night a dance was given. Hamats!a and others H. M. was my hamats!a.

The second day a xwéxwe dance with the shells was given to me by the chief of Cape Mudge. I gave him a gas boat and

---

Source: "Kwakiutl," in Edward Spicer (ed.) *Perspectives in American Indian Culture Change*. (Chicago: University of Chicago Press, 1958), pp. 470-72. Reprinted by permission of the publisher. Title supplied by editor.

---

* See Franz Boas, "The Potlatch," reprinted on pp. 72-80 of this volume.

$50 cash. Altogether that was worth $500. I paid him back double. He also gave some names. The same day I gave Hudson's Bay blankets. I started giving out the property. First the canoes. Two pool tables were given to two chiefs. It hurt them. They said it was the same as breaking a copper. The pool tables were worth $350 apiece. Then bracelets, gas lights, violins, guitars were given to the more important people. Then 24 canoes, some of them big ones, and four gas boats.

I gave a whole pile to my own people. Return for favours. Dresses to the women, bracelets and shawls. Sweaters and shirts to the young people. To all those who had helped. Boats brought the stuff over from Alert Bay to Village Island by night (This was to evade the Agent). This included 300 oak trunks, the pool tables and the sewing machines.

Then I gave button blankets, shawls and common blankets. There were 400 of the real old Hudson's Bay blankets. I gave these away with the xwéxwe dances. I also gave lots of small change with the Hudson's Bay blankets. I threw it away for the kids to get. There were also basins, maybe a thousand of them, glasses, washtubs, teapots and cups given to the women in the order of their positions.

The third day I don't remember what happened.

The fourth day I gave furniture: boxes, trunks, sewing machines, gramophones, bedsteads and bureaus.

The fifth day I gave away cash.

The sixth day I gave away about 1000 sacks of flour worth $3 a sack. I also gave sugar.

Everyone admits that that was the biggest yet. I am proud to say our people (Nimpkish) are ahead, although we are the third, Kwag·uł, *Mamaleleqala,* Nəmgəs. *So I am a big man in those days. Nothing now. In the old days this was my weapon and I could call down anyone. All the chiefs say now in a gathering, "You cannot expect that we can ever get up to you. You are a great mountain"* [Field notes 1951].

Because potlatching was for the purpose of establishing and aggrandizing social worth, there is a tendency to depreciate statements made about a potlatch by the potlatch-giver himself. In this case, however, other informants who were not

related to the potlatch-giver confirm the report as does the potlatch account book.

Since a constant expansion in potlatching could not take place without a concurrent expansion in the amount of wealth, the system was in delicate balance. It was to end as a system when Kwakiutl earnings from European sources dried up. This began in the 1920's and continued unremittingly through the Great Depression of the 30's. Even before the 20's there were some signs of strain, signs that the expansion in earnings was not quite keeping up with the constant increases demanded by the potlatch, especially the potlatch connected with the purchase of a copper. In the Hunt history of twenty-one coppers there are several coppers which were getting so expensive by 1900 that they could be sold and purchased only with difficulty. One, for example, was bought originally from a Tsimshian in 1864. It changed hands about every seven years and went from 100 to 250 to 500 blankets and approximately doubled thereafter on every exchange. By the time its price was about 4,000 blankets several men held it temporarily with an option in hopes of raising the rest of the property needed for title. The man who finally bought it faced the same difficulty in getting buyers. By the time the price was about 8,000 blankets the device of an immediate sale at the same price was used (a type of sale that did not bring much credit to the short-time owner of the copper). By the time the history ends the proper price of the copper was 16,000 blankets, and there had been no clear prospect of sale for some time.

Lagius Gives Me a Copper

CLELLAN S. FORD

When Alfred* was about three years old, Chief Lagius, my wife's father, bought a valuable copper. He paid over fourteen thousand blankets[1] for it, and gave it to me in payment for the blankets we give him when I got married to his daughter. A man, when his daughter marries and he don't pay, it is a disgrace to him and the daughter and her husband. He is saying to the son of the daughter, "Your grandfather never gave any copper, or articles, or name to your father." I handed this copper over to my brother, and he sold it and gave a potlatch with it years after that.

I and my brother were helping him to buy this copper. Lagius' share in paying for this copper was four thousand blankets. Chief Lagius and his wife gathered about six hundred button blankets – blankets with buttons on them in bird and whale designs – four hundred silver bracelets, sixty dance headdresses, some boxes, brass bracelets, beads, wooden bowls, boxes with sea-otter teeth in them, and gave all these things to me. Those things they call *hawanaka.* This means they have come to me with canoes full of stuff, and the copper represents the mast of this canoe. I gave all that away myself at a potlatch here at Alert Bay. In that potlatch Lagius gave me the copper, and I turned it over to my brother. I called all the tribes together for the potlatch, and it took me two days to give these things around. I only

---

Source: Clellan S. Ford, *Smoke from Their Fires: The Life of a Kwakiutl Chief.* (New Haven: Yale University Press, 1941), pp. 168-82. Reprinted by permission of the publisher.

---

* Alfred is the son of Charlie Nowell, a Kwakiutl Chief and author of this autobiography.–[ed.]

[1] The blankets used in this transaction were single blankets worth fifty cents apiece.

invited the other tribes; the Fort Rupert tribes were left behind.

Lagius and me decide to give a potlatch so he could give me the copper. It is according to the customs of the Indians that the chief's daughter should have a copper given to her husband by her parents, and also the goods that they brought. But before that he generally gives me some money or blankets to give a small potlatch, or he buys some food from the store and give it to me to give a small feast just for my own people. When I came to Alert Bay, he buys some food from the cannery store and give it to me, and I give a feast with it to the Alert Bay people. After that, every time we have a new baby, he give me money to give a potlatch to give a name to this new baby about four days after it is born, and the same when the baby begins to eat, and on his tenth month there has to be a feast or a potlatch and Lagius helps me out – either with his own money or the money I give to him.

This is the story of how Lagius bought the copper which he gave to me after I married his daughter. The name of the copper means, "to clean everything out of the house." Tlatli-litla, chief of the Tlowitsis, owned this copper. My brother and Lagius went to ask him to let Lagius have that copper, and say that they will give him one thousand dollars as the first payment, that is, the "pillow" of the copper. He agreed, and he called all the people to the front of the house in Alert Bay. All the different tribes were here at the time.

When all the people were gathered in front of Lagius' house, another chief, Odzistalis, spoke for the chief of the Tlowitsis, saying that the chief is now ready to get rid of his copper, which he has already bought, and say that he has seen the chief of another tribe, which he thinks is able to buy this copper. And he said, "I hand over my copper to Chief Lagius." He asked another chief to go and hand this copper over to Lagius. These were both Tlowitsis chiefs. When Lagius took hold of the copper, he says: "I have now received your copper, which you want to sell, and I'll only keep it one day, [that means one year] and then I'll buy it from you. I will give you a thousand dollars as a pillow till I pay the rest. I have been looking for a copper as big as this,

for I have been awake every night, wanting to get a copper for my daughter's husband."

Then he counted out the thousand dollars, which the Tlowitsis chief took and said to all the people: "This money is ready to be loaned out. At the time Lagius will pay for my copper, I will collect this money, which is to be paid 100 per cent back to me, and then it will be paid back to Lagius." Lagius also stood up and say he has some money to loan out if anybody wants it, which is to be paid back in the same way. I also told the people that I have money to loan out. My brother also says he has money to loan out.

When Lagius or I or my brother loan out blankets, before we pay for the copper, we loan to anybody that wants them. Maybe they want to buy some food. Maybe they owe somebody else some money, and the owner of that money wants to collect from him; if he is unable to pay himself, he asks for the amount he is shy, to pay. Or maybe he wants to sleep with a girl and wants to get the money for that. So he goes to one of us and asks us for the money. He then uses it for whatever he wants. Then comes the time when we call in our money, because we are going to buy the copper. So we go to him and ask him to pay, and we collect what we had loaned.

One thing he can do is to go to Tlatli-litla and ask him for his share in the potlatch that this chief is going to give. He can only do this if he is not a Tlowitsis, because Tlatli-litla is not going to give the Tlowitsis anything in his potlatch. So he goes to him and gets his share and then pays one of us whom he owes, and when the potlatch is given he only gets a stick, which shows that he has been paid in advance what he is to get in the potlatch. If Tlatli-litla says that you want one hundred dollars but I'm only going to give you fifty dollars in my potlatch, then this man will go to another man that is loaning out money and say, "You loan me fifty dollars and I'll pay it back double." Or he may say, "I'll pay you 50 per cent or 25 per cent," depending on how long he is going to keep the money, and will point out when he is going to pay it.

Sometimes it happens that a man remembers something that was owed to his father or grandfather by another man's

father or grandfather, and he goes to that man and asks him to loan him some money, and when that man comes to collect it, he says, "No, your grandfather owed my grandfather that and never paid." They will argue about it if the man doesn't know anything about it. I know a man from the Tenaktak that always says he doesn't know anything about what his father owes to somebody else. When he is asked to pay what his father owes, he says, "Why should I pay what I don't know anything about?" What can the other person say? But everybody is afraid to loan him anything, and nobody will borrow from him either. Nobody trusts him.[2]

When it was all collected, we told the Tlowitsis chief that Lagius is ready to buy the copper. Tlatli-litla gave a feast and called all the people of different tribes into Lagius' house. While they were eating, Odzistalis, the other chief, stood up and told the people that he is now going to ask Lagius to pay for the copper, for the time is up. Lagius says, "I am all ready any day that you want me to pay for it." Odzistalis says, "We want you to pay for that copper tomorrow. Lagius says, "You better not sleep tomorrow morning, you better get up early, because we will start early in the morning."

The next morning, some men come along the houses and say: "Wake up. Wake up. Come and watch the chief who is going to buy the copper." When they all had their breakfast, they all come and sat down in the front of Lagius' house. Lagius, at the same time, had a lot of young men to take out the blankets from his house and pile it in rows – a hundred blankets to each pile, starting from his house in both ways, for his house was on the middle of the village. What Tlatli-litla paid for his copper was four thousand blankets, and this was all put down. The "pillow," which was now two thousand dollars, was returned to us the morning that we started to buy the copper. That made the four thousand blankets that we could start with.

[2] Here are sanctions that enforce payment of debts. One who does not pay what he owes is economically ostracized. Unable to lend or to borrow, he cannot participate in Kwakiutl social life. The principal means of obtaining gratifications – sex, food, and social prestige – is all but taken from him.

Odzistalis stood up and says: "I have now seen all the blankets that we have been paid for the copper, and we are not satisfied with the amount that we have seen. Knowing that you are a chief and are willing to add more value to the copper, we will ask a chief of the Mamaleleqalas to ask for more," and he calls him up and he spoke and says: "I don't see what I am going to say, for in my part I am satisfied with all these blankets that are in a row, but for the sake of the Chief Lagius' name we all realize that he wants to pay more. So I am asking you, Chief Lagius, to pay more – whatever you think is the right amount for my position." He was the head chief of the Mamaleleqalas, and Lagius brought out two hundred blankets and a copper worth a thousand blankets. He counted the blankets and says, "Now there is added one thousand and two hundred blankets."

Then Nigia, the next Mamaleleqala chief, was called by Odzistalis to speak. He got two hundred blankets and a canoe worth four hundred blankets, but he stood up again and said: "Thank you! Thank you! But you gave my chum one thousand two hundred, and I expect to get one thousand two hundred blankets, too," and he says: "I have brought out this copper that I have paid for not long ago, and you all know the value of it. Now you gain two thousand four hundred, which is double what your chum gained." Nigia stood up and laughed and said, "Thank you; that is what I want." Then the chief of the third clan was asked to get up, and he asked for more in the same way. When he got through, Lagius got some more blankets and a canoe. The chief of the fourth clan of the Mamaleleqalas was asked to stand up and ask for more, and he gained two hundred blankets and a canoe.

Then they started with the Tenaktak. They didn't ask the Kwakiutl or Nimkis tribes because we was on the other side – the buyers of the copper. They asked the head chief of the Tenaktak to get up and ask for more, and he received two hundred blankets and a canoe. Then the second chief of the same tribe was asked to get up and ask for more, and he received two hundred blankets and a canoe, and so it went on for every chief of every clan in the Tenaktak. Then the Matilspe, the Tsawatenox, the Kwekwesotenox,

the Gwawaenox, the Hakwames. Each chief received two hundred blankets and a canoe.

Now Odzistalis got up and said, "All of you tribes have asked the chief for more, but Tlatli-litla isn't satisfied yet, and so we will return to the Mamaleleqalas." And one of them was asked to stand up, and he asked for some more. We sat down for a long time and talk together and say, "We don't know what he is thinking of; all the different chiefs has asked for more, and now he is starting it all over again." Finally my brother stood up and says: "I don't understand what you are trying to get at, for all the chiefs of different tribes have asked for more. We don't know how many more men you are going to ask to stand up. So the best way is for you to just tell us how many more blankets you want. If we could give you what you ask for, we will do it. If not, that is all there is to it. We won't give any more than what we can afford to give."

So the two chiefs of the Mamaleleqalas was asked to get up. Tlatli-litla told these chiefs how much more he wants, that he wants three thousand blankets more. They were afraid to tell us how much they want, and they stand up a long time talking. The one tells the other to do the talking, and Nigia says, "You do the talking." They are afraid, for it is a disgrace to them if they don't get what they ask for.

Finally Nigia begin to say: "This is not our own words. They are put into our mouths to speak by the owner of the copper. We have been afraid to tell you how much more he wants, for we know it is too much. This is the first time that such an amount has been asked for, but we feel, Chief Lagius and Chief Owadi, that there is nothing impossible for you to do. Nothing is too hard for you, so we will let you know what the chief says." He says, "There will be the boxes, and there will be the blankets that they wear when they give the potlatch, and there will be the belts and there will be the feather for the head, which all comes to three thousand blankets."[3]

All the people that was sitting down watching start a humming sound just like a bee, for they were all saying that

[3] In symbolic terms Lagius is being asked to contribute more blankets – some to represent the boxes, some the belts, and so on.

it was too much. My brother got up and said: "Now we know what you want. So this is why you wanted to start over again, because you want that much. You say that you want three thousand blankets more. Ee-ee-ee-ee-ee-ee, Ee-ee-ee-ee-ee-ee, where will we get that much? That is too much. The best way for us to do is to return the copper to you, and I will gather these blankets up and give a potlatch with it." Saying that, Owadi walked home, leaving the people there still talking.

The Tlowitsis people stood there looking down for a long time. Lagius gets up and says: "Well, chiefs of your tribes, we have heard the amount of blankets that you still want. I, on my part, feel the same as Owadi feels. This has never happened in buying a copper before. I thought at first that I wanted to get up and walk home, but what I think now is for you to gather these blankets up and look after them yourselves, and we will try and get some more blankets, although it won't be three thousand – maybe half of that." The Tlowitsis chief, Odzistalis, got up and says: "What you say, Chief Lagius, makes things easier for us, because we were frightened that you and Owadi talk together to say that you will return our copper. That made us scared. But the way you now speak, that makes us feel better, and we will gather up the blankets and look after them ourselves." They gathered them up, and that was all for the day.

I went to my brother and asked him how many more blankets he has got. We walked in his house, and he begin to count them. There was one thousand five hundred blankets that he had. I told him that I'll give seven thousand and fifty dollars. Lagius also has over a thousand blankets, besides canoes and another copper, and my brother also had some more canoes. All these together was worth over five thousand blankets. I wrote it all down and showed it to Lagius. He got up in his house and says, "Ah-h-h-h-h-h-h, Oo-oo-oo-oo-oo-oo, Oo-oo-oo-oo," in a loud voice. He says: "Where will Lagius be, if I fail to buy the copper? Where will I be tomorrow? I'll be going somewhere north or south for shame."

Then he went out of his house and speak in a loud voice, and tell everybody to be sure and get up early in the next

morning and say, "Ah-h-h-h." And Odzistalis came out of the house where he was and says, "I have heard you, Lagius, and you are telling us to get up early in the morning." He says, "I will be bathing all night without going to sleep, and I'll be the first man to go and wake the people up." The next morning he was the one who woke up all the people and say that Lagius is going to give more. When they all finished their breakfasts, they all came to the outside of Lagius' house, and my brother says, "Now we will try again and give some more, but if you ask more than we can afford to give, that will be the last." And he called the young men to go and get the blankets from his house. They throw the rolls of blankets out of the window, and there was one thousand blankets.

When he finished that, I got my five hundred dollars that amounts to one thousand blankets, and Lagius also brought out one thousand blankets. Lagius says, "Wa-a-a-a-a-a, you have three thousand blankets and everything you ask for – your belts and blankets and boxes and feathers is all covered now." Odzistalis got up and spoke: "I knew in the beginning that Owadi didn't mean what he says, and I knew that Lagius didn't agree with what Owadi said. That is why we kept quiet, for we knew those two chiefs was just fooling us and trying to scare us. Now we have our three thousand blankets and that is done. The copper is yours, Lagius, and you can do what you want with it. The copper is no more ours." And he says, "Wa-a-a-a-a-a-a-a."

My brother says: "You say 'Wa-a-a-a-a-a.' I'll see if I can find about five pairs of blankets in my house that is dropped down somewhere." He called the young men to follow him and brought out two hundred blankets, and he says: "Wa-a-a-a-a-a. That is finished." Odzistalis got up again and said: "I've already said Wa-a-a-a-a-a. Bring out that little image whose name is 'ready to throw.' "[4] So they brought it out and stood it in the middle of the road. "Now we will call our grandson," he says. "Let all the people look at him." He got Alfred, who was a little boy, and he cried and didn't want to come. Tlatli-litla promised him fifty

[4] This was a little statue of a man about three feet high.

cents an hour for standing there. So they put him on top of the little statue. Then Tlatli-litla says: "All you Kwakiutls look at your chief who is standing here now. He is now in the midst of us all. Nimkis, look at your chief. He is now right in our midst." And he turned to his own people and says, "Tlowitsis, look at your chief." And they begin to sing the oldest song they have.

Then Lagius got up and says, "Now, my grandson, you will stand right in the midst of all the people that knows you." Then he turned to the Alert Bays and asked the young men to follow him, and my brother went toward his house and called the Fort Rupert young men to follow him. I and my wife went inside and got a hundred dollars. Lagius was talking on the back side of the road, and Owadi was talking on the other side, and I had a man to talk for me on the front side – all at the same time. The Tlowitsis people didn't know which to listen to, and they was just looking around. When we get through counting that, Lagius says, "Owadi, do you feel that you are getting crazy like I am, to see who is standing in the midst of us? And we all went in again, and kept on doing that again and again, till we had finished all the five thousand blankets we had. The people never said a thing; they was just looking around. Then Lagius says: "Wa-a-a-a-a. Now I know I have your copper. It is mine now. Now I can do anything I like." And he brought it out and showed it to the people. Then he turn around and says, "Owadi, I don't want to keep this copper for myself. You better get up early tomorrow morning and tell the people to get up early, for I am going to give this copper to your brother."

When we bought it, Lagius' money and my money, my brother keep track of how much we paid. We also keep track of how much he paid. All the amount we paid for the copper was 14,500 blankets. Lagius is the only loser. He paid four times, besides all the things he gave, what I paid him when I married his daughter – four thousand blankets for one thousand blankets. Three or four days after he sold the copper, Tlatli-litla gave a potlatch to all the tribes except the Tlowitsis and distributed these blankets and money around.

The next day we all came together, and Lagius told all the people that the copper was on the back of my wife. It was tied on her back, and fifty ten-dollar bank notes was sewed on the blanket she was wearing. That money means it is the shoulder strap she is holding the copper with. The copper was given to me, and also the strap of five hundred dollars, and that day I gave the five hundred dollars away to all the other tribes, except to the Fort Ruperts. When he gave me the copper, Lagius got up and told all the people that he was giving it to me, and at the same time, he gave me a name, Hamdzidagame, which means, "you are the man that feeds other people." This name belonged to Mrs. Lagius' uncle, the chief of the Tlowitsis.

When I gave the potlatch with the strap from the copper, I changed my name to Hamdzidagame, which was the name Lagius gave me, and I gave Alfred the name Melide, which means, "people are satisfied with olachen grease." At the same time, I put him in third position in my clan, where I was, and I went to the lower one – the ninth. From then on I received the gifts to him in potlatch myself and took care of him, but it was his position just the same. The same year, at Alert Bay, Johnny Whanuk also gave my brother, Owadi, articles for marriage, because my brother had married his sister. With these articles my brother gives a potlatch, calling all the same tribes that I called. At the same time he told all the people that Alfred's name will be "giving away of big coppers," and my brother put him in number one position in our clan, and my brother went down to his other position lower where he had another name. This was the sixth position in our clan, but he continued to get gifts for Alfred in the first position and take care of them until Alfred would be old enough to take them himself. If my brother had died before Alfred, then Alfred would have been the head chief.

In a marriage they have a box covered with a blanket, with red bark on it. When Lagius paid me the copper and all those things, he brought me a box, saying that masks are in there and all different kinds of dances. I can open the box when I give a winter dance and use his mask and dances. The masks all have their dances. I still have my

box unopened, because I haven't given a winter ceremonial yet. Lagius also give me a little totem pole with all his crests on it. It was about seven feet long, and he always used it whenever he was giving a speech. I use it every time I give a speech. At the visit of King George at Vancouver some of our people went down. I wasn't feeling well and didn't go. Tom Johnson went with other people. He came to me to borrow my blanket and hat – a mask hat – and my totem-pole walking stick. He used that in Vancouver, and the stick was stolen from him there. A man wrote and say he saw this same stick in the States used by an Indian called Mathias from North Vancouver. The Indian agents are still trying to find out where this stick is.

At the time Lagius gave me this copper, he told all the people that he was going to give me different kinds of articles – that he was going to *hawanaka*, which means he is going to put things in a canoe for me to take back to Fort Rupert to my home. He brought out one beaded blanket, one button blanket, one silver bracelet, a headdress like the ones you see with ermine skins on the back, and other things. He says: "These are the kind I am going to give you, and you will call the people together and give them away. This copper will be the mast to your canoe." Then he went and collected all those things he promised me and gave them to me – dishes, pails, sticks with otter teeth in them, about six hundred of those. Any girl that doesn't have that kind, it is a disgrace to her; when she quarrels with other women, they say she has no teeth, and is not fit to quarrel with – she has no teeth to bite with. And he gave me some bracelets and a lot of those big beads – strings of them. I gave away all these things in a potlatch to all the tribes except the Fort Ruperts.

At my potlatch, I handed my copper over to my brother to sell, so he could give a potlatch. He took it and sold it for more than we paid for it. He sold it to a chief from the Nimkis tribe who was buying it for his daughter's husband. When they come to buy it, my brother wanted more, but he and his daughter's husband says: "We haven't got any more. We will ask you to let us have our share in the potlatch in advance." They come and mention their relatives' names

asking for their share. My brother gave each of this man's relatives one hundred blankets, and the Nimkis chief received one hundred blankets. When it comes to the one that the copper is being buyed for, my brother counted ten piles of one hundred blankets and says, "Those are for him." They counted all these blankets and paid them back to my brother to pay more for the copper. At the time my brother gave his potlatch he just had a stick and say, "So-and-so, you have already had your share." This man sold the copper to give a potlatch, and in his potlatch he give my brother a thousand blankets, remembering how much my brother gave him in his potlatch. My brother loaned these thousand blankets out to other people, always mentioning my name. He is going to collect later to pay for my copper, which he has already sold. My brother died before he paid me for the copper, but the stuff he loaned out is still out. If it weren't for the Indian Act, I could collect in my brother's place and pay myself. As it is, all that he loaned out is lost to me through the Indian Act.

When Tlatli-litla gave the potlatch with the blankets that we paid him for the copper, he used a crest which he got from the Kwekwesotenox – a big cradle ornamented with shells, ermine skins, and red bark about eight feet long. Early in the morning before daylight he called all the Kwekwesotenox into the house which he was using at the time of his potlatch. The Kwekwesotenox had about a hundred rattles – about three feet long, hollow inside, three to four inches in diameter and painted. They begin to rattle those, and Alfred was put into the cradle. Somebody else made the noise of a baby crying, and all the people are making the rattles go to stop him from crying. A man begin to sing a baby's lullaby. Then all the people standing on the front begin to sing it too.

All the people from different houses were awake, wondering what the noise was. Some women came in with only a nightgown on to see what was happening, and they all want to come to the house and stop the baby from crying. Some of the people were so sleepy they didn't know what they were doing, and just got up and came to the house. The Kwekwesotenox started over again, and after they got through

they got my wife to go and stand beside her uncle, Tlatli-litla. The speaker, Odzistalis, told the three men that was standing behind the cradle to bring down the child, so Alfred was lifted out of the cradle and was brought down. He had a chief's headdress on him and shells hanging from the front of him – four shells in a row. The speaker says, "Now we have seen the baby of the chief's daughter." And he called my wife's name. "We are all lucky to have a male baby which you all see now standing here. This baby's name is Yatlalasogwelaq." The name means that everybody has to go and rock him. No position went with this name.

After they left Alert Bay, Tlatli-litla went home and came back again and called all the tribes to go to his village, for his wife is going to give him the articles to give away. At this potlatch, when he received those articles from his wife, he again put up this cradle and went through the same thing that was done at Alert Bay with Alfred. When he was through, his speaker, Odzistalis, stood up and says: "Now you have seen that cradle there. The noble baby is sleeping in that cradle, and nobody is allowed to come on the front of this house and make any noise for four days, lest this baby should be awakened and begin to cry. For if he does awaken because somebody is making a noise outside, there will be trouble."

The next day there was a potlatch on the other end of the village, and there was a quarrel about positions by the Fort Ruperts. There was a man half Mamaleleqala and half Fort Rupert who wanted to change his position, but the chiefs of Fort Rupert didn't want him to. The uncles of this man brought out their coppers – coppers they had broken before, and they only had the crosspieces of them – and says: "You haven't allowed our chief and your chief, your nephew, to change his position, and we are going to fight and put him there. You, Whanuk, we hear you say that you don't want it. Now I am going to strike you with this copper to make you shut up." And he threw the copper on the ground saying, "You, Wilson, we have also heard that you are another one who don't want our nephew to change his position, and here is another copper for you, and I am giving it to you to make you shut up." They put these two coppers together and says

to the young men to take these out to the deep water there and drown them. That means that they want to drown old Whanuk and Charley Wilson.

After this they went to the houses where they were staying. Tlatli-litla went into a Matilspe chief's house. I was amongst the people that was eating there. He came and stood at the place close to the fire and says: "I have come into your house to see you, for I know you have a big copper. Do you still keep that copper?" Maxwagila says, "Yes." Tlatli-litla says: "Bring it out to me. I want to see it." Maxwagila went into his bedroom and brought the copper out and handed it to him. Tlatli-litla looked at the copper, turning it over and over four times looking at the back and the front of it. Then he says, "What is the name of this copper?" Maxwagila says, "The name of this copper is Dentalayu." This name means "people are quarrelling about this copper," because it cost so much. Tlatli-litla says, "I will buy this from you." Maxwagila says, "That will be all right; take it away." And right on that place where Tlatli-litla stand, he begin to say right away, "Haw, haw, haw, haw." He goes around the house, and then he says: "I have told you not to make any noise in front of my house, where the baby is sleeping. You have awakened him up, and he is crying now. You have already been warned not to make any noise in front of my house. There is a sure thing that there will be trouble, and also that there is danger to the people that hears the noise and death to those people."

Then he went out and made a fire in his community house and all the people was called together. This was the second day of his potlatch, and they got this little statue that we mentioned before and put this statue on the rear end of the house and then put this copper on top of it. He told the people that he didn't want to do anything like breaking a copper. "That was why I warned you not to come near my house and wake the baby up, but since you have wakened him up, today I am going to break this big copper for you two that have been making the noise." And he cut half the top off and another corner from the bottom and gave one part to each of the Mamaleleqala chiefs that threw their

coppers into the water. Then he says: "Hap-hap-hap! I've eaten you. You are all in my belly now."

This was a wonderful thing that he did. When we came to Alert Bay about six months after that and all the people were here to a potlatch, one of those Mamaleleqala chiefs died. He wasn't sick at all – he just dropped down. The other one went to Fraser River that summer, and he also died there without being sick – just dropped down dead. They worried too much about how they are going to get a copper big enough to break for this chief that has broken a copper for them, and that is why they died. They tried even since Tlatli-litla break this copper for them to get a copper from the owners of other coppers, but they were too old to be trusted with a copper, and were thought unable to buy any more coppers.

PART FOUR

RANK AND CLASS: VIEWPOINTS

Rank, Wealth, and Kinship in Northwest Coast Society

PHILIP DRUCKER

Northwest Coast society was organized on no idealistic premises of the equality of man. Each individual had his place in the arbitrarily calibrated social structure of his community. However, the casual designation so often encountered of this social pattern of ranked statuses as a "class" or "caste" system with nobles, commoners, and slaves, is a crude over-simplification, except as regards the division of society into freemen and slaves. It will be the aim of this paper first to show that there were no social classes among the freemen, but rather an unbroken series of graduated statuses, and second, to investigate the principles underlying this gradation of rank.

For a working definition of a social class we may take the dictionary formulation: "Class: A group of persons, things, qualities, or activities having common characteristics or attributes"; or, "a group of individuals ranked together as possessing common characteristics or as having the same status."[1] Thus, the fundamental requirement of a class,

Source: *American Anthropologist*, n.s., 41 (January-March, 1939), 55-64. Reprinted by permission of the publisher.

[1] Webster's *New International Dictionary of the English Language* (2nd ed., unabridged, G. and C. Merriam Co., Springfield, Mass., 1936).

socially speaking, is the sharing by its members of some trait or traits which set them off as a distinct entity within their society. This common attribute, we may expect, will direct specific attitudes and behaviour by them and toward them as a group. Where such attributes distinctive of social *groups* were lacking, we are not justified in speaking of a class system.

If we survey Northwest Coast society as a whole, we find that two great social classes existed everywhere: freemen and slaves. The distinguishing criterion, condition of servitude (whether by capture, birth, or debt does not matter here) placed every individual in one or the other group. As a member of his group he enjoyed certain rights or was subject to certain disabilities – depending on which group he was in – and by virtue of his membership was the object of esteem or scorn, and was entitled to scorn or esteem those of the other class. That slaves were sometimes treated with kindness and given certain concessions made no difference in their class membership; they were still slaves, and as such belonged in a sphere apart from the free.

As a matter of fact, the slaves had so little societal importance in the area that they scarcely need be considered in problems relating to the social structure. "Society," in the native view, consisted of the freemen of a particular group. Slaves, like the natives' dogs, or better still, like canoes and sea otter skins and blankets, were elements of the social configuration but had no active part to play in group life. Their participation was purely passive, like that of a stage-prop carried on and off the boards by the real actors. Their principal significance was to serve as foils for the high and mighty, impressing the inequality of status on native consciousness.

If we seek groupings among the freemen comparable to the division into free and slaves we fail utterly to find them. I do not, of course, mean that all freemen were equals among themselves; but there was no class of nobility set off distinct from a class of "commoners," much less a three- or four-fold class system. We search in vain for any diagnostic

traits defining groups within the society of freemen.[2] There were individuals reckoned high and there were those considered lowly, true enough. Those of high rank abstained from menial tasks such as fetching wood and water, they wore costly ornaments and finer garb, and strutted in the spotlight on every ritual occasion. But these were not class prerogatives. They were not restricted to a certain group; there was no point in the social scale above which they were permitted and below which prohibited.[3]

To compare the role of the highest rank member of a Northwest Coast social group with that of the lowliest member gives an impression of a remarkably vast difference in cultural participation. The significant point is that the difference lay in extent of participation, not kind. One less high than the highest in rank, participated less fully in ostentatious activities. A person a grade above the lowest partici-

[2] Dr Murdock has seen such a criterion among the Haida, in the kind and number of potlatches given by one's parents (George Peter Murdock, *Rank and Potlatch Among the Haida.* Yale University Publications in Anthropology, No. 13 [New Haven: Yale University Press, 1936]). While it is possible that the Haida differed from all their neighbours on the coast in tending to synthesize social patterns into neat categories (and this seems unlikely, to judge by Swanton's rich data, and the present writer's brief acquaintance with these people), another explanation appears more probable. For reasons to be enlarged on in another place (footnote 9) it would seem that within late historic times the nature of the Haida potlatch has altered even more than that of other groups, though all have been affected – the modifying factors seem to be an increase in surplus goods (through European trade) and decimation of the population. For the period of adjustment to these new conditions, in the case of the Haida from about 1850 until the abandonment of the potlatch yet more recently under European influence, Murdock's interpretation must stand unchallenged. The bases of the social order must have been quite different formerly, however, if the Haida shared the broad patterns underlying societal organization of the entire area.

[3] The only institution which resulted in a cleavage of the freeborn social unit was that of the dancing societies ("secret societies") of the Kwakiutl tribes and their immediate neighbours. Even there, so far as modern informants know, there was no well-defined alignment of the populace into potential members and non-members. It appears that the head of a family owning a number of dance performances distributed them among his kin; the point at which the family stock of individual dances was exhausted defined the limits of the initiated and uninitiated groups.

pated in these a bit more than the one on the bottom rung. And thus the manifestations of statuses of high and low degree shaded into each other.

What actually occurred was that each society consisted not of two or more social classes, but of a complete series of statuses graded relatively, one for each individual of the group. No two individuals were precisely equal in rank, in fact, equivalences would pose insuperable difficulties. This is brought out most clearly in the potlatch. Barnett's keen analysis has brought out the prime function of the potlatch in validating status; all I want to do here is to point out the mechanics of the procedure. In the distribution of the potlatch gifts, it was manifestly necessary to give them out one by one, else a mad scramble would result. Invariably the giving was in order of rank. The highest ranking individual of the recipient group was named first, and given his allotted share; then the second highest, and so on down the line. This order of giving was, from southeast Alaska to the mouth of the Columbia, the most important expression of the concept of rank. For two recipients to be of equal status would throw the whole affair out of gear, obviously, for neither would submit to being called after the other. An event in recent Nootkan history reveals the difficulties involved in such a situation.

During the latter half of the last century, apparently about eighty years ago, the Tlupana Arm tribe, consisting of several local groups who wintered at ō'is, moved down to Friendly Cove, joining the Moachat ("Nootka"). The head man of ō'is stood first in the tribe; he had married a close kinswoman of the Moachat chief, and because of this relationship the latter offered him and his tribe a place at Friendly Cove. (The Tlupana Arm groups had been seriously reduced in numbers both through wars and the usual historic-period causes.) In addition, the Moachat chief "shared" his potlatch-seat with his kinsman. For a time, when one potlatched the joint tribe, he had to give simultaneously to the Moachat and Tlupana first chiefs, and by analogy, to both second chiefs, and so on down the line.

This was extremely confusing; both names and both gifts had to be called out simultaneously. No one was satisfied. Finally the Moachat chief in second place gave a potlatch at which he gave to all the Moachat chiefs, from first to last, then began with the Tlupana Arm chiefs. The first chief of the Moachat then tried to establish another order: himself and the Tlupana first chief; the second of Moachat, then the second of Tlupana; the third of Moachat, then the third of Tlupana, etc.

This did not meet with favour; the Moachat second chief was really receiving third, the third fifth, and so on. Nor would the Moachat chiefs approve of a plan to give simultaneously to both first chiefs, then to all the Moachat chiefs and after them the Tlupana men. They insisted on following the lead of the second chief, each giving to his own first chief (Moachat) and his fellows first, then to the Tlupana chiefs. The Moachat chiefs were rich, and did most of the potlatching; whether the Tlupana chiefs desisted because of poverty or from tact I do not know. There came to be considerable feeling over the situation. Finally the first chief of Tlupana potlatched, announcing that henceforth he would receive after the Moachat chiefs (and of course his subordinates received after him), so everything was settled. The whole difficulty was, in the informant's view, that the Moachat first chief "had been trying to violate all the rules of the potlatch" in interfering with the established order of receiving.

In short, there were no classes of statuses in Northwest Coast society. Each individual had his own particular status in the graduated series from high to low; each person's status had its own attributes which were not quite like those of anyone else. To insist upon the use of the term "class system" for Northwest Coast society means that we must say that each individual was in a class by himself.

Before undertaking an analysis of the factors contributing to rank, it will be necessary to define briefly the social units within which rank was regulated. First of all, a survey of the source material indicates very clearly that the primary social unit was the local group, a group of people sharing rights to

the utilization of economically important places and occupying a common village. Even among the Northern Nootkans, Southern Kwakiutl, and some Coast Tsimshian, where confederacies of these local groups formed larger units at the winter villages, the smaller divisions retained their economic autonomy and moreover manifested it in rituals, for the local groups were the usual participating units.

When we come to examine the constitution of the typical local group of the area, a more striking fact appears: everywhere this social division was no more and no less than an extended family (slaves of course excluded) and was so considered by its members. The individual of highest rank in the social unit was related to the lowliest, distantly, it is true, but nevertheless related. So ties of blood as well as common residence and common economic resources welded the group together.

Now while the economic resources – fishing, hunting, and gathering grounds – pertained to the local group as a whole, titularly they belonged to individuals. We have to do here with two overlapping and apparently not well differentiated concepts of property-right. Characteristically, a man is said to have "owned" an economically important tract. This "ownership" was expressed by his "giving permission," as natives usually put it, to his fellows to exploit the locality each season. At the same time fellow-members of his local group – his relatives – had an inalienable right to exploit the tract. The present writer time and again has heard statements by informants from northwest California to Tlingit country to the effect that a certain man "owned" a particular place, for example, a fishing-site, and that his permission was required before other members of his society could use it. Nonetheless no instance was ever heard of an "owner" refusing to give the necessary permission. Such a thing is inconceivable to the natives. The situation is perfectly clear to the Indians, if not to us. Actually, individual ownership in these cases does not mean exclusive right of use, but a sort of stewardship, and the right to *direct* the exploitation of the economic tract by the local group. The latter it was who held exclusive right.

Nootkan custom illustrated the nature of such rights very clearly. Almost every inch of Nootkan territory, the rarely visited mountainous back-country, the rich long-shore fishing and hunting grounds, and the sea as far out as the eye could reach, was "owned" by someone or other. An owner's right consisted in the right to the first yield of his place each season – the first catch or two of salmon, the first picking of salmon-berries, etc. When the season came the owner called on his group to aid him in building the weir or picking the berries, then he used the yield of the first harvest for a feast given to his group, at which he stated his hereditary right (of custodianship) to the place, then bade the people to avail themselves of its products. Any and all of them might do so. (Outsiders were prohibited from exploiting these owned places, except where they could claim kinship to the owner, i.e., for the time identify themselves with his local group.) The essence of the individual "ownership," was thus simply a recognition of the custodian's right.

The individual "ownership" or stewardship of economic areas was regarded as highly important, giving, as it did, a measure of authority to the incumbent of the position – political authority of a sort, and thus prestige. The rights were inherited according to local rules of inheritance (by the sister's son among Tlingit, Haida, Tsimshian, and Xaisla; by the son elsewhere in the area), so that it came about that in every Northwest Coast society economic wealth was in the hands of the direct descendants of a single line. Due to disinclination to divide these holdings equally among a group of brothers, the bulk of the economic tracts of a local group was under the custodianship of a single individual at any one time: the eldest heir of the past "owner." This was as true in northwest California as in the regions north of the Columbia where the principle of primogeniture was so explicitly phrased. Thus, the economic possessions of a Northwest Coast society were chiefly in the custody of, or nominally "owned" by, a line of eldest sons of eldest sons (or the matrilineal counterpart of such a line). By virtue of their stewardship these men were elevated to prominence. Directing utilization of the natural resources as they did,

they were the acknowledged heads of the groups – the heads of the extended families.[4]

The extended family heads are the individuals referred to commonly, as the "chiefs."[5] The close relatives of the chiefs were not lacking in prestige, however, not only because they were intimately associated with the head of the social group, but in addition they customarily held various minor properties, in lands and other things as well.[6] They were ranked according to their nearness to the chief. In the course of a few generations, as the secondary lines of descent diverged more and more from the direct line, and as patrimonies dwindled, descendants of the chief's brothers could claim but a low rank. Nonetheless by virtue of their kinship to the head of the village they retained certain rights and privileges. The rights of utilization of economic tracts by all group members may be reckoned an expression of this recognition of blood-relationship, as was, in the north, the right to receive at potlatches even though in a low place. The significance of these last-named facts is that status in its minimum terms – membership in society – was derived from kinship and expressed in terms of wealth.

Thus far our survey has dealt with the broader aspects of the problem. It appears that social position on the Northwest Coast was determined by two linked factors: heredity and wealth. It remains to be seen how the basic pattern was worked out in each of the major subdivisions of the area.

[4] Dr. Linton has called my attention to the important fact that since the "claims" included all the available territory along the coast it was impossible to gain social prominence by taking up a new claim in virgin territory, i.e., by pioneering. Though once there must have been a frontier, it long ago disappeared, just as has ours in recent times.

[5] It is not, of course, legitimate to refer to the head chiefs of the Northwest Coast as a "social class," for there was but one in each social unit. The effect of confederation of local groups (Northern Nootkans, Kwakiutl) makes this clear: the chiefs of the several constituent units did not form a class of equals, but were arranged in a ranked series.

[6] The statement recorded by Boas in a family tradition that the youngest of the five brothers "was like a slave and a dog" should be regarded as an exaggeration for the sake of the plot, and not be taken literally. We have similar incidents in our fairy-tales – the princess Snow White was forced to work as a scullery maid – which no one takes seriously for sociologic interpretations.

Naturally, in an area as extensive as the Northwest Coast, one would expect to find varied manifestations of the fundamental trends of areal culture. We find a sharp cultural break just south of the Columbia River mouth marking off two sub-areas. The focus of the southern sub-area lay in northwestern California. The northern portion of the coast may be further divided into culturally homogeneous blocs by a boundary drawn across northwestern Washington and around the Straits of Georgia, approximately the northern limits of Coast Salish territory (excepting the Bella Coola).[7] We shall consider the manifestations of the concept of graduated status of each of these divisions in turn.

In peripheral northwestern California, where we might expect to find areal patterns expressed in simplest terms, we find that rank was determined primarily by possession of wealth. The reckoning of status according to one's mother's bride-price savours of the hereditary principle, but the cultural accent was on wealth-holding rather than on blood. Nevertheless social position in this region was hereditary, for the simple reason that the status-giving fortunes were inherited, not earned anew each generation. It must be owned that these statuses were only loosely seriated within the group; the elaborate gradation found in the north was unknown. The outstanding figure in each local society was the head of an extended family who by virtue of his capital directed many activities. His custodianship of economically important sites made him pre-eminent in matters relating to the food quest; his capital of token goods gave him a voice in ritual affairs, for he had to equip the dancers in the wealth display performances, and in the social life, where he contributed to marriage payments and weregild. Next to this proud figure stood close kinsmen, brothers, cousins, and the like, who basked in reflected glory, as they, according to nearness of kinship, could draw on the resources of the head of the group when necessary. Grading into this group were

[7] The cultural divisions outlined here have been established by the writer in a synthesis of trait distributions of the entire area, as part of the University of California Culture Element Survey program. There are still smaller blocs, within the two major and two secondary divisions, which could be pointed out, but they have little bearing on the present problem.

lesser men who depended on what scraps of riches they might possess, the amount of bride-price paid for their mothers, and their favour in the eyes of their "big friend." (These are not, of course, categories representing distinct social classes, for they shaded imperceptibly into each other).

From the Columbia to the Straits of Georgia the basis of status was the same as in the south – hereditary wealth – although the fact of heredity was stressed more and more as one proceeds northward. Similarly, more precise systems of ranking within each society are suggested, as we enter the domain of the potlatch where order of precedence becomes a matter of great concern.

It was in the societies north of the Salishan-Wakashan linguistic boundary, however, that the concept of formal status had its most luxuriant growth. The principles underlying this gradation may be brought out most clearly if we begin with a type individual to see how he attained his place in his social system. The first thing that set our individual off from his fellows was his name. Names, on the northern coasts, were very definitely hereditary property, and what is more, each name carried with it a particular social evaluation based on its traditional origin and the honour or disrepute of its bearers subsequently. That is to say, the names themselves were ranked from high to low. Each name had a particular status associated with it, a status which was expressed on formal occasions of feasting and potlatching, where the order of receiving was determined by the sequence of the names. So firmly rooted was this association of name and rank that the process of assuming a particular status, social, political, or ritual, consisted in taking (or having bestowed upon one) a certain name. The Kwakiutl, among whom the system of naming reached its most profuse elaboration, had separate names for feasts, for potlatches, and for their secret society performances.[8] A personal name was thus a key to its bearer's status and embodied all the rights, economic and ceremonial, to which he was entitled.

[8] It should be noted that the statuses of the various names to which an individual was entitled were equal; that is, one who held the secular name of highest rank had the highest feast name and the highest dance name also.

Our friend, then, by taking his real name, defined at a blow his formal status in his society. To assume his name and status two things were requisite. First of all, he had to have a right to the name in question, usually through heredity, though in some regions transfers outside of the direct line of descent might be made: in a repayment of a bride-price, for example, or the name might be captured in war, or seized if a debt was not paid. The sole purpose of the interminable discourses at naming ceremonies was to declare the right of the claimant, through heredity or other legitimate transfer, to the name in question.

The second requisite for name-taking was that it be done formally and publicly, accompanied by a distribution of goods, that is to say, a potlatch. Not only was the name itself considered wealth, and connoted wealth, but wealth in token goods was mandatory for assuming it. If our type individual was heir of the head of his social group, there was, of course, no problem. But were his name of lesser status, he would be unable to potlatch in his own right. This is one of the most significant features of the Northwest Coast wealth system; the national wealth of each society was definitely limited, and there was no way in which a poor man could make a fortune for himself – at least, not in the days before European trade inflated and completely altered the financial system.[9] Formerly, the token wealth of the entire group was concentrated in the hands of the head of the unit just as was the custodianship of economic rights. Not only did he have a certain right to surplus products (those beyond the needs of

[9] It is on this point only that the present writer is unable to agree with Murdock's interpretation of the Haida potlatch as a status-producing force (Ibid.). In early times, it would have been utterly impossible for a man of low rank to advance his own status or that of his children by potlatching because he could not possibly have accumulated enough property to potlatch with. This is obvious from the internal evidence of the ancient wealth system, and reinforced by statements of natives themselves, who often point out that before European trade made it easy for anyone to accumulate goods in quantity, even the "chiefs," with the combined resources of their entire groups behind them, were able to potlatch but rarely. In other words, only those who had hereditary right to high status, were able to assume it by potlatching. If Murdock's interpretation be taken as applying specifically to recent times, it is undoubtedly a correct and extremely penetrating analysis. This is so because two new factors entered in recent

subsistence) of the lands in his trust, but members of his group gave him the fruits of their industry: canoes, blankets, furs. The head of the group was, in a sense, custodian of the token wealth of the family just as he was custodian of the economic resources. Barnett has pointed out this significant fact in connection with the potlatch: the entire group of the nominal giver united to support the affair out of motives of group loyalty and in return for the patronage and social favours bestowed by the head of the group. It was in this patronage that we find the means by which those of lower rank assumed whatever status they had right to. Names of lower rank were formally bestowed by the chief on those who had the right to them during the course of a potlatch. Among the Nootkans (and perhaps among other groups) the correlation between the group assistance and the chief's patronage was made obvious, for it was etiquette for the chief, in announcing the new name and rank of a member of his group, to tell how much property the latter (or the latter's parents) had contributed to the total amount to be given out. Nothing is clearer than the intimate relationship between hereditary status and wealth in the northern region. Not only were the hereditary fixed rankings in society based on economic wealth, and themselves considered a form of wealth, but material wealth was necessary for their formal assumption.

In fine, throughout the Northwest Coast, possession of riches was the basis of social gradation. This wealth was inheritable, and thus status was hereditary. The northern

---

decades. First, it became possible for anyone to acquire a small fortune in trade blankets, etc., from extra-cultural (i.e., European) sources, by such a relatively simple process as killing a sea otter or two, or putting in a lucrative season on a sealing schooner. Second, due to the sharp decline of population, there came to be more high rank statuses vacant than potential incumbents. The places were fixed. One had to demonstrate an hereditary right to claim them, but in the absence of heirs in (or even close to) the direct line of descent there were normally a number of individuals about equally entitled to each place – standing in second, third, or so degree of kinship to the past incumbent. It was such people as these who could, in late times, advance their own or their offspring's status by potlatching to assume a higher rank than that to which they had been born. Anciently, such a thing would have been impossible.

and southern regions differed only in whether overt emphasis was put on wealth-holding or inheritance of wealth. In the south, possession counted for most; the fact that wealth was inherited was little stressed. In the north, the fact of inheritance dominated native consciousness, but wealth was an inevitable concomitant of high rank. Wealth and birth everywhere were absolutely inseparable factors in the determination of status. Whatever schismatic tendencies such a system of social inequality theoretically might have had were negated by the unbroken graduation of statuses from high to low, and the bonds of blood kinship which linked the head of each social unit with his humblest subordinate.

Kwakiutl Society: Rank Without Class

HELEN CODERE

The question of the presence or absence of social classes among the Kwakiutl is the main issue in a recent controversy over the value of the work of Franz Boas.* The question is not only of interest to students of social organization but also of general importance, since the course of future work will depend upon the reputation accorded Boas. If some of Boas' specific conclusions and consequently his general conclusions were erroneously devalued, it would be wasteful of scientific time and talent to fail to use them or to rediscover them. It would also be destructive from a scientific point of view to ignore or to make insufficient use of types of data that cannot be duplicated by field work among the acculturated Kwakiutl of today.

This article will try to demonstrate that Kwakiutl society was, as Boas said, a classless society in which social rank was the organizing principle. Whether or not this demonstration is successful, it should serve the secondary but still important purpose of publicizing the general nature of the data upon which Boas based his conclusions and with which others can test them and form additional hypotheses.

SOCIAL RANK AND SOCIAL CLASS

Given our company of knowledge and thought, a definition of social class does not seem to be a problem, although it is possible that a careless definition disregarding past work and involving such faulty logic as "If there are people called

Source: *American Anthropologist*, n.s., 59 (June, 1957), 473-84. Reprinted by permission of the publisher.

* Some aspects of this controversy are treated on pp. 159-65 of the present volume.

'commoners', there is a class of commoners," may have played some part in the Boas controversy. Walter Goldschmidt's definition of social class is excellent:

We may accept the minimal definition that a social class is a segment of the community, the members of which show a common social position in a hierarchical ranking. Class is differentiated from status in that the latter suggests a range and continuum, while class connotes a degree of unity and some form of homogeneity among its members.[1]. . .

We suggest that a true class-organized society is one in which the hierarchy of prestige and status is divisible into groups each with its own social, economic, attitudinal and cultural characteristics and each having differential degrees of power in community decisions. Such groups would be socially separate and their members would readily identify. We may say that a society approaches a class system if either (a) the groups are clearly identifiable, but do not differ with respect to all the characteristics noted; or (b) the groups do differ in these characteristics, but are not sharply separated.[2]

Like Goldschmidt, Talcott Parsons[3] states that social ranking must be combined with classification into social groups for the resulting system to be described as a class society or one in which social classes exist or are important. This definition has a clear-cut corollary: the two principles, ranking and classification, are independent. The presence of a social ranking principle, even in an exaggerated form, need not entail any classificatory principle. Among the Kwakiutl this is exactly the case.

KWAKIUTL SOCIAL ORGANIZATION AS SEEN BY BOAS

In 1906 Boas wrote "Society on the North Pacific Coast was divided into four classes, chiefs, nobility, common

[1] Walter Goldschmidt, "Social Class in America - A Critical Review," *American Anthropologist*, n.s., 52 (October-December, 1950), 491.
[2] *Ibid.*, p. 492.
[3] Talcott Parsons, *The Social System* (Glencoe, Illinois: The Free Press, 1951), p. 172.

people and slaves"[4]. However, this statement did not apply specifically to Kwakiutl, and Boas did not permit any of it to stand as applying to them in his later generalizations. In "The Social Organization of the Kwakiutl" published in 1920, he begins with a clear statement to the effect that earlier conclusions required revision, and from that time on he described Kwakiutl society as classless:

The Indians emphasize again and again the rule that the "house name" and the attached position and privileges can never go out of the line of primogeniture and may not be given away in marriage. The first born child must take them whether it is male or female. It is not clear, however, even from the genealogies at my disposal, what was done in former times if the parents did not hold enough seats and names to go around among their children, unless in these cases the children received names from the mother's father. At present, and for about seventy years past, this condition has probably never arisen. The inference from the general point of view of the modern Indian is that the younger lines had names of inferior rank and formed the lower classes.

It seems to me that the conditions among the Kwakiutl and the Nootka must have been quite similar insofar as a sharp line between the nobility and the common people did not exist. In one Kwakiutl tale, it is even stated that the youngest of five brothers "was not taken care of by his father and was like a slave or a dog".[5]

As usual, Boas neither oversimplified nor spent any time or publication space in augmentation or in pointing out obvious inferences, but his view of Kwakiutl society is clear and completely in line with the full detail which he and George Hunt recorded in text – the most objective way possible. The material he cites for this and other statements

[4] Franz Boas, "The Tribes of the North Pacific Coast," in Ontario Provincial Museum *Annual Archaeological Report* (Toronto: Department of Education, Ontario Provincial Museum, 1906), p. 242.

[5] Franz Boas, "The Social Organization of the Kwakiutl," in Boas, *Race, Language and Culture* (New York: The Macmillan Company, 1940), pp. 360-61.

about Kwakiutl social organization is primarily that of genealogies and family histories, as might be expected, since it has so direct a bearing on the subject. There seems to be no type of conclusion to draw from this material other than that which Boas has drawn. "Commoner" in Kwakiutl refers to a person who at the moment of speaking is either without a potlatch position, chief's position, or standing place – all these being interchangeable but "noble" terms – or applies to one who has low rank which is nevertheless a "standing place" or position. The man referred to at that moment might have passed on his position just the moment before, or he might just the next moment be a successor to a position. "Commoners" in Kwakiutl society cannot be considered a class, for they have no continuous or special function; they have no identity, continuity, or homogeneity as a group, and no distinguishing culture or subculture. Individuals can at will become commoners by retirement from potlatch positions, and they customarily did so; individuals are raised from a common to a noble position at the will of others; individuals chose to consider "common" the lower positions of noble social rank; brothers and sisters of the same parents were given positions greatly varying in social rank and the younger ones might receive a position so lowly as to be "common." The following cases from the texts are illustrative of the type of material Boas cites. They support the conclusions made and are accessible to all students of Kwakiutl social organization.

(1) A younger brother of "common" parents gives potlatches and has a potlatch name and position. Because of his cleverness at accumulating property (perhaps partly because he never married) he potlatches as frequently and impressively as the important chiefs of his tribe and they hate him because of this. He then passes on his position to a man who is not related to him in any way, but who had been friendly toward him and had not "hurt him with words." He had no seat after that, although his friend had four seats.[6] *This case demonstrates that "commoner parents" were commoner*

[6] Franz Boas, *Contributions to the Ethnology of the Kwakiutl.* Columbia University Contributions to Ethnology, vol. iii (New York: Columbia University Press, 1925), pp. 97-99.

only in the sense that they had only lowly noble positions to pass on to their children. It also demonstrates that a lowly potlatch and social position could be used in such a way as to be a serious challenge to the greatest positions in the tribe.

(II) A chief whose seat was "at the head of all the eagles," i.e. the highest in his tribe, gave his position to the young man whom "he believed to be his own son." At the public transfer of his position he tells his tribe, "You will give property to me in the last seat of my numaym*.". . . The account continues, "Now Âwaxălag·îlis gave all his privileges and his names to his prince L!aqwag·ila, after this, and Âwaxălag·îlis was now a common man* [bEgwā′nEmq!ala] *or – as it is called by the Indians – Âwaxălag·îlis was the speaker of the house of L!aqwag·ila, for he was the new chief; for the chief position was put into L!aqwag·ila by his father Âwaxălag·îlis." This case demonstrates the relativity of noble and common positions along a scale of social greatness, and not according to class divisions. If the greatest chief in the tribe steps down from his head position but retains his position in the last seat of his* numaym*, he is either a "commoner" solely by comparison with what he had been, or because the nearest he could get to membership in a class of commoners in Kwakiutl was by holding one of the more lowly noble positions.*[7]

It is upon case materials of this type that Boas bases his conclusions about Kwakiutl social organization and it is to such materials that he makes direct reference. There are, however, many Kwakiutl texts and data that do not bear so directly on social organization, and the question is whether this material consistently supports the same conclusions. These other data not only seem to confirm Boas but also seem to have been an important part of the background from which he generalized, so consistent are the results. It is impractical and unnecessary in this presentation to analyse all the types of Kwakiutl data available. There are many data on material culture, housing, village organization, owner-

[7] Franz Boas, *Ethnology of the Kwakiutl.* Based on data collected by George Hunt. Thirty-Fifth Annual Report, Bureau of American Ethnology (Washington, D.C.: Smithsonian Institution, 1921), pp. 1350-52.

ship, ceremonial life and many other topics which are also rich in detail relating to social organization. For several reasons it is the data of the some 300 pages of texts of Kwakiutl recipes that I wish to use: they refer to the every-day life of the people as well as to large public gatherings and ceremonials, they have not been used or cited in any previous analyses, they could not have been collected or edited with any biased selectivity relating to Kwakiutl social organization, and they have sufficient wealth of detail in context to be useful for the invariably difficult task of showing not only what is present but also of showing negative findings.

KWAKIUTL SOCIAL ORGANIZATION AS SEEN IN TEXTS OF KWAKIUTL RECIPES

The Kwakiutl recipes are recipes for social occasions as well as for various dishes. A member of our culture might well expect recipes to contain detailed descriptions of the techniques of food preparation, but the Kwakiutl recipes do much more than this. They specify in minute detail the social procedures and personnel involved in the acquisition, preparation, serving, and social meaning of food. We learn, for example, how a husband and wife prepared the food and the house for guests, whom they invited for certain dishes, how they served the food. We even learn whether water was served before, with, or after the meal; or whether guests were provided with spoons or were given an old mat on which to spit fish bones. Because this material is in text, and because it covers such a range of social situations and contains such detailed description of social behaviour, it is ideal for testing whether Kwakiutl social organization was along class lines. The minute detail on social behaviour can either be sorted out according to class lines or it cannot.

The Kwakiutl must have ranked high among the most social eaters of the world. Out of 155 recipes there are 120 instances in which a social situation for a meal is clearly specified. Only 24 describe the family meal of a couple and their children. The rest specify some number of guests ranging from a few friends, near relations, or housemates, to the

whole tribe or many tribes of the people. There are some survivals of such practices among the people today, and the deep nostalgia of elderly informants for the hospitality in old time living is very impressive. My own fieldnotes also contain some information on how George Hunt worked on these recipes; how he consulted his wife on those details of food preparation that he as a man would be ignorant about; how he would occasionally have difficulty in recording how a certain thing was done and would take a walk, check with various people, and refresh his memory. It is true that in most cases the recipes seem to tell only what might have been done or expected and that they do not seem to be eyewitness accounts of the social gatherings themselves. It is probable, however, that this merely seems to be the case, for not a few of them are eyewitness accounts and George Hunt's training in putting down case materials and the things he himself had seen and heard is clearly visible in his work as a whole. The recipes set forth social standards and procedures. In the unlikely possibility that they merely make up a Kwakiutl etiquette book of ideal standards and procedures, they could be expected even more to show "class" lines, if such exist. . . .

There are 91 cases of various kinds of hospitality detailed in the Kwąkiutl recipes. In an overwhelming number of these cases (77), the hospitality situation is one in which no class lines, distinctions, or behaviours exist. In these cases the host is "a man," "the host," or "the owner of the food." Since there are a few cases in which it is stated that the host is a chief, it cannot be assumed that all hosts are chiefs, but since "a man" may give feasts to many tribes, as do the chiefs, and since the bulk of the entertaining is done by "a man" or "the owner of the food," neither can it be assumed that "a man" is not a person of rank and perhaps a chief. The assumption that best fits the facts is that no particular kind or class of man is host, and that the host may be a person of high or low social rank. However, the most interesting thing about these hospitality situations is that the guests of the "man" in so many cases (49) consist of some special group which would be likely to include persons of different social rank, some group which would surely cut

across any class lines if there were classes in Kwakiutl society: old people, the men who happened at the time to be sitting out in the summer seat, strangers, "friends whom they like to invite." It might be argued that since "friends" [ᵋnēᵋnEmō'kwe] means "like one person," this would mean that persons would invite only those of their own "class," yet this is far-fetched. Everything suggests that the Kwakiutl meaning of "friend," like ours or like "those whom they like to invite," above all is sentimental and preferential of persons.

In a dozen additional cases, the guests of "the man" are relatives who would necessarily be people of differing degrees of social rank. A *numaym* is a lineage group consisting of a series of ranked social positions, plus children and adults who do not have one of the ranked positions but who may receive one as a relative of someone who has one to pass on or who may have held one and retired from it. Cases in which a man entertains his *numaym*, his housefellows, and his near relations, thus seem necessarily to be cases in which those lowly and high in social position are entertained together. Here again it is a question of social rank, not of social classes.

In sixteen further cases, a man is host to his entire tribe or to all the different (Kwakiutl) tribes, both very large categories that would include many gradations of social rank. He will invite and serve these guests in order of their rank, the highest always first, but he will omit no "class" of people nor will his procedures be sorted out according to "class" lines.

There are eight cases altogether in which hospitality is discriminatory: only the men highest in rank are invited to eat halibut skin and meat, only the men of high rank seem to be invited for blistered half-dried halibut, only the old chiefs are invited to eat plucked cheeks of salmon, "only the old chiefs are invited to eat the insides of seals," only chiefs are invited to eat a dish of mashed currants and salal-berries and in two further instances no invited guests except chiefs are mentioned. In the final case, "the common people" [bEgwānEmq!ālaEm] are invited to eat preserved salmon heads. This not only represents a great paucity of cases of

discriminatory hospitality for any society presumed to be a "class" society, but it also shows the difficulty – bordering on impossibility – of deciding where class lines could be drawn. How is it possible to discriminate on any class basis between "chiefs" and "old chiefs" and "those of high(est) rank"? Where is the line to be drawn between those of high and those of low rank, since we know that [bEgwānEmq!ala] means those with relatively low rank, not rankless persons alone, and that it can include a person who once held the highest position is his *numaym* and tribe, including an "old chief"? Why should there be no cases in which chiefs invite only chiefs, persons of high rank only those of high rank, "commoners" invite "commoners," if it is a class society? . . .

In a "class" society there can be some expectation of differences in etiquette according to class lines. The Kwakiutl recipes are remarkable for the extensive information on etiquette they contain, along with all the other types of detail that have been discussed. The main principle of Kwakiutl etiquette is that the inviting, seating, and serving of guests should be in order of their social rank. It is a rare hospitality situation when guests "sit down any way they like" and are presumably served in informal hit-or-miss fashion. In this connection it must be recalled that all the Kwakiutl tribes were ranked in order of social greatness, as were all the *numayms* within a tribe and all the individual positions within the *numaym*. A man's rank was his "standing place" or his "seat" – that is, his seat at feasts. Thus it was gradations of social rank that mattered and Kwakiutl etiquette was centred upon observing these and not upon seating or serving people at feasts according to any "class divisions." Indeed, it would have been impossible to have any "class" principle operating at the same time as the "rank" principle that is so frequently described in the accounts of feasts. If the highest ranking *numaym* of a tribe sit in the place of honour in the middle rear of the house, all its members including its lowly ones share this place of honour. But an organization along class lines would demand that all the head chiefs or "eagles" of the different *numayms* sit in one place, lesser chiefs in another, and so on. This was not the case. It was rank that determined etiquette.

Another question is whether there were differences in manners or differences in the degree of strictness about observing the rules of etiquette between those who were high and those who were low in social rank.

There was a common code of table manners which everyone, high or low, was expected to follow. There was a proper way to eat with a spoon and to drink from a water container. There were prohibitions against eating with both hands or even showing the left hand, which had to be kept under the blanket, and against drinking water with the meal, although it was always served both before and after the food. The few instances in which there seem to be special codes for the low and high ranking seem to be covered by the general code, to merge into it, or to be explained by some external fact, so that the distinction between high and low is lost.

On the face of it, the following case would seem to detail special manners for the nobility: "Noblemen, and particularly girls of noble descent, must not eat much. When eating they hardly open the mouth. They use pointed spoons from which they sip. They must not show their teeth when chewing."[8]

However, except in several types of feasts which were eating contests between rival chiefs and their followers, food was always consumed moderately and even fastidiously. The point of the eating contests was of course to embarrass the rival by making him feel and show the expected squeamishness. This is proof of the general Kwakiutl attitude of disapproval and distaste for gluttony. Still today, it is an insult to say that someone is greedy about food [mEs'us], like Raven. The parts of the Raven myth in which he displays his coarse voracity are received with embarrassed laughter of the sort that people of American-Canadian culture would reserve for Raven's sexual exploits. Much of the above case concerns daintiness in eating, which was part of the general code. Adherence to these niceties was

[8] Franz Boas, *The Kwakiutl of Vancouver Island.* Memoir of the American Museum of Natural History, vol. v, no. ii (The Jesup North Pacific Expedition), (New York: American Museum of Natural History, 1905), p. 42.

not according to any principle of rank alone, since girls of noble descent were supposed to be strictest of all in their manners. I am unable to comment from first-hand observation about pointed spoons for the nobility as against some other type for "commoners" in a way that would completely settle the matter. There are many rounded, ladle-like spoons for serving food, but all the spoons I have seen and have known to be for individual use were what I would call pointed. I recall a meal at which a soup of edible seaweed was eaten with hemlock spoons of the old type. Kwakiutl men and women of varying degrees of rank all sipped daintily from the pointed ends of the spoons. I therefore cannot see this case as distinguishing the standards or the behaviours of those who were noble and high in rank from those who were low in rank.

A somewhat similar case concerns the procedure followed by a wife when serving salmon to her husband: "This is the size [?] into which the salmon is broken when a chieftainess gives to eat to the chief. Into larger pieces breaks it the wife of a common man [bEqwanEmaxsala]."[9] It is difficult to see this as making a "class" point. What would prevent a woman who was not a chieftainess from acting like one and treating her husband as a chief; and what would prevent a chief from stating a preference for somewhat larger pieces of salmon? I have heard contemporary Kwakiutl men express familiar kinds of food preferences and prejudices, and such expressions may not be a matter of acculturation to Western ways. In any event, this case of differences in etiquette along class lines does not make much sense when it occurs in the privacy of a family meal rather than in one of the many and frequent occasions characterized by hospitality.

The following case is instructive, and clearer than the two previous cases in showing that the nobility had no monopoly on the "best" manners. This would seem to be an important matter in the definition of social classes and

[9] Franz Boas, *Ethnology of the Kwakiutl*. Based on data collected by George Hunt. Thirty-Fifth Annual Report, Bureau of American Ethnology (Washington, D.C.: Smithsonian Institution, 1921), p. 750.

of the means necessary to maintain class distinctions. If the "best" manners are accessible to all people in the society, if they are neither so complex that they require intensive education to master nor so monopolized by a definite social group that the outsider has not the means of learning what they are, then a non-class society is indicated: "She only stops when the liquid of what she is cooking is really milky. This shows that the fat of the fish is well mixed with the liquid. That is the reason why the woman dips up the liquid of what she is cooking, so that the liquid and fat of the kelp-fish should not be milky when it is given by the host to his friends, then the guests at once whisper among themselves when they leave the house of their host, and they say about the woman that she is lazy, although she may be of chief's blood and a chief's wife. However, the wives of those who are not of chief's blood do not give up trying to get milky the liquid of the kelp-fish that they are cooking."[10]

The system of manners that emerges is ideally consistent with the picture of Kwakiutl society as one in which social rank was important but one in which everyone had some degree of social rank and could anticipate holding a position of fairly high rank sometime during his life. Everyone would seem to have been able to learn and to have practised the best manners. There is nothing to suggest that great chiefs who retired from their high positions had to follow a code of manners appropriate to their more lowly stations, or that persons who came into high positions, as so many did, were unprepared in the appropriate etiquette.

[10] *Ibid.*, pp. 395-96.

Boas and the Neglect of Commoners

VERNE F. RAY – *Critique**

A major deficiency in Boas' work with the Kwakiutl was his neglect of the patterns and behaviour of the lower classes: his nearly exclusive concern with the nobility and his presentation of this picture as representative of Kwakiutl life. But Herskovits makes no point of this fact when he discusses Boas' paper on "Esoteric Doctrines" and quotes its conclusion: "It has taken many years for the study of culture of civilized people to broaden out so as to take in not only the activities of the great, but also the homely life of the masses. . . . If it is true that for a full understanding of civilized society the knowledge of the popular mind is necessary, it is doubly true in more primitive forms of society." And yet, when Ruth Benedict characterized Northwest Coast Indians as pathologically devoted to the achievement of prestige, a notion derived directly from Boas – Benedict never visited the area – he comments that, "These tendencies are so striking that the amiable qualities that appear in intimate family life are easily overlooked"; and says in another place that, "the more varying the ideas of a tribe divided into social strata, the more difficult it is to draw a valid picture that does not contain contradictions."

Boas' picture of the Kwakiutl is not only deficient because he failed to heed the cautions which he enumerates for

---

Source: "Review" of *Franz Boas: The Science of Man in the Making* by Melville J. Herskovits, in *American Anthropologist*, n.s., 57 (February, 1955), 139-40. Reprinted by permission of the publisher. Title supplied by editor.

---

* Sections of this review and of the subsequent selections which are not relevant to the "class" controversy or the "personality" controversy, which is dealt with more fully later, have been deleted.

others but also because he allowed this one-sided portrait to stand, not only for all Kwakiutl culture but for the Northwest Coast generally. His overgeneralization for the Kwakiutl and his failure to speak out in correction of the errors of his students, such as Benedict, has had the result that the ethnographic picture for the Northwest Coast as visualized, taught, and accepted by many anthropologists is that which in fact applies only to the nobility of the southern Kwakiutl. This situation, so painful to research scholars of the Northwest Coast, is not given attention by Herskovits despite the fact that this was Boas' principal area of ethnographic research.

ROBERT H. LOWIE – *Comment**

Not being a specialist on the area, I speak under correction on the first issue, for Dr. Ray knows much more about the tribes in question. However, if Drucker is right, Ray is accusing Boas of neglecting a nonexistent group. In any case, Boas, Sapir, and Olson agree that in the subarea embracing the Kwakiutl and Nootka primogeniture obtains which automatically eliminates rigid class barriers. No one, of course, has denied the importance of differences in rank.

There are several points a critic who specializes in the area might illuminate for the benefit of colleagues familiar with other regions. In a rank-obsessed population, how easy is it to obtain information from or about the rankless? (What, e.g., do we know about the distinctive beliefs of the Polynesian commoners?) Did the junior brothers in a household really differ basically in their patterns of behaviour from their elder siblings? Is it not a general phenomenon where differences in rank occur that imitation of one's betters levels differences? What parts of Kwakiutl culture were affected by social differences? Craftsmanship? Cookery? Dress and housing? Supernaturalism? In short, to what

* Source: "Boas Once More," *American Anthropologist*, n.s., 58 (February, 1956), 162. Reprinted by permission of the publisher. Title supplied by editor.

extent did Boas really distort the picture? Also, did he actually "neglect" the rankless any more than the circumstances of field work dictated? A very cursory inspection suggests that he took some cognizance of the existence of commoners – at times in a very instructive way.

VERNE F. RAY – *Rejoinder**

Dr. Lowie, in his commentary, "Boas Once More," finds reasons for questioning the validity of my criticisms of Boas' work on the Northwest Coast. Referring to my assertion that Boas neglected the patterns and behaviour of the lower classes he states that everywhere in the area primogeniture obtained with the consequence that there could be no rigid class barriers. He cites several ethnographers in support of his assertion regarding primogeniture, but I am puzzled as to what purpose, for the question concerns the reality of classes, not primogeniture or rigid class barriers. No one except Hill-Tout has contended that there are rigid class barriers; but there are masses of ethnographic data relating to the distinctions between the upper and the lower classes and the cultural disabilities suffered by the latter. The reality of the lower class and the magnitude of the cultural distance separating it from the upper class are firmly established ethnographic facts and citing Drucker to the contrary will not dispose of them. The statement to which Dr. Lowie refers is: "There was no class of nobility set off distinct from a class of 'commoners,' much less a three- or four-fold class system." But in the same paragraph Dr. Drucker adds that, "There were individuals reckoned high and there were those considered lowly, true enough."[1] (The one intervening sentence reads: "We search in vain for any diagnostic traits

* Source: *American Anthropologist*, n.s., 58 (February, 1956), 165-67. Reprinted by permission of the publisher. Title supplied by editor.

[1] Philip Drucker, "Rank, Wealth, and Kinship in Northwest Coast Society," *American Anthropologist*, n.s., 41 (January-March, 1939), and reprinted in this volume on pages 134-46.

defining groups within the society of freemen." I categorically assert that this statement is at variance with the facts; on this point I have accumulated abundant documentation which I shall present in an early paper.) This juxtaposition of statements is clearly ambiguous; let us therefore look at Drucker's expressed objectives in the paper in question, and certain other illuminating data which he has published.

He says: "It will be the aim of this paper first to show that there were no social classes among the freemen, but rather an unbroken series of graduated statuses. . . . For a working definition of a social class we may take the dictionary formulation: 'Class: . . .' ".[2] In taking the dictionary definition Drucker apparently is choosing it in preference to the meanings given to him by every tribe on the Northwest Coast with which he worked. In his culture element distribution list[3] he reports for fourteen groups that they had a "Named class of commoners." This is his element number 1452, and it is reported positively for the Nutka: 1–Hupachisat, 2–Tsishaat, 3–Clayoquot, 4–Clayoquot, list two; Kwakiutl: 5–Koskimo, 6–Kwexa, 7–Bella Bella, 8–Haihais, 9–Xaisla; Tsimshian: 10–Hartley Bay, 11–Gilutsa, 12–Gitksan-Kispiyox; Haida: 13–Massett, 14–Skedans; and Tlingit: 15–Chilkat. Nearly every other ethnographer of the Northwest Coast, from the Lower Chinook to the Chilkat, has recorded a named class of commoners and has provided the native name or names in phonetic transcription. I submit that this universality, reflected as it is in the various languages, goes a long way toward answering the question as to whether Drucker is right or wrong.

But let us examine the printed statements made by other ethnographers. Lowie mentions Boas, Sapir, and Olson, with reference to primogeniture. What do they say about social classes? Here are Boas' words: "Society on the north Pacific coast was divided into four classes, chiefs, nobility,

[2] *Ibid.*, p. 134.

[3] *Culture Element Distributions*, XXVI, Northwest Coast, Anthropological Records 9:3 (Berkeley, Calif.: University of California Press, 1950), p. 221. An abbreviated version of Drucker's *Culture Element Distributions* appears as an appendix to this volume, at p. 261.

common people and slaves."[4] The groups to which Boas refers, as indicated in the first paragraph of the paper quoted, are the Tlingit, Haida, Tsimshian, Kwakiutl, Bella Coola, Coast Salish, and Nutka. In another paper, published at the same time, Boas contrasts the Indians of the Plateau of British Columbia, explaining that among them "no hereditary nobility is found".[5] Boas was nineteen years ahead of Drucker in stating that "a sharp line between nobility and common people did not exist,"[6] but for him this fact did not negate the reality of the classes. Indeed, "among some of the noble families, we find a strong desire to retain the privileges in the narrowest limits of the family. This is done by means of endogamous marriages."[7]

Sapir: "All these tribes are characterized by a clear development of the idea of rank; . . . Three classes of society may be recognized – the nobility, the commoners, and the slaves. . . . The grading of individuals . . . applies, however, only to the nobility, the commoners and slaves not being differentiated among themselves with regard to rank."[8] In describing the Tsimshian of the Nass River, Sapir identifies "Classes of Society . . 1. cəmgiğa′t nobles, chiefs.' 2. wa·'a·′ιn 'common people.' 3. łiłi·ngit 'slaves'. . . ."[9]

Olson, writing *before* Drucker's paper: "Caste. As everywhere on the Northwest Coast, society is stratified. In general the distinction made is nobles (hai′mas), commoners (á′ngwah), and slaves (kla′kin). There are no intermediate

[4] Franz Boas, "The Tribes of the North Pacific Coast," in Ontario Provincial Museum *Annual Archaeological Report* (Toronto, Department of Education, Ontario Province Museum, 1906), p. 242.

[5] Franz Boas, "The Salish Tribes of the Interior of British Columbia," *ibid.*, p. 221.

[6] Franz Boas, "The Social Organization of the Kwakiutl," *American Anthropologist*, n.s., 22 (1920), 116.

[7] *Ibid.*, p. 117.

[8] Edward Sapir, "The Social Organization of the West Coast Tribes," *Proceedings and Transactions of the Royal Society of Canada*, Sec. 2, series 3, vol. 9 (Ottawa, 1915), pp. 359, 362. The essay is reprinted on pages 28-48 of this volume.

[9] Edward Sapir, *A Sketch of the Social Organization of the Nass River Indians*. Canada, Geological Survey, National Museum Bulletin 19 (Ottawa: King's Printer, 1915), p. 28.

classes. . . ."[10] Olson, writing *after* Drucker's paper: "Social Classes. All of the tribes of the Northwest Coast recognize and emphasize differences in rank or caste level. The Owi-Keno are no exception. But perhaps their social classes are not as rigid as among some other groups. . . . The highest class is that of the chiefs (or nobles) who are called hi'.mas. . . . Commoners are u'àmà and might be called a middle class. . . . Low class or ne'er-do-wells are xa'màla . . . and are just about slaves."[11]

Ray: "The strictest dichotomy existed between definitely upper and lower classmen but there was a wide intervening zone in which classification was far from exact. This intermediate group [consisted of] the more successful commoners and the unambitious or the remote of kin of the upper class."[12]

Lowie has said: ". . . if Drucker is right, Ray is accusing Boas of neglecting a nonexistent group." Is Drucker right? Does he know more than Boas, Sapir, Olson, and Ray combined?

A critical issue remains: Do the patterns and behaviour of the lower classes differ from those of the upper classes? Only if the answer be yes did Boas neglect an important segment of culture. I assert that the patterns do differ, and markedly so, but I grant that the literature is confusing; either position could be "proved" by selection of citations. I think that much of this confusion is due to the fact that many field workers followed Boas in giving attention to the more remarkable phases of culture with the result that the homely habits of the commoners did not come to be known. There are marked exceptions, and such evidence, together with that which can be gleaned from a critical analysis of all other ethnographic data for the area, will, I think, show the validity of my position. I am presently making such a

[10] Ronald Olson, *The Social Organization of the Haida of British Columbia.* Anthropological Records, vol. 2, no. 5 (Berkeley, Calif.: University of California, 1940), p. 182.

[11] Ronald Olson, *The Social Life of the Owikeno Kwakiutl.* Anthropological Records, vol. 14, no. 3 (Berkeley, Calif.: University of California, 1954), p. 220.

[12] Verne F. Ray, *Lower Chinook Ethnographic Notes.* University of Washington Publications in Anthropology, vol. 7 (Seattle: University of Washington Press, 1938), p. 18.

collation and analysis and I hope soon to present the results. At the same timc, I bcg other students interested in the tribes of Vancouver Island and northward to concentrate on the customs of the lower classes. If this be done, I expect that the rewards will be great and that whole new complexes may be found, e.g., there may emerge a well-developed guardian spirit concept and quest similar to that of Puget Sound. I agree with Kroeber . . . that these subcultures, if found, will have much more meaning today, in the light of the reasonably full comparative data available, than would have been the case in Boas' time.

Private Knowledge, Morality, and Social Classes Among the Coast Salish

WAYNE SUTTLES

An exchange of views in a recent issue of the *American Anthropologist* shows that social stratification on the Northwest Coast is still a live issue. The principal question is whether Northwest Coast society had, apart from slaves, distinct social classes of nobles and commoners or merely a single class of freemen within which there were only ranked individuals. The recent exchange* began with Ray's suggestion that Boas neglected the culture of the lower class among the Northwest Coast tribes. Lowie countered that if Drucker's analysis is right, there were only ranked individuals and no social classes, and hence no lower class to neglect. Ray then returned with quotations from several ethnographers who reported social classes and has promised us an analysis of the whole body of published Northwest Coast ethnography, which will demonstrate the existence of a lower class. Since this exchange, Codere has presented an analysis of some of Boas's Kwakiutl material, which seems to support Drucker's and Lowie's position – that there was no distinguishable lower class among the Kwakiutl.

One of the bases of disagreement may be simply a difference in terms or in emphasis on different factors in a definition of "class." But another basis for disagreement may lie in real differences among the various Northwest Coast societies.

In this paper I will deal with a small segment of the Northwest Coast – the area of the Coast Salish of Northern

Source: *American Anthropologist*, n.s., 60 (June, 1958), 497-506. Reprinted by permission of the publisher.

* See pages 159-65 of this volume.

Puget Sound, the Strait of Juan de Fuca, and Southern Georgia Strait. My purposes are: (1) to call attention to evidence for the existence of a distinct, though probably relatively small, lower class; (2) to postulate a relationship between class and certain Coast Salish beliefs about morality; and (3) to suggest the possibility that the Coast Salish theory of morality and the absence of any very developed system of ranked individual positions may have allowed for a sharper definition of social classes among the Coast Salish than among the supposedly more rank-obsessed Kwakiutl.

When we enquire among the Coast Salish about social classes we are likely to encounter a paradox. We find among our informants a strong feeling that social classes did indeed exist in the past. Informant after informant will tell us that there were high-class people and low-class people. Yet if we ask for an identification of the descendants of former low-class people, our informants are likely to say they do not know or refuse to talk about the matter. Later, after we establish good relations with an informant, he will probably tell us that while he is of high-class descent, certain other families are of low-class descent. When we go to members of these other families, we may be told that our new informants' families are of high-class origin but certain other families, including that of our first informant, are really of low-class descent.

This is what happened to me on the Lummi Reservation. Two persons, each associated with one of the two leading lineages, told a story accounting for a low-class origin for the other lineage. One story was an account of a known ancestor of the lineage in question; the other story was really a local adaptation of a widespread folktale. Both stories, however, demonstrated the prior residence of the narrator's lineage, the former slave or serf-like status of the other lineage at some other place, and the generosity of the teller's lineage in allowing the other to settle at Lummi. Both informants agreed, as did others, in ascribing a still lower status to the family of a pair of slaves who had been freed in the 1860's.

This situation, which could undoubtedly be encountered

in many Coast Salish communities, suggests that except for the former slaves, social class was more a myth than a reality. Perhaps the accusation of lower-class ancestry is merely part of the gossip that all families enjoy relating about all others and which enables each to make claims of superior status, none of which has any more validity than another.

But there is other evidence for the reality of social classes in the past. The best evidence comes from descriptions of village structure and intervillage relations. We encounter again and again descriptions of villages in which there was a division of residence between upper-class and lower-class people. In some villages, households of lower-class people were at one end or on one side of the village. In other villages, the lower-class people were somewhat separate and often in an exposed position where an enemy might strike first. Then we are also told of villages set quite apart but in a serf-like status as vassals of high-class villages or villages with high-class inhabitants.

Barnett reports that the Saanich village at Brentwood Bay and the Sechelt village had an upper-class section in the centre and lower-class sections at the ends. I was told that the old Semiahmoo village on Tongue Spit consisted of two rows of houses, one facing outward and the other facing inward; the outer row was occupied by upper-class people and the inner row by lower-class people. Gunther reports lower-class settlements on exposed spits among the Klallam, and Barnett reports the same thing at Nanoose and possibly Chemainus. I was told that the principal Skagit village at Snakelum Point consisted of a great stockade enclosing a long house divided into three segments, each with its own named group of high-class people; outside the stockade were "camps" of low-class people who served as "scouts" and were not allowed inside the stockade. Haeberlin and Gunther report a separate lower-class village, also unprotected, for the Snohomish. I was told of lower-class villages at Warm Beach on Port Susan, possibly vassal to the Stillaguamish or the Snohomish; at Greenbank on Whidbey Island, possibly vassal to the Skagit; and on Dugualla Bay, Whidbey Island, vassal to the Swinomish. According

to an informant, the Dugualla people had to bring fuel to the Swinomish during the coldest part of the winter. Boas, Hill-Tout and Jenness report that the Coquitlam on the Lower Fraser were vassals of the Kwantlen. And while Barnett reports that the Nanoose had a divided village, Jenness and some of my own informants regarded the Nanoose as wholly lower class. They were the group with which the Coquitlam could marry, said one. One informant told of a tradition of open conflict between the lower- and upper-class segments of a village at Oak Harbour on Whidbey Island, and something similar was hinted at for a Songish village.

This is only a rough outline of the data on residence. There is no question in my mind about the existence of a lower class in this area. Its existence is also indicated by some data on marriage and inherited privileges, and it is reflected in the native terms used.

A person of high status was called *siɛ'm.* This term is often translated as "chief," but it is clear that the whole institution of chieftainship as it now exists developed after European contact. Siɛ'm meant and still means simply "Sir" or "Madam" in address and "gentleman" or "lady" in reference. One could speak of the siɛ'm of a house, if it had one clearly recognized leader, perhaps the man who had organized the building; but not all houses had such leaders. One could also say *the* siɛ'm of the village, but the title did not imply a political office. If there was *a* siɛ'm, he was probably the wealthiest man, the leader in the potlatch. Leadership in other matters was apt to be in the hands of others, depending upon their special abilities. The plural, *siiɛ'm,* is usually translated "high-class people."

People who are not "high class" are referred to by terms which are translated as "poor people," "nothing people," or "low-class people." According to one old man, the most polite term is səsəla'yčən, the diminutive plural of "younger sibling." The term used in the Lkungeneng (Straits) and Halkomelem languages for the people of a vassal village is *st'ɛšəm*: their status is clearly distinguished from that of sk'wa'yəs, "slave." Slaves were private property, captured

or purchased; vassals were simply in a low status as a group destined to serve other villages.

Thus it appears that Coast Salish society was in fact stratified. In addition to slaves, there were at least an upper class and a lower class. The proportions of upper- to lower-class people in each community varied, just as the spatial relationship between the two groups varied. But in the area as a whole, the vassal tribes were relatively few and the villages said to have lower-class sections were in the minority. It is difficult to get information on the subject but I believe the evidence strongly suggests that, taken as a whole, the upper class considerably outnumbered the lower class.

I suggest that the structure of native society was not that of a pyramid. There was no apex of nobles, medium-sized middle class, and broad base of commoners. Instead, native society had more the shape of an inverted pear. The greater number of people belonged to an upper or respectable class, from which leaders of various sorts emerged on various occasions. Mobility within this group was fairly free. A smaller number of people belonged to a lower class, upon which the upper class imposed its will and which it treated with contempt. Movement from this lower class into the upper class was probably difficult. A still smaller group of slaves lived with their masters, who were always of the upper class.

The principle of ranking individuals or groups in a numbered series seems to have been poorly developed among these tribes; it finds its most significant expression among the Nootka and Kwakiutl in seating and receiving order at potlatching. Among these Coast Salish tribes, there were two kinds of gatherings at which gifts were given: the sλɛ′šən (from λɛ′šən, to invite), an intrahousehold or intravillage gathering at which one person as host shared an unexpected surplus of food; and the sλɛ′nəq (from λɛ′nəq, to potlatch), an intervillage gathering at which the household or village as host gave away wealth. The second of these was the potlatch proper. The reason for giving away wealth at a potlatch was to pay guests from other communities to witness a change in the status of some member of the potlatcher's family. Such changes were life crises marked by

the use of inherited privileges, or merely transfer of the privileges themselves, as in the bestowal of an ancestral name. While such changes might be marked by intragroup gatherings, the larger gathering was preferable. And while one man might lead in organizing the potlatch, it was more typically an occasion when the several leaders (siiɛ′m) of a household or village pooled their life crises, name-givings, and so forth, for a joint endeavour vis-à-vis other households and/or villages. At such an occasion, each of the hosts might have his own list of guests to whom he owed gifts from previous potlatches. Whenever gifts are given to individuals there must of course be an order of giving, but it is my strong impression that there was no permanent receiving order among these Coast Salish tribes; each host had an ad hoc order based on his own debts and his own evaluations of persons.

If we ask what gave a man high status, we are apt to find different persons emphasizing different attributes, but generally we hear first that a man must be of good birth and must be wealthy. Being of good family, of high birth, and so forth, is sometimes put negatively as "having no black marks against one" – that is, having no taint of slave ancestry, low-class ancestry, or disgraceful conduct in the family. High-class people were those who had good family trees, with a stock of good hereditary names and a few other hereditary rights.

Wealth was of course important. A man had to have wealth to give away when taking or bestowing an hereditary name or exercising some other hereditary right. But wealth was itself only the product of and the proof of possession of more important things. In some cases, wealth came from the possession of hereditary rights, as in the case of a Songish or Lummi reef-net owner; but even then, the man not only owned the right to use a net at a certain place but also usually possessed the special practical and ritual knowledge necessary for its successful operation. This knowledge was acquired from other persons, usually older kinsmen. Other kinds of ritual knowledge were a source of wealth to persons who functioned as ritualists at life crises.

But many of the activities that led to the accumulation

of wealth were due, in Coast Salish theory, to the possession of spirit power. The shaman, the warrior, the gambler, the hunter, the carpenter, all persons likely to accumulate wealth, were successful in doing so, it was thought, because they had guardian spirits which made them a shaman or a warrior or a gambler. In theory, spirits could be obtained by anyone – anyone, that is, who had the courage and endurance to fast and bathe and seek a spirit vision. Of course, some families knew better than others how to train their children for spirit questing, and the location of the best places for encountering certain spirits. But poor-boy-meets-spirit-and-makes-good stories are numerous and some of them are told of actual people, so we may assume that a man without inherited fishing sites and without ritual knowledge could also become wealthy and attain high status. Over a period of several generations there was probably a good deal of social mobility. The leaders were at various times fishermen, hunters, warriors, doctors, gamblers, ritualists – men who owed their material wealth to the possession of various types of incorporeal property.

One other possession theoretically necessary to upper-class status was a sort of private or guarded knowledge; in the Straits (Lkungeneng) language this was called snəp, usually translated "advice." Advice consisted of genealogies and family traditions revealing family greatness, gossip about other families demonstrating how inferior they are, instruction in practical matters such as how to quest for the right kind of guardian spirit, secret signals for indicating that someone is of lower-class, and a good deal of solid moral training.

If we ask what accounts for the status of a low-class person, we will probably be told that low-class people are those who don't have anything and don't know anything. One informant, who often returned to this subject, said repeatedly that low-class people were people who had "lost their history," who "had no advice" (ɑ′wənə snə′ps). High-class people preserved the knowledge of their own heritage and valued it, and possessed a knowledge of good conduct. Low-class people were those who, through their own or their forebears' misfortune or foolishness, had lost their

links with the past and their knowledge of good conduct.

The moral training contained in "advice" included such warnings as "don't lie," "don't steal," "be polite to your elders," and so on. Such injunctions are presented as knowledge restricted to us few truly high-class families. It is hard for an outsider to believe that it was not generally known that one should not lie, steal, or throw rocks at his grandmother, but this was the Coast Salish fiction.

It is important to note that morality among the Coast Salish had little if any relationship to supernaturalism. Its sanctions were social, not supernatural. Children were not told that the supernatural would punish them if they misbehaved. And since there was no organized government, they could not be told that a policeman would come for them. What they were told was that if they misbehaved, they would be called "low class." In a society that stressed private property as the Coast Salish did, it must have been very effective to present moral training as private property, in the context of secret knowledge on the gaining of wealth and the maintenance of status.

Thus the theory that knowledge of good behaviour was restricted to the upper class made a contribution to social control and was therefore of some value to society. The visible existence of a genuine lower class (even though small) served to remind one of the necessity of leading a moral life, but the myth of a lower class was more important than the reality. For this reason, many Coast Salish will let you understand that there are many low-class people lurking about, but you rarely find one yourself.

How could low-class groups have come into existence in Coast Salish society? At one time, most villages consisted each of a single lineage which regarded itself as descended from an ancestor left on the site by the Transformer, or dropped from the sky. Each prided itself on the antiquity and continuity of its traditional ties with its country – the village site, fishing sites, and other productive places – and hereditary rights to names and other privileges. Kinship was reckoned bilaterally but residence was patrilocal, so membership in such a lineage was usually through the male line. (With these qualifications, Boas's early use of the term

"gentes" for Coast Salish villages was probably quite proper.) According to one native tradition, certain vassal villages were simply lineages whose ancestors had been assigned this status by the Transformer. According to another native explanation, the vassal villages were descendants of slaves who no longer had individual masters; and according to yet another, they were the descendants of originally high-class people who had been forced by famine to sell themselves into slavery.

I see several possible factors in the formation of lower-class groups:

(1) *Private ownership of resources.* While the lineage (or village) identified itself with its country, exploitation of the most productive fishing and other sites was often in the hands of certain individuals who were able to use whatever surplus might be produced. Persons unrelated to the owners would thereby suffer some poverty. Yet some activities were unrestricted, and the development of skill – in hunting, for example – interpreted as due to the possession of spirit power might bring wealth to anyone.

(2) *Primogeniture and other limitations in inheritance.* Primogeniture was often the practice and is implied by the kinship terms, which differentiate senior and junior lines of descent. Use of the term "little younger siblings" for lower-class people suggests that historically they may be the descendants of propertyless junior lines. But of course it may also be a way of extending a fictitious kinship to them when something is to be gained by doing so. However, primogeniture was not always the practice; it seems that rights such as great names often went to the child judged to be potentially the most successful. In the case of guarded knowledge such as the genealogies and family traditions contained in "advice," the child with the best memory might be the one who could later use the knowledge and assume or bestow the ancestral names. But again, a name was perhaps valued principally in relation to what was given away at the time it was assumed, so that a person with wealth might take any known ancestral name and make it great.

(3) *Slavery.* Slave status was hereditary. If household slaves became too numerous they might be turned out to

form a separate settlement, which might then become the nucleus of a group formed by the accretion of illegitimates, orphans, tramps, and those reduced by chance to beggary.

The taint of slave ancestry was most undesirable. A person captured and made a slave could be cleansed by a *cxwlɛ'n*, "cleansing rite." Such ceremonies form an important class of inherited privileges. But while the paraphernalia and ritual knowledge required were restricted by primogeniture or other means to certain members of a lineage, the rite might be performed by the owner for any member of the lineage. Thus the only persons who could not be "cleansed" were those without close ties to families which had cleansing rites. Even after a cleansing rite had been performed, gossip about the taint of slavery was important in any rivalry and made possible implicit and private rankings not usually made explicit by seating and receiving. The mere existence of a pattern of warfare and enslavement of captives led to the social evaluation of freemen.

(4) *The social function of the myth of "advice."* Private property, the prevention of its dispersal through restrictions on inheritance, and the existence of slavery as a status into which freemen may fall, all these must have contributed to the differentiation of freemen into higher and lower. Still, there were mitigating factors with each. I believe that these causes are not quite sufficient to explain the existence of the strong feelings among the Coast Salish that there are (or were) high-class people and low-class people. And they are not quite sufficient to explain the particular structure that I infer for Coast Salish society – the inverted pear with the large upper class and the small lower class. I suggest that the additional factor needed is ideological; it is the myth that morality is the private property of the upper class.

This myth made it necessary (or at least useful) for a lower class to exist as evidence for its truth, but the myth probably also acted as a check on the growth of the lower class. If the lower class grew too large, its existence would no longer be compatible with the myth; a large lower class would be seen by the upper class as a threat to society, and the attitude of the upper class would become intolerable to the lower class. The two segments of such a community

could only split, or fight it out. According to traditions, both interclass fighting and the splitting of communities did occur. At to the latter, Snyder has described how the rather complex tribal relations in the Lower Skagit area are the result of a process by which a community would segregate into an upper and a lower class and then split to form two separate communities, each of which again became stratified. Later marriages might link the more successful families of the new community with the old community. Snyder offers no explanation as to why the division was into two parts, except to suggest an underlying duality in Coast Salish culture. I believe the hypothesis presented here supports the suggestions and clarifies the process.

Let me summarize briefly. Coast Salish society consisted of three classes: a large upper class of good people, a smaller lower class of worthless people, and a still smaller class of slaves. Within the upper class there were certainly differences in status, due mainly to differences in wealth. Wealth came to some persons because of their hereditary rights, to others because of spirit powers (and practical skills) acquired through their own efforts. Mobility upward within this larger class was quite possible. Moreover, there were neither clear divisions within the upper class, nor a series of ranked individuals. There was, however, a fairly clear line dividing the upper class from the lower class, especially when they were spatially separated. Movement upward from the lower group was evidently much more difficult; if the group became large enough, greater separation and the formation of a new community was probably the usual way out.

I suggest, then, that when Coast Salish informants speak of social mobility and tell folktales and historic accounts of poor boys who became successful, they are thinking of poor (but good) families within the upper class, which included the bulk of the population. When they speak of "low-class people" they are thinking of the smaller worthless class. And when they hint that other families who claim high status are really low, they are thinking of possible links with the worthless people. Perhaps all families had such links, but as long as a family produced an occasional great man it was secure.

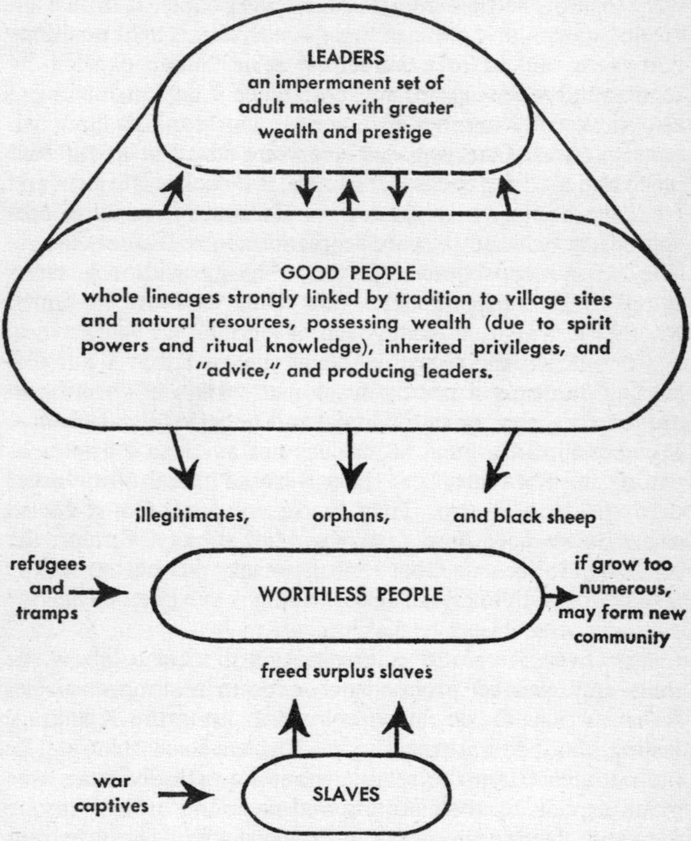

Stratification in a Coast Salish community according to the present hypothesis.

At any rate, the Coast Salish myth about "advice" may have made gossip a necessity.

Kwakiutl society seems to have been organized along somewhat different lines. There is no indication that there were separate settlements of lower-class people. Within each group, many – and perhaps most – individuals held positions that were ranked in a numerical series made explicit by seating and receiving order at potlatches. Local groups were also ranked by number in a series. This ranking had two consequences. One was that everyone stood at a different place and all differences were small; if Drucker is right (and I believe he may be right for the Kwakiutl), ranking prevented any tendency toward segregation into distinct classes. The second consequence is that ranking within a series brings into being a social unit with discernible limits, whether it is a small local group or a confederacy of tribes.

In contrast, the Coast Salish of the area that I am discussing had only a poorly-developed system of ranking in numbered series for individuals, and none for local groups. Membership in a local group was not as clear a matter as among the Kwakiutl, and there were no social units larger than the local group. Thus in one respect, Coast Salish society was more fluid than Kwakiutl society. But on the other hand, because Coast Salish society did not stress the ranking of individuals in series, it may have been easier for distinct social classes to develop.

Moreover, Kwakiutl culture does not seem to show the same emphasis on private knowledge in relation to social status as does Coast Salish culture. Among the Kwakiutl, feeling about social status seems to have been strongest at the potlatch when the relative standing of individuals was made explicit by their seating and receiving order. Among the Salish, feeling was possibly strongest when a grandparent was telling a grandchild how he should conduct himself.

I present this as one interpretation of the data at hand, in order to point out where generalizations about the Northwest Coast as a whole may be wrong. Principles of organization may be different in its different segments. We need not assume that because the Kwakiutl show the highest development of "paranoid" behaviour at potlatches, they have the

strongest development of social classes. I have suggested factors in Coast Salish organization which could have led to a greater development of social classes among them. I might also point to two other factors: the Coast Salish area under discussion had more varied and probably richer natural resources than did that of the Kwakiutl, and it supported a larger population; if resources and population are necessary to stratification, then the area might have supported a more stratified society.

Finally, I would urge that the relationship between the existence of a small class of worthless people and their society's ethical system, a relationship presented here more as hypothesis than as demonstrated fact, be studied in other primitive societies.

PART FIVE

CEREMONIALISM

The Winter Ceremonial

FRANZ BOAS

THE ORGANIZATION OF THE TRIBE

In the preceding chapter I have described a number of spirits which appear to the Indians and are supposed to bestow supernatural powers upon them. From the legends which I have told, it appears that these spirits appeared first to the ancestors of the clan, and I have stated that the same spirits continue to appear to the descendants of these mythical ancestors. The number of spirits is limited, and the same one appeared to ancestors of various clans of different tribes. But in these cases he gave each of his protégés his powers in a slightly different form. In fact each name of the nobility has a separate tradition of the acquisition of supernatural powers, and these have descended upon the bearers of the name. As indicated in some of the traditions, the spirits give new names to the men to whom they appear, but these names are in use only during the time when the spirits dwell among the Indians – that is, in winter. Therefore, from the moment when the spirits are supposed to be present, all the summer names are dropped, and the members of the nobility take their winter names.

Source: Franz Boas, *The Social Organization and Secret Societies of the Kwakiutl Indians*. Reports of the United States National Museum (Washington, D.C., 1895), pp. 418-92. Reprinted by permission of the Smithsonian Institution. Title supplied by editor. The illustrations which appeared in the original publication have been omitted in this reprint.

It is clear that with the change of name the whole social structure, which is based on the names, must break down. Instead of being grouped in clans, the Indians are now grouped according to the spirits which have initiated them. All those who are protected by BaxbakuālanuXsī'waē form one group; those who stand under Wīnā'lag·ilîs form another group, etc., and in these groups divisions are made according to the ceremonies or dances bestowed upon the person.

Thus, at the time of the beginning of the winter ceremonial the social system is completely changed. The period when the clan system is in force is called bā'xus, which term also designates those who have not been initiated by any spirit, and might be translated "profane." The period of the winter ceremonial is called ts'ē'ts'aēqa, the secrets, which term designates also the ceremonial itself. It is also called ts'ē'qa (singular of ts'ē'ts'aēqa); aik·'ē'gala (making the heart good); and g·ā'xaxaak[u] (brought down from above). The Indians express this alternating of seasons by saying that in summer the bā'xus is on top, the ts'ē'th'aēqa below, and vice versa in winter.

During this period the place of the clans is taken by a number of societies, namely, the groups of all those individuals upon whom the same or almost the same power or secret has been bestowed by one of the spirits. Thus the hā'mats'a, nū'LmaL, bear dancers, etc., form each one society, which consists of a limited number of names, because the members of the society derive each their membership from the initiation of one of the ancestors of the nobility. These ancestors have each only one representative at a time. But many of them are grouped together, as will be presently described.

It follows from these facts that a new member of a society can be admitted only when another one is dropped, whose place he then takes. The custom is analogous to the transfer of a position in the nobility to a youth; the old member transfers his rights to a young man and drops out of the ranks of the society.

The dancers (or societies) are arranged in two principal groups, whose names among the Kwakiutl proper are the

seals (mē'êmqoat) and the quē'qutsa. The former embrace a number of dancers and societies of dancers – the hā'matsa, ha'mshamtsEs, k·înqalaLala, nō'ntsîstalaL, qoē'qoasElaL, q'ō'minōqa, nā'nē, nū'LmaL. They are the highest in rank. All the others are quē'qutsa. . . .

THE DANCES AND SONGS OF THE WINTER CEREMONIAL

The object of the whole winter ceremonial is, first, to bring back the youth who is supposed to stay with the supernatural being who is the protector of his society, and then, when he has returned in a state of ecstasy, to exorcise the spirit which possesses him and to restore him from his holy madness.

These objects are attained by songs and by dances. In order to bring the youth back, members of all the secret societies perform their dances. It is believed that they will attract the attention of the absent novice, until finally one of the dances may excite him to such a degree that he will approach flying through the air. As soon as he appears his friends endeavour to capture him. Then begins the second part of the ceremony, the exorcising of the spirit; or, as the Kwakiutl call it, the taming of the novice. This is accomplished by means of songs sung in his honour, by dances performed by women in his honour, and by the endeavours of the shaman. After the novice has thus been restored to his senses, he must undergo a ceremonial purification before he is allowed to take part in the ordinary pursuits of life. The strictness and severity of this purification depend upon the character of the dance. Novices must drink water through the wing bone of an eagle, as their mouths must not touch the brim of the cup; they must suck no more and no less than four times. They must not blow hot food, else they would lose their teeth.

The songs mostly consist of four verses. Each novice, *viz*, member of a society, has his own songs. They open with a burden which varies according to the society to which they belong. This burden is sung in order to indicate the tune. Then follow the words, which, however, are interspersed with repetitions of the burden. The words are called "the

walk of the song" (or, as we should say, the words go this way). Each song is accompanied by beating of time with batons, and by a drum. The beating is sometimes so loud that it almost drowns the song. The rhythm of the tune, as well as of the beating, is exceedingly complex; but the most striking characteristic is the fact that the beating is always syncopated. The arm is raised when the tone is uttered and falls quickly afterwards. In all songs of the winter ceremonial the beating begins several bars before the singing. It is the reverse in profane songs. The beating is an intrinsic part of the songs and can not be separated from it.

The dances of the various societies differ in character, and will be described in the course of this chapter. They have all this in common, that the dancer on entering the door turns once to the left at a place between the door and the fire. Then he dances toward the right, leaving the fire at his left. In the rear of the fire he turns again to the left, and after having made a complete turn continues his course. Every time he reaches the front or the rear of the fire, he makes a turn and then continues his way in the same direction. Each dance consists of four circuits around the fire. The motions of the feet follow the rhythm of the beating, not of the song.

When a mistake is made in these songs or dances which are intended to pacify the novice, the effect is not only a renewed ecstasy of the novice, but it also excites all the older members of the various societies and thus produces a general ecstasy.

Errors in rhythm, turning the wrong way in a dance, smiling, and chewing gum are counted as mistakes. The error must be atoned for by an initiation of the person who made the mistake. When the members of the seal society observe a mistake, they jump from their seats and bite and scratch the person who made the mistake. He drops down at once and pretends to faint, and while the excited dancers surround him he disappears. This means that a spirit has taken him away in order to initiate him. The members of the seal society sit on the platform of the house or stand during the dances, that they may be certain to discover mistakes. The seal society attack and maltreat throughout the ceremonial the quē′qutsa. At the close of the winter ceremonial

they must pay an indemnity for all the damage that they may have done.

No greater misfortune, however, can happen than for one of the dancers who performs his ceremonial dance to fall. In the course of the winter ceremonial quite a hole gradually develops at the two places where the dancers turn, and it is here that they are most likely to stumble and fall.

When a hā′mats'a falls in his dance, he must lie down as though he was dead. Then the master of ceremonies calls a man whose name is E′k·îstōlîs (sand in eyes, i.e., a drowned person), whose office is hereditary. He is a quē′qutsa, and as an officer he is called ts'ā′ts'exsilaēnôx (doing secretly). He carries a large staff (k·'ē′lag·aiū), which is split like a pair of tongs, and in the interior of which some blood is hidden. With this staff he takes hold of the neck of the hā′mats'a and apparently blood is seen to flow from it. Then all the hē′lig·a lift the hā′mats'a, put him on their mat, and carry him four times around the fire. After they have gone around the fire four times his whistle is heard in the woods. When the mat is put down, it is seen that he has disappeared and that only his blankets and ornaments are left behind.

He stays away for four days and his father must make a new festival for him. When the hā′mats'a falls, everybody puts his hand over his eyes and drops his head, crying hā. As the expense of such a festival is very great, the amount equalling the return of the marriage money, but few persons are able to afford a second initiation. While nowadays every effort is made to enable the hā′mats'a's father to give the new festival, it is said that in former times the unfortunate one was killed by the other hā′mats'a, the bear dancers, and the nū′LmaL, often at the instance of his own father.

When a hā′mats'a falls in his dance, it is considered an evil omen, indicating that he will die at an early date.

The view taken by the Kwakiutl is evidently that the falling of a hā′mats'a or of another dancer is an indication of either ill will on the part of the spirit, or as a defeat of their spirit by that of another tribe. Thus I was told that at one time the Kwakiutl had invited the Ma′malēleqala for a winter ceremonial. When one of their dancers fell, their own nū′LmaL tried to kill him, and he was rescued with difficulty

by the quē'qutsa. The song which was used during his dance was never used again. They believed that the event was proof that the spirit presiding over the winter ceremonial of the Mā'malēleqala was stronger than their own.

When one of the dancers of an inferior society falls, he disappears also to be initiated, but his father does not need to go to the expense of a complete festival, as these initiations are much less expensive.

The paraphernalia of the dances consist largely of ornaments made of cedar bark, which is dyed in the juice of alder bark; of masks, whistles, and carvings of various kinds. All of these must not be seen by the profane. If any of these happened to see them, they were killed without mercy. As an example of this, I was told the following incident:

One of the quē'qutsa was preparing a carving to represent the sī'siuʟ. His daughter happened to see him at work. Then he called her into his room and dug a hole right under the fireplace. He asked her to put her head into his lap, pretending that he wanted to louse her. Then he killed her with a hammer. He put her body into the hole, covered it, and replaced the ashes. His wife looked for the girl, but he did not tell her of what he had done until the following summer, when he fell sick. Then he asked his wife to bury the remains of their daughter. As a survival of this custom, the saying remains which is used by the initiated in warning away the profane: "Go away, else we shall bury you."

By far the greater portion of the winter ceremonial is performed in a house set apart for this purpose. It is called lō'pᴇkᵘ(emptied) because it is emptied of everything that is profane. Only when dances are performed, are the uninitiated or the profane allowed to enter the house. They must stay at the left-hand side of the entrance.

Most of the dances are performed in connection with feasts. Others are shown in connection with distributions of property. As during the ceremonial the clans are suspended, the order of seats which prevails in summer is also suspended, and a new arrangement takes place. The seal society have the seats of honour in the rear of the house, and among them the highest hā'mats'a has the first seat, in the middle of the rear of the house. At both sides of the hā'mats'a society

sit the bear dancers and other members of the seal society. At the extreme ends of this society sit the nū'LmaL, the messengers of the hā'mats'a. The killer whale and rock cod societies sit in front of the seal society. They are the singers.

The hē'mElk and the whale society sit next to the nū'LmaL – the former to the left of the hā'mats'a, the others to his right. The Koskimo sit next to them near the front corners of the house. The women sit all along the sides of the house in the rear row, the chicken society farthest in the rear, the dam society and the Kē'ki'xalak[u] in front. The person who gives the feast and all his relatives are in the "kettle corner," the right-hand front corner of the house. The profane sit on the left-hand side of the door. When one tribe has invited another one, all the members of the invited tribe sit in the front part of the sides of the house. The seal society of the hosts sit in the rear, and their singers as described heretofore. The rest of the inviting tribe are in the kettle corner.

Sometimes at such occasions all the members of the seal society and of the corresponding societies of the other tribes sit in the rear of the house. Then the hā'mats'a of all the tribes sit in the middle – first those of the Kwakiutl, at each side those of the Ma'malēleqala, at their sides those of the Nimkish and Lau'itsîs. The other groups arrange themselves in the same manner, the Kwakiutl members sitting in the rear of the house; then toward the door follow the Ma'ma-lēleqala, continuing in the next row nearer the fire. Then follow the Nimkish and Lau'itsîs.

The singers sit so arranged that the rear rows are facing the fire while the front rows face backward. In their midst sits the song leader (nâ'qatē) and his two assistants (guā' nuLemē=sitting at his sides). It is the duty of the song leader to make new songs, to compose new words to old tunes, to learn quickly the songs of the returning novice, and to teach them to the singers. He also gives signals for changes in rhythm and starts the tunes. His office is hereditary in the male line. His assistants call out the words for each verse. The singers are so seated that in front of the board which serves for their back support they can spread their mats, and, when kneeling on these, have in easy reach long planks on which they beat the rhythm with batons.

These are generally of split pine wood and are made at the time of opening the feast. They are about 1½ feet long, and the singers before using them roughly smooth one end, which is used as a handle. They either beat downward, holding the baton in their hands stretched forward, or they hold it like a pestle and thump the plank with it. In former times when wood was not easily split on account of lack of steel axes, they kept the batons, which were in consequence also more nicely finished. Nowadays only the song leader and his assistants have carved or painted batons. The ordinary crude batons are generally split up at the end of the festival and used as torches for lighting the way home through the darkness of the street. It is a very pretty sight to see the numerous guests going home, each carrying his torch and lighting up the logs and canoes on the beach on the one side and the dark row of houses on the other.

I will now proceed to describe the ceremonials of various societies.

BaxbakuālanuXsī′waē, as stated above, initiates several dancers, the most important of which is the hā′mats'a, or the cannibal. He is possessed of the violent desire of eating men. The novice is taken away by this spirit and is supposed to stay at his house for a long time. The period of his absence extends over three or four months, during which time he actually stays in the woods. In the middle of this time he reappears near the village and his sharp whistle and his cries, "hāp, hāp, hāp" (eating, eating, eating), are heard. Then he comes back to fetch his k·ī′nqalaʟala, who must procure food for him. The k·ī′nqalaʟala is always one of his female relatives. Finally he returns and attacks every one upon whom he can lay his hands. He bites pieces of flesh out of the arms and chests of the people. As soon as he arrives, the servants of the hā′mats'a, the hē′lig·a (healers) or sâ′laʟila, of whom the Kwakiutl have twelve in all, run up to him, swinging rattles, the sound of which is supposed to pacify the hā′mats'a. This office is hereditary in the male line, and either four or six of them must accompany the hā′mats'a whenever he is in an ecstasy. They surround him in a close circle in order to prevent him from attacking the people and utter the pacifying cries "hōî′p, hōî′p." The rattles of the

hē'lig·a are always carved with a design which originally represented a skull. . . . In olden times, when the hā'mats'a was in a state of ecstasy, slaves were killed for him, whom he devoured. The following facts were observed by Mr. Hunt and Mr. Moffat in the early days of Fort Rupert: When a hā'mats'a had returned from the woods, a slave, a man of the Nanaimo tribe, named Xu'ntEm, was shot. They saw him running down to the beach, where he dropped. Then all the nū'LmaL of the Kuē'xa tribe went down to the beach carrying knives and lances. The bear dancers and the hā'mats'as followed them. The nū'LmaL cut the body with their knives and lances and the hā'mats'as squatted down dancing and crying "hāp, hāp." Then the bear dancers took up the flesh and, holding it like bears and growling at the same time, they gave it to the highest hā'mats'a first and then to the others.[1] In memory of this event a face representing BaxbakuālanuXsī'waē was carved in the rock on the beach at the place where the slave had been eaten. The carving is done in sandstone, which was battered down with stone hammers. Near this rock carving there are a number of others and much older ones. The Indians have no recollection of the incidents which they are to commemorate. They say that they were made at the time before animals were transformed into men.

I received another report of the killing of a slave. A female slave was asked to dance for the hā'mats'a. Before she began dancing she said: "Do not get hungry, do not eat me." She had hardly said so when her master, who was standing behind her, split her skull with an ax. She was eaten by the hā'mats'a. This happened in Newettee, and Q'ōmEna'kula, who participated in the performance, was living until a couple of years ago. He told me that it is exceedingly hard to

[1] Mr. George Hunt, who told me this story as reported to him by his father, who had been an eyewitness, added the following remarks, which are of interest as elucidating some of the views of these tribes. The slave's wife was at that time in the fort. She went out on the gallery and called out to the hā'mats'a: "I will give you five years to live. The spirit of your winter dance ceremonial is strong, but mine is stronger. You killed my husband with gun and bullet, and now I will kill you with the point of my tongue." After five years all those who had taken part in the murder were dead.

eat fresh human flesh, much more so than to eat dried corpses. The bones of the killed slaves were kept at the north side of the house, where the sun does not shine upon them. During the fourth night they were taken out of the house, tied up, weighted with a stone, and thrown into deep water, because it is believed that if they were buried they would come back and take their master's soul.

When the hā′mats'a had bitten a piece out of the arm of one of his enemies, he drank hot water after having swallowed the flesh. It was believed that this would result in the inflammation of the wound. Nowadays, when the ceremonies have lost much of their former cruelty, they do not actually bite the piece of flesh out of the arm, but merely pull the skin up with their teeth, sucking hard so as to remove as much blood as possible, and then with a small sharp knife cut off secretly a piece of skin. This is not swallowed, but hidden behind the ear until after the dance, when it is returned to the owner, in order to assure him that it will not be used against him for purposes of witchcraft.

Besides devouring slaves, the hā′mats'as also devour corpses. When a new hā′mats'a, after being initiated, returns from the woods he will sometimes carry a corpse, which is eaten after his dance. The bodies are prepared for this ceremony. The skin is cut around the wrists and ankles, as they must not eat the hands and feet. It is believed that else they would die immediately. The hā′mats'a must use for this ceremony the corpse of one of his deceased relatives, which the hē′lig·a must prepare. The Kwakiutl used to bury their dead on trees. The body was placed in a box, and these boxes were placed on branches a considerable distance up a tree. There the boxes were piled one on top of the other. The bodies, when so exposed to the action of the freely circulating air, mostly mummify. A corpse is taken down from the tree and is soaked in salt water. The hē′lig·a takes hemlock twigs, the leaves of which have been removed, and pushes them under the skin, gradually removing all the decayed flesh until nothing but the skin remains. After this is done the body is placed on top of the small hut in which the novice (g·ī′yakila) is living while he is staying in the woods. The hands of the body hang down. Its belly is cut open and

spread with sticks. The hā'mats'a keeps a fire under it and smokes it. Four days before he returns to the village he sends for all the old hā'mats'as. When they come, he tells them: "These are my travelling provisions, which I received from BaxbakuālanuXsī'waē." He asks them to point out what shares they desire to have when he will return. They take the body down and place it on a clean mat. Each points out what he desires to have. . . . His k·ĭ'nqalaʟala returns with him. She carries the corpse which has been prepared. She goes backward, facing the hā'mats'a. When she reaches the right side of the fire, the hā'mats'a enters the house. He stoops so that his face is close to the ground. On entering, he turns four times, descends to the middle of the house, and when he is four steps away from the door, he turns again four times. When the k·ĭ'nqalaʟala reaches the rear of the house, she turns again. A drum is placed in the middle of the rear of the house, bottom up. The k·ĭ'nqalaʟala pretends to put the corpse on the drum, but walks past it, the hā'mats'a following her. At the door she turns again, proceeds around the fire, and when she reaches the drum a second time, she turns again and pretends to put the body down. At this time all the old hā'mats'as, who have been outside the house, jump down from the roof and rush in through the doors. They are all naked and follow the k·ĭ'nqalaʟala in a state of high excitement. When they have run around the fire four times, the body is put down on the drum.

The master of ceremonies begins to cut it and distributes the flesh among the hā'mats'a. But first the k·ĭ'nqalaʟala takes four bites. The people count how many bites each of them swallows. They are not allowed to chew the flesh, but they bolt it. The k·ĭ'nqalaʟala brings them water to drink in between.

After this part of the ceremony is finished, the hē'lig·a rise, each takes one hā'mats'a at the head, and they drag them to the salt water. They go into the water until it reaches up to their waists, and, facing the rising sun, they dip the hā'mats'a four times under water. Every time he rises again he cries hāp. Then they go back to the house. Their excitement has left them. They dance during the following nights.

They look downcast and do not utter their peculiar cries, hāp, hāp. . . .

GHOST DANCE

I stated earlier how the ghost dance of the L'ā'sq'ēnôx originated. There are a number of traditions of similar character explaining the origin of the ceremony among various tribes. All these traditions contain descriptions of a visit to the world of the ghosts, which is believed to be located under our world. Then the visitor was given the secrets of the ghost dance and other magical gifts. This dance is a mimical representation of a visit to the lower world. The dancer wears the head ring and neck ring, which are set with skulls, indicating that the ghosts have initiated him. Elaborate preparations are made for this dance. During the days preceding it the members of the seal society hold close watch that nobody enters the dancing house in which they remain assembled. Then a ditch is dug behind the fire, and speaking tubes made of kelp are laid under the floor of the house so as to terminate in the fire. The ghost dancer appears, led by a rope by one attendant. He goes around the fire four times, summoning the ghosts. After he has made the fourth circuit he slowly disappears in the ditch near the fire. The people try to hold him by the rope, but apparently he sinks out of reach. Then many voices are heard coming from out of the fire – actually the voices of people hidden in the bedrooms who speak through the kelp tubes. It is announced that the ghosts have taken the dancer away, who will return after a certain number of days. When the time of his return is at hand, another dance is held. A carving representing a ghost is seen to rise from out of the ground carrying the dancer.

Song of the Ghost Dancer

1. *I went down to the under world with the chief of the ghosts. Therefore I have supernatural power.*
2. *The chief of the ghosts made me dance. Therefore I have supernatural power.*
3. *He put a beautiful ornament on to my forehead. Therefore I have supernatural power.*

The ghost dancer of the La′Lasiqoala wears a head ring set with four feathers and a thick veil of cedar bark falling over his face.

I have two of his songs:

I.

1. *I came to see you. Why are you making an uproar, ghosts? you who take away man's reason. You are coming up from the sea and call our names in order to take our senses, you famous ones who take away man's reason.*

II.

1. *You sent us everything from out of the under world, ghosts! who take away man's senses.*
2. *You heard that we were hungry, ghosts! who take away man's senses.*
3. *We shall receive plenty from you, ghosts! who take away man's senses. . . .*

Finally, I will describe the dances instituted by Wīnā′-lag·ilîs, namely the mā′maq'a, t'ō′X'uît, hawī′nalaL, and ā″mlala. All of these wear ornaments of hemlock; no red cedar bark. They are all considered war dances.

MĀ′MAQ'A

The mā′maq'a, or thrower, performs a dance in which he is supposed to throw disease into the people. He enters the house naked except for a head ring, neck ring, waistband, bracelets, and anklets of hemlock. His hands are laid flat to his haunches. Thus he runs with short, quick steps around the fire, looking upward with sudden movements of his head, first to the right, then to the left. When doing so, he is looking for his supernatural power to come to him. All of a sudden he claps his hands together and holds the palms flat one to the other. Thus he moves his hands somewhat like a swimmer, up and then in a long circle forward, downward, and, drawing them close to his body, up again. Now he is holding his supernatural power, "the worm of the mā′-maq'a," between his palms. During all this time he is continuing his circuit in short, quick steps, but he no longer

looks upward. Gradually he takes his palms apart, and between them is seen the "mā'maq'a's worm." This is cither a small carved sī'siuL, or snake, or it is a stick which is covered with bark. The stick consists of several tubes which fit into each other, so that the dancer can lengthen and shorten it. While the worm is thus seen to increase and decrease in size, the mā'maq'a resumes his motions of throwing, moving the closed palms in circles, as described above. Suddenly he seems to throw the implement which he is holding. At once all the people stoop and hide under their blankets. The implement has disappeared. He repeats the performance. The second time when he throws the worm, it is seen to fly in the air. Actually there is a second one of the same shape as the implement that was seen in the mā'maq'a's hands. This is attached to a long string, which is stretched across the rear of the house where the seal society are sitting. Two men are holding the string, one on each side of the house, and hidden in the bedrooms. By pulling the rope and tightening and slackening it the worm is seen to fly up and down and from the right to the left. While it is flying there the mā'maq'a moves to the right and to the left in front of it, his hands stretched forward, the palms upward, the elbows to the side, always moving with short, quick steps. Finally the flying worm disappears and the mā'maq'a catches it again. Then he resumes his motions of throwing and finally seems to throw it into himself. He almost collapses, and tries to rid himself of the disease-bringing object by vomiting. Blood is seen to flow from his mouth and down his whole body. This is sometimes procured by biting the inside of the cheek or by breaking a small bladder containing blood which the dancer holds in his mouth. After prolonged efforts he vomits the worm. At once he is hale and well and proceeds in his dance. Now he throws the fourth time. The worm flies into some of the people, who at once jump up and rush toward the fire, where they fall down lifeless. Blood is streaming out of their mouths. The mā'maq'a continues to dance around them, blows upon them until finally they are carried away like dead. The mā'maq'a follows them and either he or the shaman restores them to life. During all this ceremony the

singers beat the boards rapidly and silently, only stopping when the mā′maq'a does not dance. His song is sung after he has finished his dance. At the close of the dancing season the mā′maq'a indemnifies his victims by the payment of a few blankets.

Sometimes instead of throwing the disease, he throws a harpoon head. There are also two of these used in the ceremony. One is held and shown by the mā′maq'a. It is a real point of a sealing harpoon. The other has no blade, but is provided with two hooks to hook it to the skin. The person with whom the mā′maq'a has an understanding, hooks this second harpoon head to his skin and opens at the same time a small bag containing blood, which seems to flow from the wound. Later on the mā′maq'a pulls it out and exchanges it quickly for his own harpoon head.

There are still other performances of the mā′maq'a, one of which consists in throwing a number of ducks into a kettle that is filled with water. I am told that wooden carved ducks are tied to the bottom of the kettle and released by a helper as soon as the mā′maq'a throws. . . .

T'ŌX′UÎT

The t'ō′X'uît is almost always danced by women. The dancer is decorated in the same way as the mā′maq'a. . . .

She holds her elbows close to her sides, the forearms forward, palms upward. She walks around the fire limping, raising both hands slightly with every second step, as though she was trying to conjure something up from underground. She is followed by four attendants. Her spirit is in most cases the sī′siuL, and him she is conjuring. She moves around the fire four times, and now the ground opens in the rear of the house and out comes a huge sī′siuL. Its horns are moving and its tongues are playing. This carving is either raised by means of strings which pass over the beams of the house or by men who lift it from underneath. A carving of this sort was exhibited at the World's Columbian Exposition, and has been transferred to the Field Columbian Museum. As soon as it appears there is a great commotion in the rear of the house so that it can not be seen very distinctly. . . .

Still other t'ō'X'uît will conjure up a small sī'siuL, which flies through the air like that of the mā'maq'a. At other times the t'ō'X'uît will succeed in bringing the sī'siuL up just far enough for its horns to show. She tries to grasp it and it takes her down to the underworld. Then her friends try to hold her, but she disappears. Her attendant, who holds on to her, sinks into the ground with his forearms and seems to be carried all through the house by the woman who is moving underground. He is plowing the floor with his arms. This is done by burying a stout rope about 8 inches below the surface and covering it with loose dirt. The man pulls himself along this rope.

Still other t'ōX'uît invite the people to kill them. The dancer says "hup, hup," moving the edge of her palm along her throat, meaning, "Cut my neck!" or she moves the tips of the fingers of both hands down her stomach, meaning "Open my belly!" or she moves them along her head, shoulders, or other parts of her body. Finally, she is placed on a seat behind the fire and one of her attendants complies with her request. He will appear to drive a wedge through her head from one temple to the other. The wedge is first shown to the people and then secretly exchanged for another one, which consists of two parts attached to a wooden band that is slipped over her head and covered with hair. Thus it seems that the butt is standing out on one side, the point having passed through her skull. At the same time bladders containing blood, which are attached to the band, are burst, and the blood is seen to flow down her face. She also bites her cheeks or bursts a small bag containing blood which she holds in her mouth, so that it flows out of her mouth. A pair of seal's eyes are hidden in her hair and let down over her own eyes when the wedge is driven in, so that it looks as though her eyes were coming out of their sockets. Then she rises and walks around the fire to show the wedge sticking in her head. After one circuit she is seated again, the wedge is removed, and she is hale and sound. On other occasions the head or shoulder is struck with a paddle which seems to split it, and on being withdrawn leaves a bloody line, which looks like a wound. In this case the paddle is secretly exchanged for another one which is so

notched as to fit her head or shoulder. She walks around the fire showing it, and then it is removed.

Other t'ōX'uît request their attendants to kill them with a spear. She is seated in the rear of the house, and the spear which has been shown to the people is secretly exchanged for another one the point of which can be pushed into its shaft. The spear is put under the arm of the t'ō'X'uît, and apparently pushed slowly into her body. As it enters, blood is seen to flow from the wound. The blood is in this case also kept in a small bladder, which is attached to the skin. When it seems to have entered the full breadth of the body, the skin on the opposite side is seen to be pushed out by the point, and blood flows also from that point. As a matter of fact, a hook which is attached to the hemlock ring on the dancer's arm is fastened to the skin, which is pulled up by a slow motion of the arm. At the same time the hook breaks a bladder containing blood.

In some dances the head of the dancer is cut off, and the person who cuts it shows a carved human head bearing the expression of death, which he holds by its hair. These heads are as nearly portraits of the dancer as the art of the carver will permit.

Sometimes the t'ō'X'uît is burnt. A box which has a double bottom is prepared for this performance. The dancer lies down flat in the rear of the house and the box is laid down sideways, so that she may be pushed into it from behind. At the place where she is lying down a pit is dug, in which she hides, while being concealed from the view of the people by the box which stands in front of her. After the pit has been covered again, the box is raised, closed, and thrown into the fire. Before the box is brought in, a skeleton has been put between its two bottoms. While the box is burning, the song of the dancer is heard coming from the fire. From the pit in which she hides a speaking tube of kelp is laid under the floor to the fireplace, and through it she sings. When the fire has died down, the charred bones are found in the ashes. They are collected, laid on a new mat and for four days the people sing over them. The mat is so placed that it lies over the mouth of another speaking tube. The shaman tries to resuscitate her, and after four

days a voice is heard coming forth from the bones. Then they are covered with a mat. The woman crawls up from out of the ditch, into which the bones are thrown, while she lies down in their place. She begins to move, and when the mat is removed, she is seen to have returned to life. In many of these dances, after the performer has been killed, the d'ᴇ'ntsîq arises from under ground. It consists of a series of flat, carved boards connected on their narrow sides by plugs which pass through rings of spruce root or through tubes cut out of cedar. The joints are somewhat loose, so that the whole can be given an undulating motion forward and backward. It has two or three points on top, and mica is glued on its painting. It is intended to represent the sī'siuʟ, but I am not able to interpret the carving in detail. The characteristic figure of the sī'siuʟ certainly does not appear on it.

Charlie Nowell Recalls the Winter Ceremonies

CLELLAN S. FORD

When I was quite a big boy, a chief of our tribe called all the chiefs of the Fort Ruperts and told them he was going to give a *tsitsika.* The winter ceremonial is called *tsitsika,* which means "everything is not real." When the winter comes, we always have this ceremonial. After they get through with drying dog salmon, they all go home to their own villages. He asked all the chiefs to decide when the whistle was going to be sounded which will make known to the other people that the ceremony is going to be held. This whistle of many wooden whistles was heard in back of the houses four times that night. At the fourth time the sound of this whistle came into the house of the chief, and then two men go around to the houses and tell the people to come to the chief's house, for the big birds that make this whistling has come into his house. All the people go in there – men, women, and children. The Kwekas will be in the back end of the house, and a big fire in the centre of the house.

One man stands up and says: "We have come in here to meet the big birds that has come into this house, and we are now going to start with the first ceremony in this particular dance." The Kwekas all stand up. A man that knows the songs and the way the things are to be spoken starts to say, "Hi-i-i-i-i-i-i-i-i," in a long voice, and all the rest of the Kwekas say, "Hi-i-i-i, hi-hi-hi-hi." There is four different ways they go through. Before they begin to sing the songs, the women or children or men that is going to dance comes

---

Source: Clellan S. Ford, *Smoke from Their Fires: The Life of a Kwakiutl Chief.* (New Haven: Yale University Press, 1941), pp. 110-21. Reprinted by permission of the publisher. Title supplied by editor.

out. The women have their hair hanging on their faces, so the people won't recognize them, and those that are going to be taken away by the big birds come up behind the singers and stand up to show themselves. They are supposed to be taken away, but they really stay home. That is the first lie. The Kwekas shout out four times, "Wa!" Then they sing songs, and the chief stands up and tells the people that this Kweka chief is going to have this *tsitsika*, and asks the people to be ready to have a good time. Then they all go home.

Four days after that, we all went to the house of Omhede. He has the part of the dance to call all the people to his house to give to every person the red cedar bark which they wear in the ceremonial as a headband. When all the people get into the house, he says, "We will now call the one who has the most magic power." So some people bring her in. She wears a big red bark band on her head, and the people are around her holding a ring of red bark, and she is in the middle. They go around the house four times with this woman and stop at the right side entrance. This woman was the niece of Omhede, the only man among the Kwekas that owned this part of the ceremony.

They also called for a man named Likiosa, who is the only one among the Kwekas that could cut this big ring of red cedar bark in half. He came in and went around the house four times, and at the fourth time he comes before this ring and trys to cut it. As he cuts it, the red bark begins to squeak and make a noise; the magic in this red bark is making the noise. Then they open the red bark, and the woman was shown in the middle. They put the bark on mats and cut it up in lengths to fit our heads. Then Omhede stands up and holds a rattle and red bark in his hand and says, "O-o-o-o-i," four times, using the rattle all the time. His face is painted with black charcoal, and he begin to sing his song by himself, shaking his rattle all the time. Then he stops still and everybody keeps quiet – even the children. The song is supposed to give more power to the red bark. Then the red bark is given around, first to the Hamatsas (Cannibals) and then to the other people – men, women, and children. The cedar bark has been beaten very fine so it

becomes almost like wool, and this was given around to everybody. They wiped their faces with it, which means that they are wiping away all the ordinary human being. Then the fat of a mountain goat is cut to pieces and was given around to everybody and they put this fat on their faces. That is ready for them every time they are going to paint their faces with dried red or black powder. Then they pick up four dishes of eagle down, and they say, "Go and put it on everyone's head." Everybody now has their red bark around their head and they put the eagle down on their head. After that some of the chiefs make speeches, saying: "You will take care. Don't do anything against the rules of this ceremony. We are going to start on a narrow plank which means, if you do anything wrong, you will fall, that is, you will die, and so everybody has to be careful not to look around and not to do anything against the rules, so that we might go through the ceremony safely which is a very important thing. This is the only path you will walk in – not in any other. If you miss this path, there is death in doing it." That seems to be real, but it is only a thing that they use. Then the Cannibals sing their songs. After that they go home and go to bed.

The next night they all go into the Kweka chief's house. Sometimes it is this night and sometimes the fourth night after that. This is the first time all the masks that they use in the winter dance shows. First of all they call a man to carry a box and take it up to where the singers are. He goes around the house four times before he puts this box down amongst the singers. When he puts it down he presses it down and the box makes a squeaky noise, which means that the box has magic in it. After that they call another man that will come and begin to strike at this box. All the singers begin to strike it and beat the board. Then he beckons to them to stop beating the box. Then all the noises for the different masks are heard by all the people in the house. They make each noise that they make in the winter dance, and at the fourth time they beat the box, the screen behind the singers comes down and right on the back of the screen all kinds of masks is shown in one time – all the masks owned by all the Fort Ruperts. That means all these masks

could be shown by anybody in Fort Rupert that wants to show them. After that the singers begin to sing to quiet these masks, so they won't show up without the consent of their owners. They have a special song for that saying that the masks are mad from the beating, and now they should be quiet.

That night there is about ten or more men goes around to every house and calls out everybody's name that are in the house and says that so-and-so is going to give a feast tomorrow morning. This is to stop anybody that might go away tomorrow morning from going, for everybody is called to this feast. Early in the morning they come along and say, "We are calling you now to the feast of so-and-so." When they are all in the house, two young men from the Kwakiutl stand up and say, "Now we are turning around and we are the chiefs and the others that were chiefs have nothing to do with it. We are going to have all the fun we can have." They pretend to be fighting with the other boys who pretend to be crazy and pretend to be animals. The Grizzly Bears are chased by the boys to touch their backsides which is supposed not to be touched. The Grizzly Bears don't allow anybody to touch it, and if they turn their backsides toward the people they say, "I see that backside of yours," and the Bear goes and tries to hide it. Crazy men – I was one of them at another winter ceremonial – could pick up stones and throw them at others and spears and anything we could get hold of to hit other people with if we were let to do it, but we don't bother the Hamatsas because they are the chiefs of all the Crazy Men and the Grizzly Bears and others. These Crazy Men don't let anybody say anything about their nose. If anybody touches it or talks about it, I get a stone or a spear and pretend to try to hit them with it. It seems that you really don't want your nose to be touched.

The Hamatsas are supposed to be cannibals that goes to other people and kills them to eat their flesh. In eating them, I don't think they were eating them, but just pretending. My old people was telling me that when Hamatsas was eating the dead bodies, they wasn't eating them at all. They was pretending and putting the flesh in a basket concealed in their bodies. But they say that some of them did it, but

these are the ones that didn't know any better. At the last time they was eating the dead flesh, they say two of the Hamatsas died right in the room, and that the corpse they ate was poisonous. Others of them got awful sick and nearly died too. When they get fierce they bit pieces out of the arms of those they come up against. When they bit a piece off another's arm, they have to give him something for it – maybe a canoe – maybe blankets or something the next day after he gets through dancing.

Sometimes the Crazy Men and Grizzly Bears and Hamatsas goes right into the houses and upsets things – especially the water buckets so they won't drink any water that day. And others guard the wells, and don't let anybody get near. Sometimes they pour water on the fires so they won't cook. "Let them starve," they say. Then somebody goes and gives them food and this quiets them down. Or singing songs will quiet them down so that they just walk around like other men.

This goes on for many days and many nights, sometimes right along during the winter. Every time there is nobody else gives a feast, the Kweka chief gives a feast, and any time nobody else gives a dance, he gives a dance. At the Kweka chief's fourth dance everybody dances during that night, dancing their own dances, starting from the head of the Kwakiutl, Peter Knox's granddaughter, then the head of the Walas Kwakiutl, and the second clan of the Kwakiutl, and then the head of the second clan of the Walas Kwakiutl, and so on, all except the Kwekas who has hired them to come and dance for them. Every time anyone comes in to dance, he or she is paid by the Kweka chief's wife. They come in through the door of the house and come in front of the singers and dance, and while she is dancing, she dances around and then goes out and then she gets clothing or something from the Kweka chief's wife.

At the Kweka chief's house, I did my dance – the Warrior dance. I had spruce twigs thrust through the flesh on my thighs by one of the men. He first put a sharp iron through. Then when they took the iron out he put the twig through and put a knot in the twig to hold it together, and the same way in two places on by back. That hurted a little bit, and

then they tied a rope onto the twigs and tied it onto the frame of a double-headed snake mask. And they have three poles and lift me up by lifting the mask, and the ropes lifted me and take me along the beach toward the Kweka chief's house. All the time I say, "Hi-i-i-i-i-i-i-i-i, Hi-hi-hi-hi," and all those that has the same dance comes close around watching and make the same noise with me. They were the only ones supposed to come close. They all have their knives with them, cutting their foreheads. When we got to the front of the house, they put up a rope on the house and pulled me up to the roof, and all the singers were under me, holding up their hands while I was pulled up toward the roof of the house. When I got up to the roof, they pulled me to the back end, and put me through the hole in the roof and I was there hanging up till all the peoples came in. When they all came in, they lowered me down. But when I was hanging up there they all sing my song, and at the words "Cut with your knife," I cut my forehead and the blood came down all over me. I showed the knife to the people smiling, and then take the knife and cut, cut, cut my forehead still smiling to show the people how brave I am. When I am lowered down, they take off the frame and the rope is holded by several men, and they begin to pull while I am dancing while they sing my song. Then they begin to say, after the song is ended, shouting, "Go to war." And then they begin to pull the ropes and try to break the twigs out of my leg and back. Two strong men come on my both sides to hold me so that when my skin breaks, I don't fall. When they couldn't break my skin, they took my knife away from me and cut my skin, and when they have pulled the rope away, the Grizzly Bears they say, "Wo-o-o-o-o-o-o-o-o." Everybody was standing in the house at the time, and I go around the house after all the ropes is off and go back of the screen and stayed there, and in the night when they begin to dance again, they have small paddles all painted with red – that is the blood of the people I am supposed to have killed. Hanging around tied with white thread and a needle stuck in me all over, holding each one of these little paddles, holding a double-headed snake made out of yellow cedar wood in my hands all carved, and I come out and dance. That's all I have on when I dance

that night. Hemlock branches is around my head. I go back again and I am finished my dance. All the time before this I was staying in the house for I was supposed to be out in the woods. I was just sitting down there, sometimes go to sleep. I eat because they bring me something all the time when they eat. I had to wait till nighttime to go to the beach to the toilet so nobody see me. I had to go through the back door and then go to where there is no houses. While I was doing the dance, I didn't hardly feel any pain at all.

In my brother's winter dance, I was the Grizzly Bear. I wore a grizzly-bear skin, and a mask carved like a bear. That could be used at winter dance and at potlatches during the summer. When that mask opens up, it becomes a double-headed snake. The carved man's face inside is all dressed up with abalone shells inside – abalone shells for the eye-balls. This is used when it is opened in potlatches in the summer-time. When I danced, I didn't open it. This Grizzly Bear mask is the only bear mask that can be used both winter and summer. The man inside it is the crest that shows in the summertime. In the winter dance, I could have used another Bear mask as long as it didn't open and show the man inside it. It is the same as any other Bear mask. I went with all the people to watch them dance the night they all danced together and I sat on the side. A Hamatsa came and pulled me by the arm and took me outside. That means I am gone into the woods.

The next morning the Hamatsas and the rest of the people came and got me, and I was dressed up in my Bear's clothing, and I came back to my brother's house and I go around acting like a fierce bear, crawling on the ground and pulling the earth and throwing it all over the place. Each night for four nights I do this. During the daytime I stay behind the screen, and in the meantime eat all the time. When I go out and run around, I go into the other houses. My brother told me once to go to a new canoe and break it up, and so I did. It means I can do anything – break anything without any trouble, because I have a chief that backs me, and as I go around the houses doing all these things, a man comes with me and keeps track of everything I break. I go into a house and pull down a cupboard and bust all the dishes, and the

owners never say a word because they know it's going to be paid for. He pays for all those things right after we get through the fourth night, and we are tamed down. I had a lot of fun. I run after men and women and they run away from me. When I'm tired, I sometimes let someone else go in my skin while I rest, because the boys want their Bear to go around all the time. In the old days, it was only the chief's sons that could be these things – Hamatsas, Grizzly Bears, Warriors, and Crazy Men.[1]

Another good dance is the Towidi – a woman that comes around the house slowly, and when she gets up to the front of the singers, she stands up and face the fire while all the people are sitting down and says, "Will some of you bring me a knife?" – that is to cut her head off. Nobody brings her one, and then she turns and says, "Bring me a hammer to crush in my head." Each time she says that she always turns around and face the singers, and the people ask each other who has the hammer, and nobody has it. Then she says, "Bring me a paddle to chop my head in two." And nobody has a paddle. Old ones but not new enough. And then she says: "Bring me a box, one of the Indian boxes, and put me inside it. Put the cover on and put the box and me into the fire and burn me up." They all try to find a box big enough, but none is big enough. And then the chief says to the singers, "Beat your board with your sticks, and let us see what she will do." And she go from one end of the house to the other pretending to try to catch something that she alone can see. When she catches it the chief says, "Stop beating that board." The chief listens but she don't say nothing so they beat it again. She does the same thing four times. Then when she catches something it whistles when she moves her hand and she throws it among the singers, and there at once there is a lot of whistling among the singers and then a big snake will come out that reaches to both sides of the house,

[1] Here the function of the winter ceremonial as an outlet for pent-up aggressions becomes clear. But even here there are limits: the people who are bitten by the Cannibals and whose goods are damaged by the Grizzly Bears will be paid for their losses. It would probably be too dangerous to remove all restraints and permit the dancers complete freedom in their expressions of aggression.

and she come along with a wood made like a sword and there is a man on the centre of this serpent – a man's face. And she comes there and strikes the man's head with it and it splits and the two sides of the serpent spread apart, and then it comes together again and begins to go down and is supposed to go under the ground. Then the people begin to sing her song, and she goes around the house and back behind the screen and stays there. She does this only one night.

A girl, a chief's daughter, had a dance, a Towidi, and as she was brought to the front of the dance house from the woods, while she was dancing and everybody was watching, she turned the wrong way, and all the people start saying what she had done, and one of our chiefs stood and was talking about the thing she has done and says: "What shall we do with her? Shall we kill her?" Some of the Crazy Men came close to her with their axes and pretended they were going to kill her, and the Grizzly Bears came with their claws and stood around her, and she was just standing there pale. My brother says: "We better not kill her here. The best way is to tie a rock on her neck and take her out in the water and drown her." And so they shoved a canoe down to the water, and all the Grizzly Bears, the Crazy Men, and others went into this canoe, and while they were doing this, everybody was watching them, the clothing of this girl and the hemlock branches were taken off her and put on a boy her own size, while this girl was between a group of men that took her into the house without anybody seeing her.

The boy in the clothing of the girl was led to the canoe and got on to it still singing her song, and when they paddled out about twenty feet off shore, they tied her neck with a rope and tied it on a boom chain which they let down on the side of the canoe facing all the people. Then they left this "girl" and place her on the side of the canoe while she was still singing her song, and pushed her overboard. All the people in the canoe shout, "Woo-oo-oo-oo-oo-oo-oo, hi-hi." And all the people on shore that was watching, the relations of this girl, was told to sing their songs, but none of them could. They all say that their throat was blocked, and they couldn't make any sound, and there was four women wearing Wolf masks that sat down close to the water and begin to

cry, because the thing seemed to be real. Nobody see how it was done. They had a rope on the other side of the canoe and when they pushed her overboard, the front side of the men on the other side was pulling this boy up and give him his own clothing and blankets, and then they came on shore and jump out of the canoe one by one until there was nobody in the canoe, and the people keep watching and see that the girl didn't come out. I was one of those people that took the girl into the house, and, when we got in there, her husband was in bed there crying to beat hell. It looked so real that everybody cried that didn't know how it was done. This is one of the reasons the winter ceremonial is called lies; it looks real, but it isn't true. I was a Grizzly Bear that time. Oh, she was scared! When she went to her husband, he asked her what happened to her. Her reply was: "I don't know. I don't remember when I went in the canoe, and, when I came here, I was so scared I went unconscious."

There was another Towidi who was asking for a box to be burned. They put her in the box while all the people saw her put in there in her blue blanket and tied the box, and then they put the box on the fire and poured on the olachen grease. The fire burned and the box burned, and she was still singing inside, and then the box go up in flames, and they can see her burning there in her blue blanket, and all her relatives just cry and cry. Although they know it is not real, it looks so real they can't help it. It was all a trick. There was a hole under the box with a tunnel leading out of the house, and the woman went out of the box and put a seal in her place wrapped in a blue blanket, and then someone sang into the fire through a kelp tube, her song. Oh, it looked real!

There was another one ask for a knife. That is the first thing that they ask for. They turn four times and ask for different kinds of tools to kill themselves with. The one that ask for the knife at the fourth time, a man came around with a knife, went around the house with it, took out some of the black charcoal from the fire, smashed it and put it all over his face, and, when he got to the front end of the house, he begin to speak to the people, and he says, "Take hold of her and lay her on a board." They brought a short board and laid the board on the ground, and he came around to her

and took his knife and aimed for her neck four times, and, on the fourth time, he took hold of her hair and pulled her head back and cut it right off. Holding her by the hair, he turned around and put the head in his blanket, and went around looking fierce, and when he got to the front end of the house, close to the door, he sat down there and took this head and put it on the ground there facing the fire. And he went away from her and walked away from the head while the head was still standing on the ground there, and the mouth kept opening and the face twitching as if there was still life in that head, and the man came around and picked it up and put it under his blanket again, and he go to another side of the house, and put the head on a box, showing the people it is the same face as this woman has, and he went to the rear end of the house and put it down on the ground again, so the people on the front end will see it. And everybody with their mouths open – wide-eyed – because the head is still moving its face and then the fourth time he goes to the body of it and puts it back, and then they wrapped her up and put her on the place where she is going to be for four days. By the way the head acts it makes a noise and everybody thinks it is a real head, because it is the same looking as the head of this woman.

Here, too, they had a tunnel under the house, and the man that cut the head off is the only man that knows where the tunnel is. When he went there to set this mask down that he got away from the body, there was a man in there that takes up the board that covers the hole. When the killer puts the mask down, the woman that was supposed to be killed comes up and sets her head up. They say she had a hard time breathing because the boards were tight around her neck, and when the man goes to the top to take the head off, he only takes off the cedar branches that is on top of her head. While he is walking slow around the house she walks under the tunnel to where the box is and puts her head up there.

PART SIX

DEVIANCE AND NORMALITY

Crime and Punishment in Tlingit Society

KALERVO OBERG

Every Tlingit is born into one of three matrilineal phratries. He is either a Tlaienedi, a Shinkukedi, or a Nekadi. If he is a Tlaienedi, he calls himself a Raven; if a Shinkukedi, a Wolf; if a Nekadi, an Eagle. The Nekadi, however, are so few in number that they may be neglected, and we may speak of the Tlingit as Ravens and Wolves, each person referring to a member of the other phratry as his opposite. The members of a phratry consider themselves blood relatives and prohibit marriage within the group. A phratry possesses no territory, has no property, no political unity, no chiefs. While members of a phratry perform certain types of labour and ceremonies for their opposites, it is not the phratry that acts as a unit.

What is more important to a Tlingit is the fact that he is born a member of a clan. This clan has a name denoting its place of origin, a story of its genesis, a history of its migrations. The crests of the phratries have become securely established through a tradition reaching back to the mythical beginnings of the Tlingit people. The crests of the clans, on the other hand, are not on so secure a foundation. A clan possesses a number of these crests or emblems which it has gained in numerous ways throughout its history and the right

Source: *American Anthropologist,* n.s., 36 (April-June, 1934), 145-56. Reprinted by permission of the publisher.

to them is often questioned by other clans of the same phratry. These crests, along with songs, dances, legends, and face paintings, are jealously guarded by the clans. But the clan as a whole has no property.

The local division of the clan, however, possesses definite territories for hunting and fishing, houses in the village, and has a chief or ceremonial leader. While labour, ceremonies and potlatches are performed by members of one phratry for the members of the other, it is the clan that forms the active nucleus. In practice it is a wife's clan that builds a man's house or buries him. It is a clan that invites clans of the opposite side to a potlatch. It is a clan that carries on feuds and sees that customary law is enforced.

From what has been said it would seem that the clan was a group of great solidarity, and theoretically this is true. In practice, however, this solidarity is weakened by individual status. Within the clan every person has his or her rank which is definitely known. The people of higher status, the *anyeti*, wield considerable power through their position and wealth, and are able to decide legal issues to their own advantage at the expense of their less important kinsmen.

In the matter of crime and punishment, the relation of the individual and the clan comes out clearly. Theoretically, crime against an individual did not exist. The loss of an individual by murder, the loss of property by theft, or shame brought to a member of a clan, were clan losses and the clan demanded an equivalent in revenge. That is to say, if a man of low rank killed a man of high rank in another clan, the murderer often went free while one of his more important kinsmen suffered death in his stead. Slight differences in status could be overcome by payments of property, but the general demand in case of murder was the life of a man of equal rank. In some instances the offending clan was of lower status and therefore none of its members could compensate for a crime committed against an important clan. It was therefore necessary to select a clan of the offender's phratry that could show some relationship to the offending clan; but in this case war usually followed, as this procedure was not legally established. In general, it made no difference whether the opposing clans were in the same phratry or in

opposite phratries. Some of the bitterest feuds were between the Ganaktedi and Tluknakadi, both of the same phratry.

Thus a clan appears to be the group of greatest unity, soildarity, and integration. There was no penalty within the clan for murder, adultery, or theft. A clan punished its members by death only when shame was brought to its honour. Crimes of this nature were incest, witchcraft, marriage with a slave, and prostitution.

Murder among the Tlingit was punishable by death when committed outside the clan. The number of murders, however, was not excessive until the advent of liquor. In the old days rivalry over women and disputes about individual privileges during potlatches sometimes led to murder. Murder was generally committed in the heat of argument, and if clansmen of both sides were present, a general fight was prevented by a chief of high rank stepping between the angry clansmen with an important crest in his hand. It was considered a desecration of the emblem or crest if fighting occurred under these circumstances.

Immediately after a murder was committed spokesmen from both clans met to decide who was to die in compensation for the murder. If the murdered man happened to be of low rank and of poor reputation, a payment of goods could satisfy the injured clan. But if the murdered man was of high rank, a man of equal standing was demanded from the murderer's clan. There was generally much haggling over the rank of the murdered man and the rank of the one who was to die in compensation. These disputes always appeared in the peace dance which followed the complete settlement of the crime. The man selected as compensation prepared to die willingly. He was given much time to prepare himself through fasting and praying. The execution took place before his house.

On the day set for the execution, the man put on all his ceremonial robes and displayed all his crests and emblems. He came out of his house, stood at the doorway, and related his history, stressing the deeds that he and his ancestors had performed. All the villagers were gathered around for this solemn occasion. He then looked across to the clan whom his death was to satisfy to observe the man who had been

selected to kill him. If this man was great and honourable he would step forth gladly; but if the man was of low rank he would return to the house and wait until a man of his own rank or higher was selected to kill him. When this was done he stepped forth boldly with his spear in his hand, singing a girl's puberty song. He feigned attack but permitted himself to be killed. To die thus for the honour of one's clan was considered an act of great bravery and the body was laid out in state as that of a great warrior. His soul went to Kiwa-Kawaw, "highest heaven."

The actual murderer, if a man of great rank and wealth, often went free, but if the man was of low rank and came from a poor house he went as a slave to that house in his clan which had given up a man in compensation for the murder. If property was passed as partial payment to the murdered man's clan, the actual murderer could be handed over as a slave. Even if the murderer was not forced into slavery, his position was an uncomfortable one. There was a feeling of very close unity among clansmen and when one had brought shame to his own clan, he felt the matter keenly and for a time led a miserable life.

Among a people who divided themselves into two exogamic groups, incest was bound to be a constant occurrence and facts well bear this out. There are many known cases where a man and woman of the same phratry fell in love and lived together until found out. Songs tell of the pathetic and forlorn hopes of these forbidden lovers. The penalty for incest was death, both persons being killed by their respective clansmen. In spite of this penalty incest was common enough to make the law less rigorously enforced. In cases where the man who committed incest was of high rank, exile was imposed. The man would then go to settle among the interior people or among the Tsimshian or Haida. When the white people came with their law, the Indians soon realized that it permitted marriage between people who were not blood relatives, and they were quick to take advantage of this when it suited their purpose. The Indians claimed that this was one of their first social customs to give way before the whites and many of the young people rejoiced at the new freedom. When an illegal marriage occurred the couple went

to the white settlement for protection. A peculiar case of this nature occurred immediately after American occupation, when a famous chief of the Daklawedi clan of Kake left his wife and took a woman of his own phratry. He was too powerful to be immediately killed, and had time to flee to Wrangell, where he had the protection of American law. Later his wife died and he married a woman of the opposite phratry. He could then have returned to Kake but preferred to live in Wrangell, as he feared the stigma attached to one who marries his own "sister." At present marriage within the exogamic group is common, but in the more conservative villages marriages of this type are frowned on and the couples become outcasts.

Like murder, adultery was not punishable within the clan. If a wife committed adultery with her husband's kinsman and was caught by her husband, he would ignore the matter; but if they were caught by someone else, the wife could do one of two things. She could continue having secret relations with this man and endure the social stigma attached to this, or she could keep the man as a second husband. In this circumstance the husband could do nothing but share his wife with the other man, who often lived in the same house and was his cousin or nephew in our sense. There was, however, no marriage ceremony; but the young man was not permitted to marry another woman as long as the wife wished to keep him. This custom was common among Tlingit of high rank and the natives rationalized it as a means of keeping the idle women of the rich satisfied and at home.

Adultery, when it occurred between a woman and a man who was not of the husband's clan, was punishable by death, both guilty persons being killed by the husband. If he were fond of his wife, he might forgive her; but in this case the wife's kinsmen must pay him property to clear his honour. If the adulterer escaped, there was no way of bringing him to task except by pursuit by the husband. In case the adulterer was a man of very high rank, the husband's own clansmen paid him goods to pacify him, for demanding the life of a very high man was a serious matter. When property was given to the husband by both his wife's clan and his own clan the transaction was known as *tuwatuk'ayawaci*, "they

wipe the shame from my face." Before reparation was paid, the husband remained indoors and came out only after a gathering had taken place at his house in which the property was transferred to him.

If a man of low rank had illicit connections with a woman of high rank the matter was very serious. First, the wife's clansmen killed two of the man's clansmen having rank between that of the man and the woman. This was to show that the wife's clan was highly insulted and incensed, and would not let the matter drop. The man's clan was then expected to offer for slaying one of its men of rank equal to that of the woman. If they would not do this, a feud might arise between the two clans which might last for a long time and might involve other clans, as in the quarrel between the Sitka and Wrangell people over a woman. In case the man's clan now offered a man, equal in rank to the woman, the woman's clan would be satisfied and would compensate the man's clan with property for the killing of the first two men. The adulterer was often handed over to the woman's side as a slave in partial payment or he became a slave to his own clan in order to compensate for the loss he brought about. During all these activities the husband remained indoors and came out only after a full settlement had been made.

If a woman of high rank became lax in her conduct and ran around with numerous men, her uncle might ask one of her brothers to kill her, which he was obliged to do. If a man of low rank had illicit connections with a girl of high rank, the father of the girl demanded either the man slain or a great deal of property. If the man was of as high a rank as the girl, her father could force them to marry. But if the girl was already promised to another man, the father was given a number of blankets.

Theoretically, stealing did not exist within the clan. Natural resources were held in common and food was but loosely guarded by the various house groups within the clan. If a man took a tool or a weapon that belonged to a member of his own clan, he was forced to return it. If a man of low rank was caught stealing from another clan, the injured clan could kill him. If he was of high rank, his own clan would make reparation by a payment of goods. If, by some chance, a

man of very high rank was caught stealing, he was said to be bewitched. Then a shamanistic performance was held over him to discover the sorcerer who had forced him to steal in order to injure his social position. The sorcerer when discovered was killed and the crime thus compensated.

If anyone beside the clansmen or those invited were caught taking fish from clan territories, or if they were caught hunting there, they could be killed. This was also true if anyone trespassed on clan domain or used their trade routes. Sometimes when a powerful party came to fish on another clan's territory, the owning clan would invite the transgressors to a feast, treat them well, and give them presents. This they did to shame the aggressors, who generally withdrew after such treatment. If a man was hungry he could shoot an animal in someone else's territory, but he was forced to give the hide or pelt to the owning clan.

Adopting the crest of another clan was considered stealing, but the aggressor always claimed the right to the crest through some event in the past. Conflict over the use of crests led to war between the clans or was settled by the opinion of the phratry or the transfer of property.

The penalty for assault was payment in goods. A high-ranking Tlingit was very sensitive about his appearance and if in a dispute someone struck him so as to cause marks on his face, he would remain indoors until the marks were healed and until a public payment had been made to him by the clan of his assailant. If a man of high status injured his face by falling in the street of his village, he would remain indoors until the marks had healed; then he would give a small feast to his own clan. This was to compensate his clan for the shame brought to it by his disfigurement.

If a man was injured or accidentally killed while out hunting with the members of another clan, this clan would have to compensate the dead or injured man's clan by a payment of goods. If the man killed was of very high rank and his death could be shown to be due to the carelessness of his hosts, then the dead man's clan could demand that a man of the hosts' clan be killed.

If a person was injured by a dog belonging to another clan, the owner of the dog would compensate for the injury

by a payment of goods to the injured man. Harm coming to pass through another clan's property had very wide ramifications and was always settled by a payment of goods. Falling twice before a man's house would entitle the one who fell to ask for a payment of goods. Catching a chill in another man's house, injuring one's self with another man's tools, or becoming angry or irritable due to contact with others, would give a right to a small payment of goods, provided these injuries were caused by members of another clan.

Another example of this appears in the case of suicide. If it could be shown that a man had committed suicide because his wife had treated him badly, then a man of his wife's clan could be selected and killed. Therefore a Tlingit woman was very careful how she treated her husband. This punishment was also meted out to others who caused a man to commit suicide.

Many articles, such as canoes, tools, traps, weapons, and such lesser ceremonial gear as masks and dancing shirts, were owned by individuals. Other individuals, either within the clan or outside, could borrow these, provided they brought them back or replaced them at some later date. If the borrower failed to return the article within a reasonable time, the lender could disseminate stories of ridicule about him. These stories were somewhat in the nature of the paddle songs of the Tsimshian, but not so highly stylized, and like the paddle songs they heaped ridicule upon the debtor until he came to terms. These stories were used only when it was well known that the debtor was able to pay but refused for selfish reasons. If these stories did not have the desired effect, the creditor could discuss the matter with members of his own clan. If the debtor belonged to the same clan and was in a position to pay, the social pressure of the clan was sufficient to bring him to terms. If, however, he was unable to pay and there was little likelihood of his ever being able to pay, the clan would permit the creditor to take the debtor as a debt slave.

The debt slave, when a clansman, was not treated exactly like a chattel slave. True enough, he lost his freedom and status, but it was understood that when he had worked long

enough to repay the debt, he would be freed and would regain his former status. A debt slave was not sold or given away at a potlatch unless he belonged to another clan.

If the debtor belonged to another clan, a different procedure took place after ridicule ceased to have effect. The creditor would have a crest of the debtor's clan made which he placed on the front of his own house or on a totem pole. Among the Tlingit clan crests were jealously guarded, and the fact that another clan had taken one brought great shame to the clan to which it belonged. All the people in the village would at once notice it and the story come out. The debtor's clan was now dishonoured and would make considerable efforts to pay the debt. Usually a wealthy house group paid the debt and took the debtor as a debt slave, thus saving the honour of the clan.

The taking of an important clan crest was always resorted to in the case of a prestige potlatch. If a clan refused to give a return potlatch to another clan of the opposite phratry, the creditor clan could take a crest and keep it until payment was made.

Names could be used in place of crests for debt exactions. Names, like crests, were clan property and were not supposed to go outside the clan. An interesting case of name adoption occurred at Klukwan. It happened that a Chilcat Indian was engaged by Lieutenant Schwatka as a guide when he made his famous trip into the interior. Schwatka had promised the Indian a certain sum of money which, it is said, he did not pay. The Indian promptly took Schwatka's name, which is still in use among the people of Klukwan. The name is now pronounced Swatki and is of great importance in the Daklawedi clan of Klukwan. During wars between clans, names and even crests were taken in payment to bring about the equality which is a prerequisite of peace. Names sometimes remained permanently in a foreign clan, but crests were sooner or later brought back.

The above is a brief summary of the main types of Tlingit crimes and their punishment. From this summary certain social characteristics stand out prominently. The first of these is the importance of a clan as a sovereign group. The second is the importance of individual status. How crime is

to be punished depends largely upon the rank of the criminal. Men of high rank could often escape death through a payment of goods. Every man and woman had a valuation in terms of goods. As the status of a clan was judged largely by the amount of goods it gave away at its last prestige potlatch, so was the status of an individual determined by the amount of goods he gave for his wife. The bride price evaluated both the husband and the wife. The bride price formed the basis for settlement made in terms of goods. There were no fixed fines, since the bride prices varied with the wealth of the community and the status of the individuals. There has been no attempt made here to describe actual punishment in terms of such and such a quantity of goods, but rather the social forces governing the amount of goods given in reparation for the crime.

Closely allied with the criminal act was the shameful act. The fundamental differentiation seems to be determined by the type of social prohibition. Criminal acts were politically or legally prohibited; shameful acts were connected either with etiquette, morals, religion, and economy, or all combined. For the purpose of this paper it is also important to differentiate the criminal act from the shameful act on the basis of the nature of the punishment. While crime was punishable by measures taken against the life and property of the individuals of a clan, the shameful act was punished by ridicule. But so effective was ridicule, that the performer of a shameful act, as in the case of blunders at ceremonials, often died as a result of social disapproval.

We must here distinguish between acts that brought shame to the performer and acts that were performed to shame someone else. One could shame an important chief by seating him in a corner or by calling him by his boyhood rather than by his honourable name. But these were crimes and might lead to serious difficulties between the clans of the respective men. Any crime, of course, brought shame to the injured clan. It is the act shameful to the performer that is under consideration here. Among the Tlingit propriety was of the utmost importance. The *anyeti* or nobility thought of themselves as being eminent because they and their ancestors had never performed shameful acts. An important man

could permanently lower himself by repeated shameful acts. Quite often men destined for chieftainship were ignored because they had in some way shamed themselves.

A member of the *anyeti* would shame himself if he fell down in public, or otherwise bruised or injured his person. He would shame himself if he were caught doing menial labour, such as cleaning fish or carrying wood or water. He would be shamed if he were caught in an altercation with a slave or a man of low rank, or if he were caught seated in a sprawling position, or if he went to an important meeting without the proper clothes. In every case ridicule could be heaped upon him but the important man prevented this by giving a feast, inviting all the individuals who had seen him. This saved his honour, for it was a great shame to ridicule one's host.

Among the Tlingit one could enjoy the hospitality of a member of his own phratry for an unlimited length of time, but it was considered a great shame to abuse this hospitality. It was shameful to publicly dispute the word of a man older than yourself. It was shameful to have sex relations in your own clan with a woman of inferior rank, but not necessarily so if the woman was of your own rank. It was shameful to be seen near your mother-in-law. Individuals of high rank were shamed if people of low rank saw them nude. It was shameful to be seen defecating or urinating, but it was not shameful to talk about these things in public, nor was it shameful to talk about sexual matters. It was also shameful to break the customary ways of hunting, fishing, and eating.

A shameful act was generally sufficient reason for preventing people performing it. But among the Tlingit, as among other people, there were certain individuals who dared shame in order to gain their ends. It was these who were brought to terms by ridicule. Ridicule had many forms. The most effective consisted in making the offender of the proprieties the laughing stock of the village by disseminating songs and stories about him. Such songs and stories were often composed by paid song makers. Another form was the making of ludicrous wooden likenesses of the offender and placing them in prominent locations. Sometimes elaborate totem poles were carved with this motive in mind. Mimicry

was also resorted to in bringing an offender to terms, or he might be called a white man, which every Tlingit considered the height of public censure.

Another point worth stressing is the fact that the criminal was permitted to be at large pending the settlement of the crime, while the injured party always remained indoors until his honour was cleared.

There are other social usages that are so closely connected with crime and punishment that we must discuss them here. The Tlingit used the sweat bath primarily for cleansing, curing, and for shamanistic performances before a war, but it had another function as well, that of a kind of court house.

Among the northern Tlingit the sweat bath was an excavation in the floor of the house into which heated stones were thrown. They then went in and sat on a platform, covering the opening with a mat. Water was thrown on the hot stones to create clouds of steam. Among the southern Tlingit the sweat bath was a corner of the house walled off for the purpose. There was nothing sacred about the sweat bath, both women and children were permitted to use it, and when it was not thus used it was a store room.

When onc of the important house owners wanted to discuss clan matters with other elders of the clan, he would prepare his sweat bath and invite them. While in the bath they carried on their discussions, and if there were any young men in the clan who were misbehaving, they were called in and reprimanded. These admonitions revolved largely around marriage regulations, which demanded that a man marry a girl equal in rank to himself.

Witchcraft and shamanism were also closely connected with crime. Sorcery was a powerful method of working harm to individuals. The Tlingit believed that people could be harmed if a certain procedure was followed. Thus if a piece of some dead person's body, such as a bone or hair was put into a man's food, he would become ill. Performing spells over objects closely associated with a man's body could also bring him harm. Some sorcerers could inject sticks or stones into a man's body to bring about illness or death. A sorcerer could also bring one bad luck in hunting, fishing, or in love, and could even make another person commit crimes such as

stealing or murder. Most members of a Tlingit community went about in great fear of witchcraft. It was said that if a sorcerer were discovered in action he would be killed immediately by his own clansmen. An interesting fact is that no informant had ever heard of a witch or sorcerer being caught in action. They were always caught by the aid of dreams or by engaging a shaman.

If a man believed that he was bewitched he would take careful notice of his dreams. If he observed, in his dream, an individual trying to hurt him, then that individual must be the sorcerer, and steps would be taken to bring about the death of the evil-doer. In cases when dreams failed to reveal the sorcerer, the shaman would be resorted to. The shaman would hold a performance to discover the sorcerer. The unfortunate man would then be tied with his hands and feet together behind his back and left on the beach or thrown into a pit where he died, or he might be killed outright by being choked to death between two logs.

The employment of shamans in the discovery of crimes such as murder and stealing lent itself to abuse among the Tlingit. Men would steal and later claim that they had been bewitched by a slave and thus escape the penalty. Rivals were often exterminated by paying the shaman to name them as sorcerers in cases of murder where the murderer escaped detection and in cases of illness.

Taking into account the importance of status and the use of shamans in crime detection, it appears that there was a law for the strong and a law for the weak. Men of high rank and great wealth could, through the shaman, commit crimes and still escape punishment. People of low status and slaves were in constant fear of the powerful families and the shamans they employed.

There is still another phase of the Tlingit legal pattern which must be discussed, namely the peace dance. After the settlement of a dispute by execution or by payment of goods, the whole matter was closed by a peace dance.

The whole village attended the dance, which was usually performed in the open air. The two performing clans lined up opposite one another and each picked out a number of messengers and attendants. Then the important men on

each side called out, "Come exchange with me." Four men of high status would volunteer from each side. Then the messengers dashed across to the opposite side as if to attack and brought in the hostages who had offered themselves. After this exchange the attitude of the performers changed. Every act then symbolized peace. The hostages were called kowakan, "deer," because the deer is the most harmless of animals. Each hostage took a special name signifying peace, humility, happiness, and plenty, such as "woman," "salmon-trap," "humming-bird," "robin." They fasted four days in the houses of the most important chiefs or clansmen. They were not permitted to do anything for themselves, having attendants. On the fourth day their fingers were tied together and they ate with their left hands, because the left hand was weak in fighting. Their food was eaten from stone slabs, to signify that peace would be lasting. The hostages were at first dressed poorly and sang sad songs. The nature of the songs revealed the mood of the two clans, and the natives listened closely to them to tell if both parties were satisfied or still bearing ill will toward one another.

During the last day the hostages put on the clothes representing the objects after which they were named. Then they spoke to the clans, addressing themselves to the daughters of the clans, thus showing the highest respect. The hostages then danced, imitating the person, bird, animal, or object after which they had been named. After the dance, eagle-down was placed on the heads of the hostages as a token of peace, and the messengers led them back to their own clans. In this way peace was publicly proclaimed and settlements took on the weight of public sanction.

The Patterns of the Culture

PHILIP DRUCKER

It is interesting to review the sanctioned patterns of social behaviour which functioned as prime determinants in the personality formation of the bearers of the culture, or to phrase the matter in another way, the social patterns that defined the culturally approved personality type or types. Our discussion of social life has brought out a variety of traits and sanctions which were of importance in this regard. In ordinary social situations the predominant pattern required avoidance of aggressive behaviour and included a strong feeling against physical violence in conflict situations. Our data from social life reveal a people who regarded as ideal the individual noted for mildness of temper. This was more than a vague ideal. The many cases recorded of social situations show that for chiefs of high and low degree, and commoners as well, the amiable, non-aggressive individual held the esteem of his fellows, and – this is important – because of their esteem secured their very essential co-operation in economic and ceremonial matters. Person after person of whom informants tell, and who were regarded as estimable, were in all their lives involved in no conflicts more serious than the "swearings," the verbal quarrels in which angered people indulged. It appears that these vituperative outbursts usually provided sufficient outlet for overwrought emotions. To come to blows, to tussle with an adversary, was to overstep bounds of propriety. To carry physical conflicts into the rituals associated with status and hereditary honours, that is, the potlatches, was con-

Source: Philip Drucker, *The Northern and Central Nootkan Tribes* (Washington, D.C., Bureau of American Ethnology, 1951), Bulletin 144, pp. 453-57. Reprinted by permission of the publisher.

sidered disgraceful. In other words aggressiveness was not fostered; it was inhibited at every turn. That it was pretty thoroughly stifled, not just repressed on the overt level, is indicated by the relatively low frequency of witchcraft. The black arts were practised, it is true, but less than among many Indian groups in which the culture provided more outlets for aggressive tendencies than did the Nootkan one.

In harmony with its own ideals, the culture provided no formal mechanism supplying force to deal with nonconformists. There were no police powers to regulate social behaviour (there were ceremonial police to punish tabu-breakers during the Shamans' Dance). Anyone – and everyone – intervened to separate quarrellers who came to grips. Any close kinsman whose age and level-headedness inspired respect set about placating an angry person, advising him to forget his grievance. Any person high in public esteem would take it on himself to reprimand a malefactor. The weight of public opinion thus expressed was implemented by knowledge that people would pointedly cease to help the nonconformist in his daily affairs. Were he a chief they moved out of his house. They could not send him into exile, but they could make life so unpleasant that he would have to move away of his own accord. Thus it was that public opinion served as a control on the quarrelsome, self-assertive, and rebellious. It was not 100 per cent effective, but it had a very high degree of effectiveness.

The reasons for this pacific pattern of social behaviour are not altogether clear. I believe that the absence of the wergild complex was one factor, negative in a way, of course. At least, attention was not focused on injuries as it was among people who exacted compensation for injury – the Tlingit, Haida, and Tsimshian, for example, and the northwest Californians. Lacking the concept that something had to be done about a wrong – a payment exacted or vengeance wreaked – the Nootkans, after loudly and profanely expounding their displeasure, nearly always let the matter drop. Thus we hear from them so many anticlimactic conculsions to instances of conflict. Wrongs that elsewhere often stirred men to drastic action, such as witchcraft, adultery, and the like, usually ended after an exchange of

insults. Informants say of the principals, "They just let the matter go. They weren't friends for awhile, and didn't speak to each other, but after a bit they forgot about it."

Another factor that may have had a more positive effect was the interaction of several traits: first, the absolute ownership of all important economic and ceremonial rights by the chiefs; second, the clear recognition that cooperation of many individuals was necessary to exploit these rights; and, third, the fluidity of group membership and rules of residence. In other words both the chief and his tenants knew that the former's effective performance of his role, his greatness, depended on the assistance of his tenants. If he offended them and treated them ill, they would help him but little, or even move away. This was the reason for the advice to young chiefs to "be good to their people, treat them kindly, and give them many feasts to make them happy." A person of low rank could be made to feel the pressure of unfavourable opinion as easily as a chief, or perhaps more easily. There is, of course, little that is novel in a society in which one class rules and owns, and another class does the productive work. There are many such in the world. The exceptional feature was not the symbiotic relationship, but in other aspects of their relationship: the freedom of the lower class to affiliate themselves with whatever chief they pleased (on the pretext of some remote, or perhaps fictional kinship), and the very practical recognition of the fact that the chief had to consider their welfare and treat them well to win their aid. Young chiefs were told time and again, "That is the way with a chief. If his tenants are good to him, and help him, working for him and giving him wealth, then he can make his name great. If his tenants don't care for him, he is nothing, no matter how high a name he has."

I have deliberately left warfare out of consideration up to this point. For one thing, intertribal warfare had been abandoned at the time to which most of the present information refers. If we now step over the time boundary to consider the cultural scene when the ruthless wars were fought, we note first of all that along with the complex of weapons, head-taking, tactics, and the rest went a set of attitudes that were completely and thoroughly the opposite of peacetime

social behaviour. Violence was honoured, savagery and sadism esteemed. Yet the evidence very plainly indicates that the attitudes of war were kept separate from those of ordinary social intercourse, just as the war chief kept his whale-bone club and his "medicines" for war in a separate box, to be taken out at certain times. We have as evidence the clear statements of observers during the fighting days – Sproat, Jewitt, Moziño, and others – that the same lack of violence characterized relationships within the group in their day as in the times my informants described. That warfare did not provide a necessary outlet for otherwise repressed aggressive tendencies is clear from the fact that with the coming of peace, the Nootkans did not develop new outlets – they did not become more prone to violence in intra-group situations.

Concomitant with the major social attitude were two others of different order of importance. The main trend served to regulate the contacts between the individuals in day-to-day life; these others came to expression elsewhere. The first was a very keen interest in ceremonialism. As has been noted in connection with the importance of chief's ritual prerogatives, one receives the impression that ceremonics were the axis about which all life revolves. Modern Nootkans say, "That's all they used to do all winter long in the old days; have Shamans' Dances, potlatches, and feasts. That was all they cared about." And they often add a bit wistfully, "They always were having a good time; not like us today." The Nootkans are not, of course, unique in the area in their emphasis on ritual. Just what effect this may have had on the rest of the culture is difficult to say. The neighbouring Kwakiutl had just as much interest in ritual elaboration. Nevertheless, the contrast between the groups from Cape Flattery northward and those to the south of that point and inland, where ritual was at a minimum, is worth noting.

The second subordinate strand characteristic of Nootka life was their very well-developed sense of humour. They were and still are a light-hearted people, quick with a jest or a laugh. The subject matter of their jokes is often ribald; favourite anecdotes are still told with glee at feasts and

other gatherings. Horseplay and buffoonery were used to give relief to the seriousness of the Shamans' Dance. Nootkan satire, exemplified in some of the clown performances and in the *t'ama* songs, was of a rather high order. This may seem a strange matter to stress, yet it was so prominent an aspect of daily and ritual life that it gave the typical personality a cast quite different from the gloomy sullen one sometimes pictured as characteristic of the Northwest Coast.

This appraisal of the Nootkan personality – non-aggressive, rather amiable, disliking and disapproving violence in conflict situations, with a deep interest in that type of ceremonial that was essentially a theatrical performance, and a keen and lively sense of humour – differs radically from that depicted for the neighbouring and closely related Southern Kwakiutl. Only in the warfare situation, in which the Nootkan social values were drastically altered with aggressiveness substituted for mildness and sadism for amiability, do the two personality types correspond. In view of the remarkably close general cultural similarity between the two nations, this contrast is the more surprising. Our Nootkan data is too full and their pattern is too clean-cut for there to be any doubt regarding the correctness of our appraisal. Possible explanations for the differences between the Nootkan personality pattern and the "Dionysian" one of Benedict's appraisal of the Kwakiutl, are these: The appraisal of the Kwakiutl pattern may be considerably overdrawn. There are numerous points in Ford's recently published Kwakiutl study that indicate that the Southern Kwakiutl had many other fields of interest in addition to the one of competitive potlatching so stressed in Benedict's analysis. Such interests as that in ceremonialism for its own sake, similar to that of the Nootkans; in humorous situations; and strong sexual interest; all seem to have had an important place in Kwakiutl life to judge by Ford's account. Indeed, in the material of Boas which Benedict used as source material, there are to be found numerous hints as to the importance of these same fields of interest. Mention might be made of the feature of horseplay and buffoonery during the dancing society rituals (which both Nootkan and Kwakiutl informants have assured me were of the same ribald sort that

delighted Nootkan audiences). The use of terms of endearment in ordinary address and in ceremonial speeches, occurs time and again in the texts. Such traits as these do not seem in keeping with the sullen vindictive "meglomaniac paranoid" personality that Benedict defines.

There is another possible basis for some of the contrast between Nootkan and Kwakiutl personality patterns. It may be that the Fort Rupert tribes, whom Boas studied, may themselves be an anomalous group among other Southern Kwakiutl. The reason for this may lie in the fact that the Fort Rupert tribes who assembled in historic times at the Hudson Bay Company post were faced with the knotty problem of integrating their respective series of ranked chiefs into a single order of precedence. . . . The concept of the competitive potlatch which the Fort Rupert tribes carried to extreme lengths may very well have grown out of this historical situation. As a matter of fact, information from them and from the closely related groups of Quatsino Sound indicate very strongly that this is so.

At this range and with the present lacunae in basic information, it is difficult to say which of these explanations bearing on Benedict's interpretation of Kwakiutl personal norms is correct. Probably both need to be taken into account. It is hoped that material can still be collected from the various Southern Kwakiutl tribes which will aid in the solution of this problem.

The Amiable Side of Kwakiutl Life: The Potlatch and the Play Potlatch

HELEN CODERE

Field work among the Kwakiutl in 1951 produced evidence of a kind of potlatching, play potlatching or potlatching for fun, that has never been described but is of the greatest importance for an understanding of Kwakiutl life. The existence of playfulness in relation to potlatching requires reinterpretation of the character both of this institution and of the people participitating in it. The 1951 field data include much new material on home life, child-rearing, and humour that supports Boas' claim that the private life of the Kwakiutl possessed many amiable features, but it is the aim of this presentation to show that even in the public life of the ceremonials and potlatches there was mirth and friendliness.

A summary of the relevant interpretations of Kwakiutl life will be given, followed by an examination of Boas' first-hand account of the winter dances and potlatches of 1895-96 in which there are incidents of fun-making. The new material on play potlatching will be submitted and, in conclusion, the evidence will be discussed in relation to necessary reinterpretations of Kwakiutl life and general theoretical implications.

BOAS' "ATROCIOUS BUT AMIABLE" KWAKIUTL AND BENEDICT'S "PARANOID AND MEGALOMANIAC" KWAKIUTL

Ruth Benedict's presentation of Kwakiutl character and culture[1] has received the widest publicity and general ac-

Source: *American Anthropologist*, n.s., 58 (April, 1956), 334-51. Reprinted by permission of the publisher.

[1] Ruth Benedict, *Patterns of Culture* (Boston: Houghton Mifflin Company, 1934), pp. 173-221.

ceptance. The picture she drew is so well known and so consistent and free of the complications of qualification that it is unnecessary to review it in detail; a few of her characterizing phrases will serve as sufficient reminders:

The object of a Kwakiutl enterprise was to show oneself superior to one's rivals. This will to superiority they exhibited in the most uninhibited fashion. It found expression in uncensored self-glorification and ridicule of all comers. Judged by the standards of other cultures the speeches of their chiefs at their potlatches are unabashed megalomania [p. 190].

These hymns of self-glorification were sung by the chief's retainers upon all great occasions, and they are the most characteristic expressions of their culture. All the motivations they recognized centred around the will to superiority. Their social organization, their economic institutions, their religion, birth and death, were all channels for its expression [p. 191].

They recognized only one gamut of emotion, that which swings between victory and shame. . . . Knowing but the one gamut they used it for every occasion, even the most unlikely [p. 215].

The megalomanic paranoid trend . . . [they made] *the essential attribute of ideal man . . .* [p. 222].

Franz Boas' response[2] to this character portrait of the Kwakiutl is comparatively little known, but, in spite of its brevity and incompleteness, it sets problems of great interest and utility for students of culture:

Evidently, the wider the scope of the leading motive of culture the more it will appear as characteristic of the whole culture, but we must not be deceived into believing that it will give us an exhaustive picture of all the sides of that culture.

As an example I may refer again to the Indians of the Northwest Coast of America. The leading motive of their lives is the limitless pursuit of gaining social prestige and of

[2] Franz Boas, "Die Individualität Primitive Kulturen": *Reine und Angewandte Soziologie*. Volume in honour of Ferdinand Tönnies. (G. Albrecht, Leipzig, 1936), p. 267.

holding on to what has been gained, and the intense feeling of inferiority and shame if even the slightest part of prestige has been lost. This is manifest not only in the attempts to attain a coveted high position, but equally in the endeavour to be considered the most atrocious member of the tribe. Rank and wealth are valued most highly, but there are also cases of criminals (in the sense of the culture we are discussing) who vie with each other in committing atrocities. A loss of prestige in either sense is a source of shame which must be made good by some action re-establishing the lost respect. If it is not possible it leads to suicide. Art consists in the glorification of the family crest or of family histories. A pretense of excessive conservatism, often contradicted by obvious changes of behaviour, is closely allied with the jealous watch over all privileges.

These tendencies are so striking that the amiable qualities that appear in intimate family life are easily overlooked. These are not by any means absent. In contrast to the jealousy with which prerogatives are guarded, everyone within the family circle belittles his position. Husband and wife address each other as "You whose slave I am," or "You whose dog I am." Parents and grandparents designate themselves in the same way when talking to their children, who in turn use nicknames when addressing their parents and grandparents.[3]

Boas' criticism of Benedict centres on a denial of her thesis that a culture, or, at least, some cultures, can be described in terms of a dominant character or leading motif. In relation to Benedict's interpretation of Kwakiutl character, Boas' criticism states points of significant difference but is actually very mild, brief, and even self-contradictory. He is in agreement with the substantial part of Benedict's characterization when he states that "the leading motive" of the Kwakiutl is "the limitless pursuit of gaining social prestige." If anything, he outdoes Benedict in his use of the characterizing word "atrocious," for its connotations, or the connotations of some of the possible translation choices

[3] Franz Boas, "The Methods of Research" in Franz Boas (ed.), *General Anthropology* (New York: D. C. Heath and Company, 1938), pp. 684-685.

like "vicious" or "evil," seem to go further than some of Benedict's stronger words, such as "paranoid." On the sharp point of difference – the simultaneous presence of other and contradictory qualities in Kwakiutl life – the evidence he cites as revealing "amiable" qualities is slight, unclear, and unimpressive. Nevertheless, it is clear that there is a basic conflict of opinion about Kwakiutl life and the Kwakiutl people.

Were there no need to conserve space, it would be valuable to consider at length how this conflict of opinion could have arisen and stayed unresolved between two persons of such stature in anthropology, such close and continuous association, and such humaneness. Such consideration would, however, involve the entire field of anthropology, basic questions concerning the collection and interpretation of data, and the entire content of the several lifetimes' work of both Boas and Benedict. The conclusion could, I think, be stated in turns of phrase borrowed from Kwakiutl: no one in anthropology has yet written, or is for some time likely to write, in such a way as to end with, "It is finished" rather than, "Here is where I shall stop my words."

It is clear, however, that Boas presented relatively little material to work with on the more amiable side of Kwakiutl life, that Benedict ignored such materials as were present as perhaps being far out of the range of the norms of behaviour, and that both Boas with his "atrocious but amiable" Kwakiutl and Benedict with her "paranoid" Kwakiutl took the structural material at face value for purposes of determining the meanings and qualities of the culture.

Although there will follow a full section showing how Boas' published materials demand a different interpretation from that Benedict – and even Boas in his few interpretative comments – placed upon them, it may be useful to examine a brief illustration at this point. Boas points to such family usages as, "You whose dog I am" or, "You whose slave I am" as his sole specific evidence of "the amiable qualities that appear in intimate family life." As it stands, it is difficult, if not impossible, to see how this is satisfying or sufficient proof of the point, and the interested student will

gain little additional light from a search of the literature for there is no section in it on such usages, or such usages in context. There are merely vocabulary, footnotc, and text references that do not give the emotional tone of the situations in which the usages occur. Nevertheless, it is arresting material and demands to be explained or, at least, to be taken into account. In spite of the extreme degree of Kwakiutl acculturation evident in 1951, some of these usages were present in the context of human interrelationship, and their meaning can be recovered and detailed. For example, one set of great-grandchildren called their great-grandfather "Doggy Face" (^{E}wátsEmalE), and two other great-grandchildren related through a second daughter called him "Doggy Collar" (Malú). These terms are in the same category as those given by Boas and differ from the proper kinship word for grandfather. The remarkable thing about the relationship between the great-grandchildren, a boy of eight and a girl of six, and their "Malú" was its symmetrical comradeship. Facts that the relationship seemed to take no notice of were a gap of over seventy years in age, the blindness of the old man, his general infirmity in contrast to the bounce of the children, and his past high rank among his people and, in other contexts, his still proud consciousness that he had held great names and done great things in the potlatch. The children showed no deference, constraint, or separateness, and he exacted none. If the little girl hid his indispensable cane, he laughed with her as he fumbled for it in the corners of the hallway. All three thought it a very funny joke on him when in his blindness he missed the low settee and sat down heavily on the floor. He played with apparent enthusiasm a childish pokey teasing game with his great-granddaughter, and on several evenings of the week that the writer was there his great-grandson's last occupation of the day was to curl up on the couch with head and shoulders in the old man's lap to hear his stories of "Mink" with an attention as casual as that the old men was giving to his storytelling, which was sometimes very lively and full of dramatization and sometimes so softly reminiscent that it seemed he was speaking mostly to himself. He startled the writer on one of these occasions by calling her name

and saying, "This is the way my grandfather used to tell stories to me."

He was a child with them, but only in the sense that all adults could be expected to be wholeheartedly playful on a childish level if there were certain additional expectations, for instance, that adults, like children, can be easily diverted and need be under no obligation to keep things going beyond the point when interest wanders. He and the children seemed to share equivalent expectations about human attention. To a member of our society, the incidents of hiding his walking stick or laughing when he missed a couch and sat on the floor seem cruel or at least callous, but in our society an equalitarian relationship between young and old or hale and infirm would be rare if not unthinkable. This relationship was equalitarian also in its emotional balance, as far as could be seen. It was warm but casual on both sides, without any high degree of intensity or any emotional loading that would seem to be particular to one of the "two kinds" of people involved. In a week's observation of the old man he was never seen to be rueful about his age or disabilities, and this was especially remarkable in his relationship with the children for we are used to seeing the old express enviousness, sometimes quite hostile enviousness, in relation to the young, just as we are used to seeing children with a swagger or a glint in their eyes that says, "You just wait!" One young woman told of how two of her grandparents kept asking her to call them by one of these "Doggy" names. She said that she just could not do it, that she loved them and respected them too much. This is particularly interesting because, in this case, her grandparents had been her sociological parents and there had been all the intensity of emotional ties and all the ambivalences that might be expected in the relationship. Symmetry and equalitarianism in the relation were therefore impossible.

These cases detail certain amiable features in Kwakiutl living, yet it is understandable that in Boas' published material Benedict missed or glossed over such verbal usages and that Boas, with a knowledge of them in context, thought them to be telling evidence. It seems equally understandable why Boas did not record details of a case such as that of

"Malú," for as proof of a point it has embarrassing inadequacies to anyone committed to the scientific tradition. It seems to the writer that, although some objective detailing of situation has been done, what has mostly been done is merely an expansion of Boas' response labelling of the situation as "amiable." A response labelling is, however, relevant when the qualities of a people are being discussed, and there may be a special hazard in the fact that the psychiatric and anthropological vocabulary is far more developed and "objective" in relation to all the negative, cross-grained, and reprehensible qualities to which reporters and interpreters respond than in relation to the fine qualities people seem to have. It is less easy to understand why Boas failed to refer to other evidences of "amiable" features in Kwakiutl life, such as those connected with potlatching, why Benedict ignored certain materials available in the published accounts and why there has been no review of the evidence in connection with the widespread and continually developing interest in culture and personality interpretations.

"AMIABLE" FEATURES PRESENT IN THE 1895-96 POTLATCHES OF THE KWAKIUTL AS DESCRIBED BY BOAS

It is precisely in respect to potlatching that such interpretative judgments of the character of Kwakiutl life as "atrocious," "paranoid," "rivalrous," and "grossly competitive" have been made. Qualifications of this sharp delineation have largely taken the form of noting that a certain amount of cooperation on the level of the family or *numaym* was required in order to sustain and enhance the rivalry of the potlatch and social system. Additional and fundamental qualifications are required, either if the accounts are looked at freshly and in a way undetermined by previous interpretations or if those data in the accounts that do not fit such interpretations are not glossed over as being unimportant and overwhelmed by other data. Boas' 1895-96 description has been selected for examination because it is the most detailed, play-by-play eye-witness account of Kwakiutl potlatching and winter ceremonial.

Some of the skits and incidents that formed part of the ten days of winter ceremonials and potlatches were plain

fun-making, and there is nothing in the account to indicate that the fun-making was not a true part of the proceedings, for all instances of it were right in sequence with other dramatizations and potlatches. They occurred after as well as before the distribution of eagle-down that signals such sacred tone as there was in the winter dances, and they were particular to no one group such as a "clown" group or one of the three participating Kwakiutl tribes or any of their subdivisions. There are five extremely clear instances of fun-making.

To anyone who would regard Kwakiutl as impelled by an unqualified straining for self-maximization and glorification and triumphing over rivals the following skit would seem peculiar indeed:

> *A man rose who acted as though he was a Haida. He delivered a speech, during which he made violent gestures, imitating the sound of the Haïda language. An interpreter who stood next to him translated the pretended meaning of his speech, which was supposed to be of the nature of thanks to the host for the soap berries, because they were one of the principal food articles of the Haida, and because the speaker was pleased to eat the kind of food to which he was accustomed in his own country. He continued, saying that he carried a box filled with food which he was going to give to the person who would pronounce his name. Then the host's daughter was called upon, and was asked to say his name. He began, G.a'tsō, which she repeated; Sē'as, which she also repeated; then followed, spoken very rapidly, Qoagā'ñ Gustatē'ñ Gusgitatē'ñ Gusoa't Qoag·ē'ns Quqā'-xsla. Then she said: "I can not say this; I must go to school in order to learn it." The Haida asked her to go to school with him for four nights; then she would know it. The girl's father interrupted them, saying that he wanted to wash his daughter before she went to school with him.*[4]

Boas notes that this "joke has been known for about eight years and is often repeated." The joke is no more broad or

[4] Franz Boas, *The Social Organization and the Secret Societies of the Kwakiutl Indians.* Reports of the United States National Museum (Washington, D.C., 1895), p. 546.

subtle than the meaning of the entire incident in humanizing the character of the Kwakiutl and their institutions. Kwakiutl hosts were, above all, the individuals allowed to make grandiloquent speeches and to strike heroically stuffy postures, and their behaviour and speeches have been pointed to again and again as central proof of such main themes in Kwakiutl life as a "will to self-glorification," "bombastic," "triumphing over rivals," and so on down the "paranoid" list. Here is a Kwakiutl host who takes a full part in the presentation of a skit in which the type of food he has just given his guests is joked about and in which his daughter, and himself by reflection, is allowed to look foolish and all too human. No one in this skit would seem to care about the kind of false stuff-shirt dignity that must be vigilantly protected in order to be maintained.

Two other skits are of particular interest because they are potlatches, but potlatches given in a humorous frame of reference. This would seem impossible in an unqualified view of Kwakiutl society as obsessed with social prestige that had to be maintained and validated by potlatching. Such view makes potlatching a deadly serious business.

After this was done [after a potlatch distribution in connection with a winter dance presentation was made], *a messenger entered the house and said: "Some strangers are on the beach." The speaker of the Nā'q' oaqtôq sent a man out, who took a torch and went down to the beach. Soon he returned and informed the speaker that some white men had landed and asked to be permitted to enter. The speaker sent for them, and the messengers came back leading a young Indian girl, who was dressed up in European costume, with a gaudy hat, a velvet skirt, and a silk blouse. Then they asked Nō'Lq'auLEla what he thought of her; if he thought she was wealthy. They asked him to send her back if she should be poor. He looked at her and said: "I can easily distinguish rich and poor and I see she is wealthy. Let her stay here." Then the speaker looked at her and said: "Oh, that is Mrs. Nū'le." They led her to the rear of the house and asked if she carried anything in her pocket. She*

produced a roll of silver quarter dollars which the speaker took and distributed among the people.[5]

Now the door opened, and four men dressed as policemen entered . . . .

The last of these acted the judge and carried a book. He sent the policemen around asking if everybody was present, and KuLE'm asked, "Are all here?" The people replied, "Yes." Then the two other policemen went around, looked at everybody, and stated that one person was missing. They went out, and soon returned leading the old woman Gudo'-yo, whose hands were fastened with handcuffs. Then they pretended to hold court over her on account of her absence. The judge pretended to read the law on the case, and fined her $70. She replied that she was poor; that she was able to pay in blankets but had no ready money. KuLe'm, who acted the interpreter, pretended to translate what she had said into English, and the payment of 70 blankets was accepted. Then the friends of Gudo'yo turned against the judge and said: "That is always your way, policemen. As soon as you see anyone who has money, you arrest him and fine him." She was unchained, and the policemen went back to the door. [Boas notes here that "this performance was first introduced in 1865, and has been kept up since that time.]"

They called K·ēx· and his friends, the killer whales, and told them to fetch the 70 blankets. The cousin of the old woman, who was the speaker of the Maa'mtag·ila, told them where to go, and soon they returned. Gudo'yo's sister, Lē'mElxa'lag·ilîs followed them, dancing. All the people were singing a ha'mshamtsEs song for her. The blankets were distributed in her name. The mā'maq'a of the Nā'q'oa-tôq received his share first: then the other members of his tribe, and afterwards the Koskimo beginning with the hā'mats'a. While this was going on, button blankets and bracelets tied to sticks were being carried into the house. A G·ē'xsEm, whose daughter had married Lē'Lelälak[u]*, a G·ī'g·îlqam of the Kuē'xa was going to repay the purchase money of his daughter.*[6]*. . .*

[5] *Ibid.*, pp. 559-60.
[6] *Ibid.*, pp. 562-63.

Let us consider some arguments against the claim that these two incidents display a rather lighthearted approach to potlatching. The two incidents are in the full context of apparently very serious winter dance presentations and potlatch distributions. Can they be accounted for as comic relief necessary to sustain a seriousness so heavy that it would otherwise be unbearable? Skipping the fact that such an argument would mean a shift of ground from a conception of potlatching as an institution in which there was no levity at all, it seems impossible to discover in what way they form any different kind of potlatching except in their connection with a skit that does anything but make a point of inflating the honour and glory of the donor. The humour of these skits is not uncomplicated. In both incidents the European is lampooned or derided, but in both cases the giver of the potlatch is identified with the European. Careful study of both the pattern and the content of the various types of event occurring in these ten days of festivities (feasts, dances, speeches, potlatches, fun-making) does not reveal these and other instances of fun-making as "comic relief" occurring at any discernibly special or meaningful time. The first follows a winter dance ceremonial ending with a potlatch and is followed by another winter dance. The second follows a winter dance, speech, and potlatch and is, as the quotation above indicates, followed by a potlatch. This is, however, the standard pattern of the entire ten days, and there is nothing that singles out the events of fun-making. They do not seem to occur just before or after moments of particular tension or moments of easing of tension. They were not initiated by members of either the most or the least exalted Kwakiutl group. The same individuals seem to have been involved in both the skit potlatches and the apparently serious potlatches. The amount of property distributed in the skit potlatches is not at all out of line with the amount distributed in other potlatches, except for the fact that there is one serious potlatch during these ten days that overshadows all the rest, serious and skit potlatches alike.

Of the two remaining instances of fun-making in this 1895-96 account both form a part of the winter dance ceremonials. Although Kwakiutl winter dancing should be

considered separately at some time in relation to the interpretations of Kwakiutl character based upon it, it can be considered here as the context of potlatching, and it can be noted that as the context it was relieved by fun-making. One episode is so briefly described that its nature as fun must depend upon the fact that Boas labelled it as such. Boas tells of the opening of the winter dance ceremonials, how all three tribes gathered, feasted, sang their songs in turn, teased a Fool Dancer, and how, while the people were eating their second feast course, "the different societies uttered their cries:

"The hens are pecking!"
"The great seals keep chewing."
"The food of the great killer-whale is sweet."
"The food of the foolish boys is sweet."
"The great rock cods are trying to get food."
"The great sea lions throw their heads downwards."
The great Mosmos said: "It will be awful.""[7]

It is admittedly more than a little difficult to see this as a jolly episode; especially is there the question of whether these society cries might have anything to do with the well-known Cannibal Dance songs of the people. Boas says, however, that, "When uttering these cries, the members of the societies lifted their spoons and seemed to enjoy the fun,"[8] and we know that it was shortly following that the pretend Haida skit was put on. Boas said there was fun and there seems no good reason to doubt his judgment of the incident; neither would it do for any member of our culture to be overskeptical about the amount of fun present in relatively noisy and simple-minded group pursuits.

The second case is far more detailed and involves ceremonial and supernatural power. The violent and atrocious character of Kwakiutl supernaturals and of the dance ceremonials that recreate them has been much emphasized, yet here is a case in which the character of the supernatural has some beneficent aspects and in which the portrayal creates laughter and joy. The progress of the t'ō'X'uît ceremonial is

[7] *Ibid.*, pp. 545-46.
[8] *Ibid.*, p. 546.

described. The peak of the ceremony was reached when the t'ō'X'uît, followed by the people of her tribe, went to the four houses in the village where visitors of other tribes were staying:[9]

In each house the t'ō'X'uît caught the supernatural power and threw it upon the people, as described heretofore. Every time she threw it the uproar increased. The people shook their blankets to indicate that the power had entered them. They laughed and cried, and kissed each other's wives, for during this time there is no jealousy and no quarrelling.

The series of episodes concerned with the t'ō'X'uît has complex meanings: there is the suggestion that a proper winter ceremonial cannot be put on without this performance, that the supernaturally induced laughter is mixed with tears, that it can do harm as well as good, that it is irresistible, and that it sanctions behavioural license in the name of an ideal smoothness in human relations. However, while it is impossible to consider this material as a simple demonstration of the presence of warmth and lightheartedness in Kwakiutl winter ceremonial, it would be equally impossible to derive exclusively dark interpretations of Kwakiutl winter dancing and relation to the supernatural from any body of materials of which these formed a part.

A question might arise as to whether, granting the fun-making and fun-enjoying nature of the episodes described and discussed, they have a sufficiently important place in these potlatches and ceremonials to deserve consideration. They are but five incidents in a great march of events. Going through the report and counting incidents (feasts, potlatches, speeches, and so on) the total comes to over two hundred. The percentage is certainly unimpressive. The first answer to the question is that it might be meaningless. We know neither how to measure the intensity of any incident of fun or pleasure nor how to assess its significance in relation to the other incidents of a day or an occasion; it just seems generally to count. The second answer is to suggest that the contrast between the few incidents of fun-making and the many incidents of the ten days may not be as sharp

[9] *Ibid.*, pp. 583-85.

as it appears. It would have been humanly impossible for Boas to record the entire content of ten days, and he makes no claim of having done so; in fact, in the final two days there is visible evidence of fatigue on his part, for he merely summarizes episodes and begins to note the hour of the night in a way that elicits the anthropological reader's sympathy: "12:30 A.M., 2 o'clock, 3:15, 4 o'clock."[10] Taking all these factors into account, it would seem impossible to ignore or minimize these incidents of fun or lightness.

Incidents of fun-making are by no means the sole type of incident displaying "amiable" features that is to be found in the record Boas made. Limitations of space prevent full examination and discussion of this record here, but the reader is urged to consider, for example, the numerous and impressive instances of the occurrence of courtesy and civility in connection with Kwakiutl speechmaking, a part of Kwakiutl life that has been considered to show unqualified arrogance and braggadocio. It is impossible, for example, to ignore the continual "Friends!" as the form of address and reference to those who are receiving property at a potlatch and as the form used in reply to the self-glorifying speeches of those giving the potlatch. This usage is of the most frequent occurrence in all recorded potlatch speeches. There is certainly a strong possibility that the usage is at times ironic or even sarcastic, but it is equally certain that "Friends!" might mean just what it says or that, at the very least, it indicates an awareness on the part of the potlatch donors that even at the moment of triumph there would be no triumph unless their friendly opponents were co-operating and an awareness on the part of the recipients that the situation would be reversed when it came their turn to potlatch.

GWOMIÄSÄ: THE KWAKIUTL PLAY POTLATCH

Play potlatching made use of the heavy themes of potlatching to create fun, nonsense, and congeniality. Perhaps it would be better to say that a human capacity for insight and laughter did not miss the stuffy rigidities of potlatching, for a Bergsonian theory of laughter as social criticism seems

[10] *Ibid.*, pp. 598-99 and 601-3.

operationally relevant here until, at any rate, we get a theory of society that includes laughter.

The term for the play potlatch, *gwo'miäsä*, *g̹ŭmyasē*, or *gōmiasap!a*, suggests that old capacities for playfulness seized on the relatively newer materials offered by the development of potlatching. The only use of the word in the texts is for the giving of the first potlatch for the child at ten months. Up to that time the child had the name of its birthplace, but on the painting with ochre, and the first or ochre potlatch, the child received its ochre name. The word for play potlatch comes from the word for ochre. George Hunt writes sometime after 1916:

> *And L!ēsdaq* [*the newly named child*] *gives away property to the young men – that is when the young men give to one another paddles and mats, in the way the first men used to do, for the sake of the greatness of the young man's name, but in our recent days it is different; for shirts and kerchiefs are given away by the young men for the sake of the greatness of the young man's name and nothing is given to the old men when the young men give to one another.*[11]

It can be seen from this context why the term is translated as "baby" potlatch when it applies to both the ochre potlatch and what could be called the child's training or educational potlatch, such as those described by Charles Nowell in *Smoke from Their Fires.*[12]

The term was apparently also extended to cover an old-time woman's potlatch, which was held at the same time as the big men's potlatches and involved making fun of the men and of the institution that was absorbing their interest. Daniel Cranmer said that he used to see the women clapping their hands and singing their songs for this but that the men had no part in it. Nowell was more detailed about the "play

[11] Franz Boas, *Ethnology of the Kwakiutl.* Based on data collected by George Hunt. Thirty-Fifth Annual Report, Bureau of American Ethnology (Washington, D.C.: Smithsonian Institution, 1921), p. 825.

[12] Clellan S. Ford, *Smoke from Their Fires: The Life of a Kwakiutl Chief* (New Haven: Yale University Press, 1941), pp. 86-87. Other portions of this book are reprinted on pages 119-33 and 198-208 in this volume.

potlatching of grown women." He reported that when there was a gathering of tribes the women put on play potlatches and that the men did not come to watch them. The women had their own songs for it, and they took positions according to their husbands' positions and then proceeded to mock the business of singing insulting songs and giving insulting speeches while they distributed things like wooden dishes in the earlier days and similar types of manufactured items later. He was very clear that "the insults were all for fun." The picture of Kwakiutl husbands knowing that their wives had fun at their expense does something to humanize both the people and their most renowned institution. The ochre potlatch, the baby potlatch, and the play potlatching of grown women are, however, all earlier than the play potlatching that involved everybody in a village, and they seem also to have been forms of potlatching that were discontinued much earlier and can be recalled today by at most a very few individuals.

Play potlatching for all the men, women, and children of a village was apparently very widespread, can be recalled by many living informants, and was taking place as recently as 1948. It was not such a recent development, however, that it was not being carried on at the same time as the "serious" potlatching. Older informants are saddened by the passing both of the play potlatch and of the real potlatch.

Boas certainly knew about play potlatching, although he did not publish anything about it. It was one of the many things he had still to communicate about the Kwakiutl. An elderly Kwakiutl woman recalls with evident amusement:

At Fort Rupert when Boas was up there once they had a play potlatch. They gave away handkerchiefs and soap and things like that. Small stuff. And the women gave away and received too. He gave some too. Funny names go with it. Everyone had a play potlatch name and he was given one at that time, ME'młaelatse, "Where-the-southeast-wind-comes-from." The southeast wind comes from a rock near Fort Rupert; when water is sprinkled on this rock it brings the southeast wind.

The play potlatch name is funny only if the literary allu-

sion is detailed. MEła'lanukwē, the-owner-of-the-southeast-wind, causes the always bad-smelling southeast wind to blow by breaking wind constantly. The name, therefore, is not overly dainty, but the scatological elements in this, as in other connections with play potlatching, are fairly fastidious and amusing. When, for instance, a clam buyer did not show up, a man caught with a surplus of clams gave a play potlatch in which everyone was presented with a sack of clams and a roll of toilet paper.

Earthiness, ribaldry, spoofing, and plain and simple fun seem to have been the sense of the play potlatch meeting. They were also apparently quite spontaneous occasions, although the accounts indicate that they occurred less often according to the pattern of the clam digger who was stuck with his clams than according to a feeling that the village was in the mood for some entertainment and tomfoolery. What mostly seems to have happened is that men and women put things by with the possibility of such an occasion in mind, somewhat in the spirit of a mother who keeps some children's presents tucked in a drawer.

The general spirit of the occasion is best detailed by the account of Charlie Wilson. In 1951 he was in his eighties. He was blind and slightly deaf. There are probably few accounts less directed than his, for the only possible anthropological technique was to just record whatever he happened to reminisce upon:

G̣wo'miäsä. Fight and talk with the ladies. Try to beat each other. All happy. All laugh. You know. Very good. Oh! very good.

"You not chief," she say to me. "I am a chief myself," I say. Everybody laughs.

Wáxsɔ – that is the g̣wo'miäsä name of Lizzie Wilson. It means a circular cape of yellow cedar bark.

SE'kwēla – that's Jane Hunt's g̣wo'miäsä name. It is a waterfall at Knight's Inlet. Oh, she likes that g̣wo'miäsä!

Kl!ehEn – "Sea lion," Bill Wilson's g̣wo'miäsä name. He used to come with his mother. He liked that.

We don't g̣wo'miäsä no more. Stopped ten years ago maybe. Goin', everything goin'.

Oh, you never get tired when you see them. Laugh and laugh at each other. Have a good time. Finish twelve, one o'clock at night.

Fort Rupert is, of course, the centre of all of Boas' reporting on the Kwakiutl and was also centre of the expanding potlatching and economic activity from about 1849 until about 1920. Alert Bay became the important economic and population centre afterward. However, Fort Rupert, where the Kwakiutl were highest in social rank and most active in the potlatch, was the scene of most of the play potlatch accounts collected. Two accounts that perhaps refer to the same play potlatch held only a few years ago seem to be of special interest.

The first account is that of a young woman who was brought up by her grandparents at Fort Rupert and who is much nearer to the old life than most young Kwakiutl today. She says of g̨wo′miäsä, "We sure used to have fun. We haven't done this for five years now." She then recalls the last one:

Teddybear candies, apples, suckers, oranges were given out; or some people even went as far as bringing pigs and geese and chickens and giving them away. The pigs and so on didn't really belong to those who gave them away. It was just for a joke. People pretend to be different things. The women pretend to be crows, then the men pretend to be something. They "talk Chinese" or something. The crows go 'KäxElag·a käxEläxda käx–Käx' and on and on like crows until you burst out laughing. This is for everybody from babies to old people. One family starts it [the g̨wo′miäsä] *and someone who is all dressed up is sent around to invite everyone. They give away dishes, boxes of apples, combs. The people that think of it have it planned. They think of giving a name to a grandchild or they think of something and they go and get everything. Sometimes they announce it ahead of time. Have you ever heard of M.K.? He was funny. He made funny faces and then everyone imitated him. The Du′tluba are funny too. They tell you what they are going to do and then they do it and you are not supposed to laugh. If you laugh you quit the game. Everybody but the Du′tluba*

laughs. It goes on for hours, singing songs, playing games, until everyone is too tired to sleep.

An elderly man describes what might be the same occasion, although he places it as "four years ago."

Started by giving away different coloured glass bowls from mixing bowls to the little ones. Got them from Vancouver in all different colours. We fixed the women! They couldn't beat us! We went to a chicken house and took eighteen hens and a big rooster and gave each woman one of them. The women were mad and wouldn't take them. There was a lot of snow then and the chickens all came back from the other end of the village in the snow. We teased the women and said they had killed the chickens. [The allusion seems to be that the chickens were like ghosts in the snow.] *Everyone gave everyone else bowls. Old and young men and women all gave around bowls. When the bowls were given people made speeches and sang and teased one another. We started in from one end of the village and took turns giving potlatch. Gave in order of place in the village. It was just to pass the night away. One will start it. When the one who called the feast started it, there we all stayed until we all had given a potlatch!*

Fort Rupert was by no means the only place where play potlatching occurred. One account concerns recollections of play potlatches at Harbledown Island (T'Ena'xtax):

It is women against men and vice versa. The one giving away makes a BIG *speech. One time we made a narrow place at the entrance of the house and put a line at the end of it that you had to stoop over to get in. The line was hung with all sorts of pots and pans to make a big noise. You weren't supposed to laugh, so you hid your laughing in your blanket. They gave out frying pans and said things like "Here is this frying pan worth $100 and this one worth $200." That was about thirty-forty years ago. Oh you used to get together jam bottles, tin cans – sometimes you made use of them when you got them. I gave a play potlatch once. I told Mrs. J. so she said she would help. She gathered all her glassware even good ones. Aunty did all the speech. She called me all kinds*

of things: I am the "prince" of the place and I am going to give a big potlatch, dishes worth $40 and $50; just a cup and saucer!

Gwo'miäsä are for a pastime and when you have nothing to do. The whole village comes. We used to have them all the time. The last one was given by B.M.'s brother. His wife was always so full of fun. It is still the same, but not so strong. This last one was two or three years ago now. First one started it. Invited everyone Christmas week. I did it too. I told them all the dishes in front of you are yours. Save me washing them up. Someone grabbed the sugar bowl and the butter dish as well as their own plate and cup and saucer!

Such accounts as these are but memories, imperfect and incomplete recollections of the lively moment. Because of the informality and the spontaneity of the play potlatching, these accounts are probably even more incomplete than recollections of a weighty and formal occasion so dependably structured that an individual memory would have a sure outline to follow. In spite of all that must be lost about play potlatching because of lack of an eye-witness account by an observer who tried to get down everything possible, the nature of the play potlatch is clearly revealed as fun and nonsense and potlatching for everyone irrespective of rank, sex, or age, the last with the exception that the very young seem not to have initiated the proceedings.

One informant said, "Even the big chiefs are in the play potlatches and they have more fun than anybody. There are speeches and play potlatch names for everyone and everyone has a good time." From every point of view the play potlatch seemed to have the aspect of a free-for-all. The lowly or the high-ranking might begin it; before it was done everyone was likely to have been involved. The goods distributed ranged from quite useful articles to mere favours or things like the pigs and the chickens that were not properly the donors to give so that the gift was a fraud and a joke. The war between the sexes seems to have been a frequent theme for both the speeches and what little organization of events the gathering had, a feature that does little to set off the Kwakiutl as utterly distinctive in the world! The entertainment was a combina-

tion of Halloween and Kwakiutl theatrical art but seemed always to be arranged so that young and old alike might find it amusing. Maybe the salacious songs one informant claimed were occasionally sung were above the heads of the young or they were unable to savour the lampoons of potlatch speeches at the fullest, but they were there and most of the entertainment seems to have been at the level of fairly simple and exuberant play. Most anyone could enjoy the "you are not supposed to laugh" games and pantomimes and the noisy pots-and-pans trap and the pretending to "talk Chinese" – at least for a time. It seems to the writer that, although there is warmth and laughter in Kwakiutl life today, there is nothing ready to replace this healthy and equalitarian community fun, if it were to die out as many thought it would.

The main question would seem to be how to interpret the meaning of Kwakiutl play potlatching and how to determine its place in Kwakiutl life. Play potlatching seems to be a feature of village life, as distinct from the great public life in which several villages gathered and the large and famous potlatches were given; that this means that play potlatching was done in a homely community context is, however, insupportable. Play potlatching was not done in the context of home life or family or private life. The more rivalrous and serious competitions did exist between individuals of roughly similar social rank in different villages but any one village contained several ranked lineage groups, *numayms*, and each of these *numayms* contained ranked individual standing places that had to be maintained by the individuals within the *numayms* in relation to one another. It is useful in clarifying Kwakiutl social organization to know that individuals usually refer to themselves as "one-half" from such and such a village and "one-half" from another village and "one-half" from one *numaym* and "one-half" from another. This is by no means a new usage or one that does not fit all existing descriptions of Kwakiutl social organization, and it clarifies the system nicely. Marriages were usually between individuals of different villages. Children's ranked positions could come from either parent or, in some cases, both parents. Loyalties to one village and identifications with one

village were by no means uncomplicated or undivided. The results are clear: rank order permeated family, *numaym*, the single village, and the entire series of villages alike, and there could be no private, at home, escape from it. Therefore, there is no question but that play potlatching was engaged in by the same individuals who did serious potlatching with and against each other. The residual question is rather whether the ranking and the maintaining of rank was as unqualifiedly cut-throat, serious, and competitive as has been made out, and the answer to this question would be in the negative.

CONCLUSIONS: REINTERPRETATIONS OF KWAKIUTL CHARACTER AS SEEN IN KWAKIUTL POTLATCHING

Kwakiutl potlatching has been considered the central expression of Kwakiutl character. The details of potlatching have been used repeatedly to document claims that the people, like their premier institution, were characterized by megalomania, paranoia, and, more particularly, by rivalrousness of deadly seriousness and violent intensity. Reservations about incorporating this portrait into general and scientific thinking and usage have been few in number, brief in statement, and relatively narrow in scope of distribution. There are many areas and aspects of Kwakiutl life that force a reconsideration of the nature of the people and their institutions, but, because potlatching is such a critical centre of interpretation, it has been the attempt of this study to confront this issue first of all.

Re-examination of the published first-hand descriptions of Kwakiutl potlatching shows them to contain materials that will not permit the construction of unqualified interpretations of the people and their institutions. The existence of incidents of fun-making and horseplay in connection with potlatching necessitates qualification of such characterizations as "paranoid" or "limitless pursuit of . . . social prestige," "uncensored self-glorification," "violence and rivalry that were the heart of the culture." All such generalizing would have to assume that the facts that did not support the generalization were too few, too inconsequential, or too

irrelevant to merit consideration. The facts on fun-making in the published material on potlatching are few but they are certainly not irrelevant, and it seems that, little as we know about the place of fun and laughter in society, they are not inconsequential. The new evidence on play potlatching alone would necessitate a more humanized view of the Kwakiutl. It would be useful at this point to have some full cross-cultural study of the degree to which people make fun of their most sacred and important institutions, but, lacking opportunities for immediate comparison, it seems sound to state at least that if the Kwakiutl could laugh at themselves and their potlatch they were not wholly serious about it, they were not obsessed with it and with the rivalry and competitive ranking it involved, but rather they were capable of sufficient objectivity and insight to merit characterization in terms other than those strictly appropriate to human pathology and neurosis.

The conclusions of this study concern how Kwakiutl character and life are to be interpreted or reinterpreted and how the interpretation is to be related to the widely held theoretical view that cultures are integrated wholes. The second question was set by Boas and by the conflicts of interpretations made by Boas and Benedict; it has been magnified by the contradictory Kwakiutl data presented. Boas' division of Kwakiutl life into a rivalrous and atrocious public life and an intimate family life with amiable features breaks down completely. Play potlatching, for example, extended far beyond the boundaries of intimate family life. The defeat of Boas' idea, which had the great merit of including certain paradoxical and contradictory characteristics of the Kwakiutl people, is no victory for the configurationists, whose integrated picture of Kwakiutl character and life seems to have been drawn originally and reproduced continually without sufficient reference to the whole it claimed to portray. However, Boas' division and analysis suggest a possibly important theoretical point that is related to the question of whether cultures are integrated wholes. Public and private life may not prove to be separate and contradictory in Kwakiutl or in any other culture, but

serious contradictions might always be expected to exist in any culture.

To date configurationist theory has maintained that cultures are integrated like personalities but has brought forward cases merely of neurotic integration, which is by definition a spurious integration or no integration at all. The Kwakiutl case at present seems to leave configurationists two lines or argument, neither of which would do much for the theory as it stands. The first would be a mystical claim that the Kwakiutl evidence of play potlatching and other amiable characteristics could be understood as a vacation from tension or a temporary transvaluation of the central and continuous Kwakiutl values that was necessary to maintain the harsh and serious system. Such a position would indeed be mystical. As a device for dealing with contradictory evidence it would have everything in its favour except the vital factor of demonstrability. The second line of argument open to a configurationist would seem to be to abandon the claim of speaking of true integration and to assert that a culture or cultures can possess only neurotic integration or a spurious sort of integration that is necessarily full of conflicts, contradictions, and cross-currents which achieve at best but a perilous balance. Although it has seldom been expressed by anthropologists in print, one exception being Sapir's "Culture, Genuine and Spurious,"[13] it is not infrequently said that some culture, or culture in general, is full of neuroticisms, conflicts, rationalizations, and hypocrisies, and it is acknowledged that as far as there is any basis of judgment these "bad" things can as often as not be part of "good" methods and aims. Sapir's "genuine" cultures, Periclean Athens and Elizabethan England, were possibly both real and integrated cultures. They may be idealizations that refuse to include all the historical facts, a sort of anthropological Graustark, like the idealized Hopi of Huxley, Thompson, or Collier. Rather than confuse reality with ideals and hopes about whole personalities and whole cultures, it might be far more fruitful to concede that true

[13] Edward Sapir, "Culture, Genuine and Spurious," *American Journal of Sociology*, 29 (1924), 401-29.

integration of either a functional or configurational sort is utopian and ideal, that there may be a tendency toward integration and the elimination of conflicts in culture analogous to Sullivan's tendency toward mental health in individuals but that there have so far been only differences in degrees of imperfection of integration and that all cultures contain genuine contradictions. It is necessary to concede, at least, that the Kwakiutl and their culture possess positive and amiable characteristics as well as negative ones and that the latter must be given less extreme names than those that have been used and accepted, such as "paranoid." It is therefore also necessary to concede that the Kwakiutl case is no longer support for configurationist theory and that, if some reworked configuration is in time produced, it will have to be along lines much more complex than those of simple analogy between a neurotically integrated individual personality and a whole integrated culture.

Because many other aspects and institutions of Kwakiutl life besides potlatching must be considered before any systematic and detailed reinterpretation of the culture and the people is attempted, only one very general conclusion seems justified at this time. Even in those parts of Kwakiutl life in which a competitive, paranoid, atrocious character seems most unrelieved, there is evidence that such an extreme and unqualified characterization cannot be made. A more positive statement follows the well-known and scientifically supported humanistic generalization and basis of criticism; no person or people is in truth all black or all white. Even an artistic and truthful caricature is more than black lines on white paper, suggesting shadow and complex motion. The Kwakiutl are more real, more complex, more human than they have been represented to be. Even in their potlatch, their most extreme and flagrant institution, there are elements of humour and great complexity of thought and feeling: they are not single-minded; they are not lacking in insight; they do not put themselves and their most exigent interests beyond reflective thought and criticism. Laughter and fun-making are evidence of this. If a cultural institution is laughed at, its meaning cannot be taken at face value.

Laughter must be regarded as the denial of cultural automation and the affirmation of a complex human freedom to follow, change, or create culture. There may be no explicit analysis or evaluation in fun-making. There may be no highly conscious intellectual or emotional processes in laughter. But such elements are present, and they represent not only negative and destructive but also positive and creative human qualities.

The Amiable Side of *Patterns of Culture*

VICTOR BARNOUW

While I appreciate Helen Codere's well-written corrective picture, "The Amiable Side of Kwakiutl Life," I would like to express qualifications of some aspects of her paper. To begin with, these concern the relationship between Boas' and Benedict's views of Northwest Coast culture, but they also deal with the question of cultural configurations and some related topics discussed by Codere which bear on the evaluation of Benedict's work.

After quoting a passage from Boas, which Codere refers to as his "response" to Benedict's character-portrait of the Kwakiutl, Codere concludes that "Boas' criticism of Benedict centres on a denial of her thesis that a culture, or at least some cultures, can be described in terms of a dominant character or leading motif."[1] I think this conclusion is unjustifiable. In the first place, there is no evidence that Boas had Benedict in mind in the passage quoted. The notion that he was "responding" to Benedict's views is Codere's inference, based largely, it seems, on the fact that the statement originally appeared a year or so after *Patterns of Culture* was published. However, even if Boas had been thinking of Benedict, Codere's conclusion is still inadmissible, for in the same text from which she quotes, Boas also stated: "Much clearer and of unified character is the picture of those cultures in which a dominant idea rather than the predominant occupation controls life."[2]

Source: *American Anthropologist*, n.s., 59 (June, 1957), 532-35. Reprinted by permission of the publisher.

---

[1] Helen Codere, "The Amiable Side of Kwakiutl Life: The Potlatch and the Play Potlatch," *American Anthropologist*, n.s., 58 (April, 1956), and reprinted in this volume on pp. 229-54.

[2] Franz Boas, "The Methods of Research" in Franz Boas (ed.) *General Anthropology* (New York: D. C. Heath and Company, 1938), p. 684.

That Boas considered the Kwakiutl to provide a good example of such a culture may be seen in some paragraphs of his which appeared six years before *Patterns of Culture* and four years before Benedict's *Configurations of Culture in North America*: "Wherever there is a strong, dominant trend of mind that pervades the whole cultural life it may persist over long periods and survive changes in mode of life. This is most easily observed in one-sided cultures characterized by a single controlling idea. . . . On the North Pacific Coast the importance of hereditary social rank, to be maintained by the display and lavish distribution of wealth, determines the behaviour of the individual. It is the ambition of every person to obtain high social standing for himself, his family, or for the chief of his family. Wealth is a necessary basis for social eminence and the general tone of life is determined by these ideas."[3]

In the passage quoted by Codere, Boas simply made the reservation that we need not expect to find the leading motive expressed in all aspects of the culture. As will be seen, this is also Benedict's view.

Codere claims that Benedict ignored what material there was about the more amiable side of Kwakiutl life, but this is not true. Benedict specifically drew attention to it: "In the intimacies of Kwakiutl family life, also, there is opportunity for the expression of warm affection and the easy give-and-take of cheerful human relations. Not all situations in Kwakiutl existence require equally the motives that are most characteristic of their lives."[4]

Codere, then, seems to exaggerate differences of opinion between Boas and Benedict. I see no real indication of "a basic conflict of opinion about Kwakiutl life and the Kwakiutl people."[5] Indeed, it would be surprising if there had been one between such close associates.

To be sure, Codere's presentation of the humorous features in Kwakiutl potlatching is a valuable corrective, and

[3] Franz Boas, *Anthropology and Modern Life* (New York: Norton and Co. Inc., 1928), pp. 151-52.

[4] Ruth Benedict, *Patterns of Culture* (Boston: Houghton Mifflin Company, 1934), p. 122.

[5] Helen Codere, "The Amiable Side of Kwakiutl Life: The Potlatch and the Play Potlatch," p. 232 in this volume.

her point is well taken that "The Kwakiutl are more real, more complex, more human than they have been represented to be."[6] This is in line with the less sensational emphasis in the accounts of Ford and Drucker, which seem more plausible than Benedict's highly-coloured one. However, in accepting this milder view there is a danger that we may develop a blind spot to the significance of Boas' rich material. Boas, after all, was closer in time to the living culture than later workers in this area, and his contacts with the Northwest Coast covered a period of more than forty years. Moreover, we should not let our notions of plausibility influence us too far in this connection. We have lived through the era of the Nazi regime and have some vivid evidence of the extreme forms which cultures may assume. If we had simply read about the Nazis in an anthropologist's account of a remote people, we might well reject the whole report as exaggerated.

With regard to the Northwest Coast, there is abundant evidence that the culture was characterized by a set of values and attitudes which permeated the whole life of the people. Boas is not the only one who provided evidence for this. We find similar impressions in Aurel Krause's work on the Tlingit, first published in 1885 and recently translated by Erna Gunther: "The Tlingit has a highly developed sense of ownership. He not only has his own clothes, weapons and utensils, he also has his own hunting grounds, his own trade trails which no one else may use without his permission or without paying damages. Generally everyone's property rights are respected by his tribesmen, less from a sense of justice than from fear of revenge. . . . Even in his relationship with his friends and his nearest relatives the Tlingit shows great selfishness. For every service he renders, for every gift he gives, he expects a return. . . . Vanity is one of the leading traits of Tlingit character. Nothing can hurt him more than injury to his self esteem. Jealously he is on guard to see that all his prerogatives and rights are recognized, and he looks with disdain on anyone who has lost an advantage. . . . The Indian cannot stand a peaceful, quiet existence. His great sensitivity and his strong sense of property rights are con-

[6] *Ibid.*, p. 253 in this volume.

stant cause of resentment. For every bodily injury, for any damage to his goods and property, for any infringement by strangers on his hunting or trading territory, full compensation is demanded or exacted by force."[7]

It seems to me that a revised picture of Northwest Coast culture should retain some of the insights of this sort made by Boas and Krause, although it should also incorporate modifications suggested by the work of Codere, Ford, and others. It should, I think, lay more stress than Benedict did on the element of control. Her wild picture of the Cannibal dance, for example, ignored the elements of staging and planning that were so important in these dramatic displays. Drucker tells us that the persons who were bitten by the Cannibal were not chosen at random. Arrangements were made with the victims beforehand, and they were later rewarded with gifts. Similarly, Charles Nowell explains that when he displayed aggressive ceremonial behaviour in the Bear's skin, going from house to house to smash dishes, he was accompanied by a man who kept track of everything he broke so that the owner could be compensated later. These features seem to be characteristic of the area. The enormous amount of time spent in food-getting and in the production of standardized goods shows that there was a strong "Apollonian" core in Kwakiutl society. And when we examine the magnificent art products of the Northwest Coast, we are struck by the emphasis on form. This is not a wild expressionistic art; the elements of tension and the occasional strong colours are bound by strong forms and definite outlines.

Admittedly, then, "Dionysian" is not an adequate or particularly helpful characterization for this culture; and the terms "paranoid" and "megalomanic" also seem extreme, although Kroeber has defended their use. But instead of dismissing Benedict's picture for its apparent exaggerations, it might be better to see if statements of the sort quoted by Codere cannot be restated in more acceptable terms. For

[7] Aurel Krause, *The Tlingit Indians: Results of a Trip to the Northwest Coast of America and the Bering Straits.* Translated by Erna Gunther (Seattle: American Ethnological Society, 1956), pp. 115, 116, and 169.

Benedict and Boas may have been on the track of something valid. I feel, for example, that Benedict convincingly showed that the motifs of rivalry and self-glorification appear not only in the potlatch, but also in connection with marriage and shamanism. And surely the boastful speeches of Kwakiutl chiefs quoted by Benedict are striking evidence for the attitudes she describes.

Ruth Benedict's way of phrasing things in extreme terms makes it easy enough to refute some of her statements. This has been evident in her description of Pueblo culture. Benedict claimed, for example, that drunkenness is "repulsive" to the Zuñi, and therefore that liquor has never been a problem in the Pueblos. But we learn from Smith and Roberts that "By far the most common 'crimes' at Zuñi are drunkenness and drunken driving."[8]

Benedict stated that in Zuñi whipping is never a corrective of children. "The fact that white parents use it in punishment is a matter for unending amazement."[9] And in the initiation, "The lash does not draw blood. . . . The adults repudiate with distress the idea that the whips might raise welts."[10] Here again, particularly if it is meant to apply to the Pueblos as a whole, the overstatement makes refutation a simple matter. But while errors of this sort deserve correction, some of the overstatements contain valuable insights. For instance, there is Benedict's extravagant assertion that suicide is "too violent an act, even in its most casual forms, for the Pueblos to contemplate. They have no idea what it could be."[11] Here it is sufficient for Hoebel to cite three Pueblo suicides (all after 1939) to refute her. But in this case the easy refutation that is possible should not blind us to the reality of a difference between the Pueblo and Plains tribes in their attitudes toward suicide and aggression. Benedict's overstatements tempt one to throw out the baby with the bath-water. While her errors of fact and interpretation

[8] Watson Smith and John M. Roberts, *Zuñi Law: A Field of Values*. Papers of the Peabody Museum, vol. 43, no. 1 (Cambridge, Mass.: 1954), p. 58.

[9] *Op. cit.*, p. 63.

[10] *Ibid.*, p. 83.

[11] *Ibid.*, p. 107.

should certainly be corrected, there may still be observations worth preserving here, as in her analysis of Kwakiutl culture.

This point brings me to Codere's conclusions with regard to configurations of culture. In Codere's mind, the "conflicting" data which she presents about amiable traits among the Kwakiutl invalidate or weaken the case for configurational theory. "It is therefore . . . necessary to concede that the Kwakiutl case is no longer support for configurationist theory. . . ."[12] Codere suggests that there may be only a tendency toward integration in cultures, which is never fully attained. It seems to me that this view of cultural integration is one that has generally been held. It is my impression that most anthropologists who have discussed cultural integration hold that conflicts and inconsistencies may appear within a culture. Ruth Benedict stated that "Integration . . . may take place in the face of fundamental conflicts."[13] And Ralph Linton wrote: "Cultures, like personalities, are perfectly capable of including elements and logical inconsistencies."[14] Codere's data neither damage, nor require an alteration in, the concept of cultural configuration.

Let me make a final point in summing up. Much of the early field work in the Pueblos and the Northwest Coast was done at a time that was closer than ours to "aboriginal" conditions, and this probably enabled the ethnologists of the time to get more of a "feel" of the culture than is possible now. Their impressions and hunches are therefore of great value and constitute an important part of the data they have left us. In the case of the Northwest Coast there is Boas' valuable work, which formed the basis for Benedict's description. Codere tries to see an opposition between his view of the culture and Benedict's, but I have tried to suggest that there is no basic conflict; I think that there is continuity, rather than discontinuity. And if there are exaggerations and distortions in the picture which deserve to be corrected, there may also be some insights worth preserving.

[12] Helen Codere, "The Amiable Side of Kwakiutl Life: The Potlatch and the Play Potlatch," p. 253 in this volume.

[13] *Op. cit.*, p. 210.

[14] Ralph Linton, *The Study of Man* (New York: D. Appleton-Century Co. Inc., 1936), p. 358.

APPENDIX

CULTURE ELEMENT DISTRIBUTIONS

This Appendix includes only those portions of Drucker's original list of traits which are relevant to the papers included in the present volume.

The initials at the top of each column refer to the selected Indian informants to whom Drucker circulated the trait questionnaire. The symbols used should be interpreted as follows (the quotations are from page 166 of Drucker's original text):

+	The trait is present
—	The trait is absent
(+) or (—)	"Not certain, probably present or probably absent"
S	"Sometimes, i.e. occasionally, practised"
R	"Practised, but known to be of recent introduction"

Source: Philip Drucker, *Culture Element Distributions:* XXVI Northwest Coast, Anthropological Record 9 : 3 (Berkeley, Calif.; University of California Press, 1950).

	NOOTKA				KWAKIUTL AND SALISH*							TSIMSHIAN			HAIDA		TLINGIT	
	NH	NT	NC	N2	KK	KR	KW	BC*	KO	KC	KX	TH	TG	GK	HM	HS	LS	LC
Dwelling Houses																		
Rectangular plank houses	+	+	+	+	+	+	+	+	+	+	+	+	+	+	+	+	+	+
Permanent framework, removable sheathing	+	+	+	+	+	+	—	—	—	—	(+)	—	—	—	—	—	—	—
Framework and sheathing inseparable	—	—	—	—	—	—	+	+	+	+	+	+	+	+	+	+	+	+
Sheathing horizontal	+	+	+	+	+	+	S	+	—	—	—	—	—	—	—	—	—	+
Sheathing vertical	—	—	—	—	—	—	+	S	+	+	+	+	+	+	+	+	+	—
Roof of boards	+	+	+	+	+	+	+	+	+	+	+	+	(+)	—	S	—	S	+
Roof of bark	—	—	—	—	—	—	—	—	—	—	—	—	(+)	+	+	+	S	—
Earth floor	+	+	+	+	+	+	+	+	+	+	+	+	+	+	—	—	—	—
Board floor	—	—	—	—	—	—	—	—	—	—	—	—	—	—	+	+	+	+
Central fireplace for rituals (only)	+	+	+	+	+	+	+	—	—	—	—	—	—	—	—	—	—	—
Central fireplace (everyday use)	—	—	—	—	—	—	—	+	+	+	+	+	+	+	+	+	+	+
Roof boards moved for smoke	+	+	+	+	+	+	—	—	—	—	—	—	—	—	—	—	—	—
Central smokehole	—	—	—	—	—	—	+	+	+	+	+	+	+	+	+	+	+	+
Sleeping platform around walls	+	+	+	+	+	+	+	+	+	+	+	+	+	—	+	+	+	—
Other Structures																		
Subterranean caches	—	—	—	—				+	+	+	+	+	+	+	+	+	+	+
Stockades	—	+	+	+	—	+	—	+	+	—	+	+	—	+	+	+	+	—
Sweathouses	—	—	—	—				—	—	—	—	+	+	+	+	+	+	+
Dugout Canoes																		
"Nootkan"-type canoe	+	+	+	+	R	R	—	—	—	—	—	—	—	—	—	—	—	—
"Northern"-type canoe	—	—	—	—	+	+	+	+	+	+	+	+	+	+	+	+	+	—
Dugouts of cedar	+	+	+	+	+	+	+	+	+	+	+	+	+	—	+	+	+	—
Canoe Appurtenances																		
Carved decoration	—	—	—	—	+	+	+	+	+	+	+	+	+	—	+	+	+	—
Painted decoration	—	+	+	(—)	+	+	+	+	+	+	+	+	+	—	+	+	+	—

Techniques																		
Trees chiseled down	+	+	+	+	+	+	+	+	(+)	(+)	−	−	−	−	−	−	−	−
Part split from standing tree	−	−	−	−	+	+	+	+	+	+	+	+	+	−	(−)	−	−	−
Canoes hollowed by burning	+	+			+	+	+	+	+	+	+	+	+	−	+	+	+	−
Canoes spread by steaming					+	+	+	+	+	+	+	+	+	+	+	+	+	+
Superstructures on bow and stern	+	+	+	+	+	+	+	+	+	+	+	+	+	+	+	+	+	−
Society																		
Autonomous local groups	+	+	+	+	+	+		+	+	(+)	+	+	+	+	+	+	+	+
Descent: bilateral	+	+	+	+	+	+	+	+	S	R	−	−	−	−	−	−	−	−
: patrilineal bias	+	+	+	+	+	+	+	+		(−)	−	−	−	−	−	−	−	−
Descent: matrilineal	−	−	−	−	−	−	−	−	S	+	+	+	+	+	+	+	+	+
Moieties	−	−	−	−	−	−	−	−	−	−	−	−	−	−	+	+	+	+
Crests clan owned									+	+	+	+	+	+	+	+	+	+
Names clan owned	−	−	−	−	−	−	−	−	+	+	+	+	+	+	+	+	+	+
Privileges owned	+	+	+	+	+	+	+	+	+	+	+	+	+	+	+	+	+	+
Personal names	+	+	+	+	+	+	+	+	+	+	+	+	+	+	+	+	+	+
House names					+	+		+	+	+	−	+	+	+	+	+	+	+
Canoe names					+	+	−	+	(−)	−	+	−	S	−	+	+	(+)	−
Songs, dances	+	+	+	+	+	+	+	+	+	+	+	+	+	+	+	+	+	+
Territorial rights owned	+	+	+	+	+	+	+	+	+	+	+	+	+	+	+	+	+	+
Fishing places	+	+	+	+	+	+	+	+	+	+	+	+	+	+	+	+	+	+
Hunting grounds..	(−)	−	−	−			+	+	+	+	+	+	+	+			−	−
Heriditary chiefs	+	+	+	+	+	+	+	+	+	+	+	+	+	+	+	+		+
Title for "chief"	+	+	+	+	+	+			+	+	+	+	+	+	+	+		+
Title for "chief's wife"	+	+	+	+	+	+			(+)	(+)	+	+	+	+	−	−		−
Title for "chief's heir" ("prince")	+	+	+	+	+	+			(+)	(+)	+	+	+	+	(−)	+		−
Title for "chief's daughter" ("princess")	(+)	(+)	(+)	(+)	+	+			+	+	+	+	+	+	−			−
Title for "village (and/or clan) chief"	−	−	−	−	+				+	+		+	+	+	(+)	+		+
Title for "house chief"					−	−			−	−	−	+	+	+	−	−		−
Chiefs of group or tribe ranked		+	+	+	+	+			+	+	+	+	+	+	+	+		+

	NOOTKA				KWAKIUTL AND SALISH*							TSIMSHIAN			HAIDA		TLINGIT	
	NH	NT	NC	N2	KK	KR	KW	BC*	KO	KC	KX	TH	TG	GK	HM	HS	LS	LC
Named class of commoners	+	+	+	+	+	+			+	+	+	+	+	+	+	+		+
Lived in chief's house	+	+	+	+	+	+			+	S	+	+	+	+	+	+		+
Worked for chiefs	+	+	+	+	+	+			+	+	+	+	+	+	+	+		+
Could marry into chief's family	+	−	−	−	+	S			−	S	S							
Slaves held	+	+	+	+	+	+			+	+	+	+	+	+	+	+		+
Captured in war	+	+	+	+	+	+			+	+	+	+	+	+	+	+		+
Bought and sold	+	+	+	+	+	+			+	+	+	+	+	+	+	+		+
Could marry free person	−	−	−	−	S	−			−	−	−	−	−	−	−	−		−
Could "marry" another slave	+	+	+	+	+	+						+	+	+	+	+		+
War chief	+	+	+	+	+	+	+		+	+	+	·	+	+	+	+		+
Social Customs																		
Avunculate	−	−	−	−	−	−	−	−	(−)	+	+	+	+	+	+	+	+	+
Kin avoidances	−	−	−	−	−	−	−	−	−	−	−	+	+	+	+	+	+	+
Privileged familiarity	−	−	−	−	−	−	−	−	−	−	−	+	+	+	+	+	+	+
Secret Societies																		
Winter ceremonials (i.e., specific season)	−	−	−	−	+	+	+	+	+	+	+	(+)	+	+			−	−
Performance at any time	+	+	+	+	+	−	−	−	−	−	−	(−)	−	−			−	−
Ranked series of dances	−	−	−	−	+	+	+	+	+	+	+	+	+	+		(−)	−	−
Unranked performances	+	+	+	+	−	−	−	−	−	−	−	−	−	−		(+)	−	−
Initiation by inspiration	−	−	−	−	+	+	+	+	+	+	+	+	+	+		+	−	−
Initiation by abduction	+	+	+	+	(+)	−	−	−	−	−	−	−	−	−		−	−	−
Dances																		
Cannibal dancer	−	−	−	−	+	+	+	+	+	+	+	+	(+)	−	+	+	−	−
Fire-thrower dancer	−	−	−	−		+	+	+	+	+	+	+	(+)	(−)		+	−	−
War dancer	+	+	+	+	+	+	+	(+)	+	+	−	·	−	+		+	−	−
Dog-eating dancer	−	−	−	−		−	(+)	(+)	+	+	+	+	+	+	+	+	−	−
Grizzly bear dancer	−	−	−	−	+	+	+	+	−	−	−	−	−	−		+	−	−
Shaman dancer	−	−	−	−	+	+			+	(+)	+		−	−		−	−	−

Ghost dancer	−	−	−	−	+	+	+		+	+			−	−		−	−	−
Cedarbark society insignia	+	+	+	+	+	+	+	+	+	+	+	+	+	+	+	+	−	−
Age-grade groups associated with ritual	(+)	(+)	+	+	(+)	+	−	−	−	−	−	−	−	−	−	−	−	−
Masks used in society performance	+	+	+	+	+	+	+	+	+	+	+	+	+	+		+	−	−
Potlatches																		
Function of house group or village (not clan units)	+	+	+	+	+	+	+	+	+	+	+	S	−	−	−	−	−	−
Function of clan or moiety	−	−	−	−	−	−	−	−	−	S	S	S	+	+	+	+	+	+
For secret society performance	+	+	+	+	+	+	+	+	+	+	+	−	−	−	−	−	−	−
Mortuary potlatches	+	+	+	+	+	+	+	+	+	+	+	+	+	+	+	+	+	+
For succession of heir (separate occasion)	+	+	+	+	+	+	+	+	+	+	+	+	+		−	−	−	−
For building house of heir (separate occasion)	−	−	−	−	−	−	−	−	−	−	−	−	+	+	+	+	−	+
For erecting memorial to dead chief (separate occasion)	−	−	−	−	−	−	−	−	−	S	S	+	+	+	+	+	+	R
Potlatches at life crises	+	+	+	+	+	+	+	+	+	+	+	+	+	+	+	+	+	+
Face-saving potlatches	+	+	+	+	+	+	+	+	+	+	+	+	+	+	+	+	+	+
Competitive potlatches	−	−	−	−	−	+	−	−	(−)	−	−	(−)	+		+	+	S	S
Property destroyed	−	−	−	−	−	+	−	−	(−)	−		(−)	+		+	+	+	+
Fixed order of potlatch seats	+	+	+	+	−	−	−	−	−	−	−	−	−	−	−	−	−	−
Seats according to individual rank	+	+	+	+	−	−	−	−	−	−	−	−	−	−	−	−	−	−
Tribe or clan sits as group	−	−	−	−	−	−	+	+					+	+	+	+	+	+
Fixed order of receiving	+	+	+	+	+	+	+	+	+	+	+	+	+	+	+	+	+	+
Names assumed at potlatch	+	+	+	+	+	+	+	+	+	+	+	+	+	+	+	+	+	+
Privileges assumed at potlatch	+	+	+	+	+	+	+	+	+	+	+	+	+	+	+	+	+	+
Gifts according to rank	+	+	+	+	S	S	+	+	+	+	+	+	+	+	+	+	+	+
Gifts to all guests (at major affair)	+	+	+	+	+	+	+	+	+	+	+	+	+	+	+	+	+	+
Host's wife or sister gives to women	+	+	+	+	+	+	+	+	+	+	+	+	+	+	+	+	+	+
Gifts to repay services (carving, tattooing, housebuilding, etc.)											+	+	+	+ +	+	+	+	+
Services vicariously performed											+	+	+		+	+	+	+
Fixed seating order (of individuals) at feasts	−	+	+	+	+	+	−	−	−	−	−	−	−	−	−	−	−	−

	NOOTKA				KWAKIUTL AND SALISH*							TSIMSHIAN			HAIDA		TLINGIT	
	NH	NT	NC	N2	KK	KR	KW	BC*	KO	KC	KX	TH	TG	GK	HM	HS	LS	LC
Coppers																		
Value of copper from original price	—	—	—	—	—	+	+		+	+	+	+	+	+	+	+	+	—
Value remains same (or slight increase)	—	—	—	—	—	—	(+)		S	+	+	+	+	+	+	+	+	—
Value pyramids (or doubles with each sale)	—	—	—	—	+	+	(—)		S	—	—	—	—	—	—	—	—	—
Coppers broken	—	—	—	—	+	+	+		+	+	+		+		+	+		+
Coppers displayed at potlatches	—	—	—	—	+	+	+	+	+	+	+	+	+	+	+	+	+	+
Finance																		
Slaves as wealth	+	+	+	+	+	+	+	+	+	+	+	+	+	+	+	+	+	+
Trade blankets as wealth	+	+	+	+	+	+	+	+	+	+	+	+	+	+	+	+	+	+
Skins as wealth	+	+	+	+	+	+	+	+	+	+	+	+	+	+	+	+	+	+
Loans made	—	—	—	—	+	+	+		+	+	+	+	+		+	+	+	+
For potlatching	—	—	—	—	+	+	+		+	+	+	+	+		+	+	+	+
At interest	—	—	—	—	+	+	+		+	+	+	+	+		+	+	(+)	(+)

SUGGESTIONS FOR FURTHER READING

BARNETT, H. G. *The Coast Salish of British Columbia.* University of Oregon Monographs. Studies in Anthropology, IV. Eugene, Oregon: University of Oregon Press, 1955.

BENEDICT, RUTH. *Patterns of Culture.* Boston: Houghton Mifflin Company, 1934, pp. 173-222, ("The Northwest Coast of America").

BOAS, FRANZ. *The Kwakiutl of Vancouver Island.* Memoirs of the American Museum of Natural History, VIII, pp. 307-515, New York: American Museum of Natural History, 1909.

BRITISH COLUMBIA HERITAGE SERIES: *Our Native Peoples* (Victoria: British Columbia Department of Education Curriculum Division, Social Studies Bulletins)
Introduction to Our Native Peoples, Series 1, Vol. 1, 1951
Haida, Series 1, Vol. 4, 1952
Tsimshian, Series 1, Vol. 6, 1952
Kwakiutl, Series 1, Vol. 7, 1953
Bella Coola, Series 1, Vol. 10, 1953.

COLSON, E. *The Makah Indians.* Minneapolis: University of Minnesota Press, 1953.

DRUCKER, PHILIP. *Cultures of the North Pacific Coast.* San Francisco: Chandler Publications, 1965.

DUFF, WILSON. *The Indian History of British Columbia,* Vol. I, "The Impact of the White Man." Anthropology in British Columbia, No. 4, 1964.

FORDE, C. DARYLL. *Habitat, Economy and Society: A Geographical Introduction to Ethnology.* London: Methuen & Company Limited, 1934, pp. 69-100 ("The Nootka, Kwakiutl and Other Fishing Peoples of British Columbia").

GOLDMAN, IRVING. "The Kwakiutl Indians of Vancouver Island," in Margaret Mead (ed.), *Cooperation and Competition among Primitive Peoples.* New York: McGraw-Hill Book Company, 1937, pp. 170-209.

HAWTHORN, H. B., C. S. BELSHAW, AND S. M. JAMIESON. *The Indians of British Columbia.* Toronto: University of Toronto Press, 1958.

JENNESS, DIAMOND. *Indians of Canada.* National Museum of Canada, Bulletin 65 (3rd edition). Ottawa: Queen's Printer, 1955, pp. 327-350 ("Tribes of the Pacific Coast").

KRAUSE, A. *The Tlingit Indians: Results of a Trip to the Northwest Coast of America and The Bering Straits.* (Translated by Erna Gunther) Seattle: University of Washington Press, 1956.

MURDOCK, GEORGE P. *Our Primitive Contemporaries.* New York: The Macmillan Company, 1938, pp. 221-263 ("The Haidas of British Columbia").

OLSON, R. L. *The Quinault Indians.* University of Washington Publications in Anthropology, VI. Seattle: University of Washington Press, 1936.

PETERSON, LEN. "Stand-in for a Murderer," in W. R. Goldschmidt (ed.), *Ways of Mankind: Thirteen Dramas of Peoples of the World and How They Live,* by Lister Sinclair and others. Boston: Beacon Press, 1954, pp. 11-19.

SERVICE, ELMAN. *A Profile of Primitive Culture.* New York: Harper & Brothers, 1958, pp. 200-221 ("The Nootka of British Columbia").

SWANTON, J. R. *Contributions to the Ethnology of the Haida.* Memoirs of the American Museum of Natural History, VIII, pp. 1-300. New York: American Museum of Natural History, 1909.

UNDERHILL, RUTH. *Red Man's America: A History of the Indians of the United States.* Chicago: University of Chicago Press, 1953, pp. 292-319 ("The Potlatch-givers: Tribes of the Pacific Northwest from Northern California to the Canadian Border").

NOTE ON THE EDITOR

Tom McFeat graduated from McGill University in 1950, and obtained his PH.D. from Harvard in 1957. He was engaged in field work in the Southwest (the Pueblo Indian culture) from 1953-54. Dr. McFeat was on the faculty of the University of New Brunswick from 1954-59, and it was during this period that he began field work on the culture of the Malecite Indians of the St. John River, research which he is still continuing.

From 1959-65 Tom McFeat was on the staff of the National Museum of Canada in Ottawa, and in 1964 he was appointed Chairman of the Department of Anthropology at the University of Toronto. He is now Professor Emeritus, and is a member of the Royal Society of Canada. His works include *Small-Group Cultures*, and *Highways to All Places: An Informal Ethnography of the Maliseet People*.

THE CONTRIBUTORS

FRANZ BOAS (1858-1942)
Department of Anthropology, Columbia University, New York; Professor, 1896-1937, Professor Emeritus, 1937-42.

JOHN R. JEWITT (1783-1821)
Armourer on the ship *Boston*. Captured by Nootka Indians, 1803-1805.

GILBERT MALCOLM SPROAT (1834-1913)
Commissioner of Indian Lands in British Columbia, 1876-80.

PHILIP DRUCKER
Bureau of American Ethnology, Washington, D.C., 1941-42 and 1945-55.

EDWARD SAPIR (1884-1939)
Division of Anthropology in Geological Survey of the National Museum, Ottawa, 1910-25; Department of Anthropology, Yale University, New Haven, 1931-39.

JOHN R. SWANTON (1873-1958)
Bureau of American Ethnology, Washington, D.C., 1904-44.

T. F. MCILWRAITH (1899-1964)
Department of Anthropology, University of Toronto, 1925-1964; Curator of Ethnology and director of the Royal Ontario Museum, 1927-1964.

H. G. BARNETT
Department of Anthropology, University of Oregon, Eugene.

HELEN CODERE
Department of Anthropology, Vassar College, Poughkeepsie.

RONALD OLSON
Department of Anthropology, University of California, Berkeley.

VIOLA E. GARFIELD
Department of Anthropology, University of Washington, Seattle.

CLELLAN S. FORD
Department of Anthropology, Yale University, New Haven.

VERNE F. RAY
Department of Anthropology, University of Washington, Seattle.

R. H. LOWIE (1883-1957)
Department of Anthropology, University of California, 1925-1957.

WAYNE P. SUTTLES
Department of Sociology and Anthropology, University of Nevada, Reno.

KALERVO OBERG
Institute of Inter-American Affairs, Rio de Janeiro, Brazil.

VICTOR BARNOUW
Department of Anthropology, University of Wisconsin, Milwaukee.